# Clough Williams-Ellis
## The Architect of Portmeirion

To
Gevret Sheli
for 50 marvellous years
with love

# Clough Williams-Ellis
## The Architect of Portmeirion

# A memoir by Jonah Jones

**seren**

**seren** is the book imprint
of Poetry Wales Press Ltd
First Floor, 2 Wyndham Street,
Bridgend, CF31 1EF
Wales

© Jonah Jones, 1996

A British Library Cataloguing in Publication Data record
for this book is available from the CIP Office

ISBN 1-85411-166-3

*The publisher and the author gratefully acknowledge*
*the financial support of the Arts Council of Wales*

Front cover photograph: Bruno de Hamel
Back cover photograph: Richard Tilbrook

Printed in Plantin by
WBC Book Manufacturers, Bridgend

# Contents

# List of Illustrations

# Preface

When Clough Williams-Ellis returned from service on the Western Front in the First World War he was to take up again an architectural practice that had begun round about 1905. He had enjoyed early success and his first major commission, Llangoed Hall near Brecon, was nearing completion when war broke out in 1914.

On my own return from war service in 1945 I had yet to find my feet as a freelance artist. Having lost precious years of studentship I was determined to break straight into practice. That depended very much on patrons, of course, and I owed much to Clough in those difficult early years. He soon came along with work in stone carving or lettering; a finial for a Portmeirion building perhaps, or armorial bearings for Voelas hall near Betws-y-Coed, and so on. It was the beginning of a professional association that was to last from the late forties until Clough's death in 1978. It was a privilege and pleasure to know him and to work for and with him.

He wrote a great deal during his life and his autobiography *Architect Errant* (1971) is a lively (but largely undated) account of his life and work. The loss of valuable papers in 1951 in the fire at his Meirionnydd home, Plas Brondanw, meant he had to rely mostly on memory.

Nothing has appeared since then on Clough's life, though the architectural historian Richard Haslam has recently published a valuable book on Clough's drawings. It is to be hoped that a critical assessment of Clough's buildings will be published one day.

I felt therefore that someone who knew him might fill a gap, for judging by the numbers of visitors to Portmeirion, there is a great deal of curiosity about him. There is of course much more to him than that charming folly, and I attempt to bring this out.

Happy are they who live in the dream of their own existence; to whom the guiding star of their youth still shines from afar, and into whom the spirit of the world has not entered. They have not been 'hurt by the archers', nor has the iron entered their soul. The world has no hand on them.

William Hazlitt

# Childhood

In the heavily glaciated region above Cricieth and Chwilog in Caernarfonshire there is a small village called Llangybi. Its dedication is to one of the early Celtic saints, St Cybi, who probably came from Ireland on missionary duty. The Irish packet port of Holyhead is dedicated to the same saint under the Welsh name Caergybi. Llangybi church consists of no more than a single aisle, a pattern frequent throughout the Llŷn peninsula. It is now only open for service once a month, so is usually locked, but a key can be obtained from the Rector at nearby Llanystumdwy.

On the north wall is a tall oak memorial tablet. In its original state the lettering was painted, so upon my setting up workshop after war service at the end of the forties, one of my earliest commissions was from a Mr Clough Williams-Ellis, to incise that lettering, thus rendering it less fugitive. It reads:

Courage arise He
calleth thee


Remember
John Clough Williams-ELLIS
M.A. J.P. 'Sion Pentyrch'
of Glasfryn and Brondanw
who died May 27th 1913 Aged 80
For 20 years Fellow and Tutor of
Sidney Sussex College Cambridge
and 10 years Rector of Gayton
Northants. He spent the last 25
years of a useful happy life
in literary retirement at Glasfryn
where is his burial place.
To him, his wife and surviving
four of his six sons dedicate this tablet
in love and gratitude.
Also Ellen Mabel his wife who
died April 22nd 1941 at her birth-
place Tanyrallt Tremadog aged
89 and is buried at Clynnog.

Both Glasfryn and Plas Brondanw were ancestral Williams-Ellis homes. The name 'Sion Pentyrch' was John's Welsh literary soubriquet, after the conical hill which rises behind Llangybi Church, where in those last twenty-five years of his life he was so often the celebrant.

Ellen Mabel (or 'May' as she was always known) was the

daughter of John Whitehead Greaves and Ellen Steadman. John Whitehead came originally from Birmingham, then Warwick, and finally invested wisely in the burgeoning slate quarry industry at Blaenau Ffestiniog, the source of his ultimate wealth.

John and Mabel had six sons, the first of whom, John, was killed in the Boer War, while the second ('Dico' or 'Nico') died in infancy. Of the survivors, Clough came second, after Rupert, and was followed by Edric and Martyn.

As for Gayton, it is a small place in deep Northamptonshire country, hidden away now between the A5 and the M1. Clough was born there on the twenty-fifth May, 1883, and was baptised Bertram Clough. There is an early photograph of father John and his five surviving sons (taken around 1893 and well before the eldest son John's death), all clad in Arab costume. Mother does not appear. The props are authentic; John senior puffs at a *narghila*; on an occasional table the proper *sumsumsiya* of coffee awaits their attention while they all (plus small dog also in *galabiya*) are being photographed. Rupert is seated and glowers, as he was wont to do, and is perhaps impatient to serve the coffee. The others stand firmly on both feet, except for Clough who, already looking tall and with long hunting rifle, hands on hip and quite detached, adopts a contrapostal position facing towards Edric, who was always unpredictable and might at any moment fall to his knees in prayer, as though to impress father. As to that Clough would be already critical, even actively hostile as far as he dared. For Edric did indeed show embarrassing signs of religious mania, and had to be 'looked after'. He married his nurse Meg and seems to have been something of a worry in a harmless way. None of this appears to have affected Clough's generally optimistic nature, but it must have contributed to that air of self-reliance he wore, of depending little on others, of wariness of being pigeon-holed or cramped in style or in any way deflected from his chosen course.

Despite this ecclesiastical lineage, Clough was rigorously rationalist in his attitude to religion, and till the end of his life loved impious humour, would tease anybody who professed religious faith, but never seek to hurt. It would be humour always, never malice, and on the odd occasion, when 'on parade' so to speak, he would talk of his tenuous link with Christianity. But much as he would admire Palladio, he could never share the piety of the master, whose love of white was once expressed as 'of all the colours, none is more proper for churches than white, since the purity of the colour, as of life itself, is particularly satisfying to God'. I can imagine Clough asking 'How did he know?'

Clough's earliest memory, a traumatic one as it happened, was of Queen Victoria's Jubilee in 1887, when he was four, not so much as a memory of loyalty to the Empress, but because the Gayton School celebrations were interrupted by an almighty thunderstorm. It provides an interesting insight into child psychology. I have recorded elsewhere my own early memory of a similar fright during a violent thunderstorm. In both cases there is an association with a very particular smell — in Clough's case, since he hid under the great dining-room sideboard, it was the faint smell of musty wine. In my own case, since we were caught out in open country in my grandfather's pony and trap, I always associate lightning with the smell of horses.

Although Clough admitted to being accident prone, he records in *Architect Errant* being quite reckless as a child: a pitchfork through the ear, an axe injury to the knee, being rolled on and kicked after an incautious pony jump, nearly drowning, were all an integral part of a childhood in the country. None of it induced caution. Rather it reinforced 'an innate belief in luck'. Neither he nor his five brothers were cosseted by their mother, since she shared the same happy-go-lucky attitude. His childhood upbringing bore all the marks of common sense. Northamptonshire, though hardly one of England's more celebrated landscapes, has a charming countryside, right at the heart of all that summons up Middle England: country lanes leading to obscure villages, perhaps with a fine church endowed in earlier prosperous times of the wool trade.

When still very young, Clough's family was torn from this comfortable warmth to what seemed to him 'a strange and desolate country . . . where there was no architecture and scarcely any building'. John senior was returning to Glasfryn to his 'literary retirement'. How productive he was is difficult to say, but he fails to appear in *The Oxford Companion to the Literature of Wales*.

Glasfryn lies in a very particular area of Llŷn, with its pointed volcanic cones, and the long avenue of oaks, trailing right across the neck of the peninsula, known as Lôn Goed. But children are sensitive to climate or to changes of it, and the change would be noticeable.

Clough recalled an outing proposed by his father to look at a place called Gors Marchog (Horseman's Marsh). Revealingly he remembers his childish expectations, among them a very touching and prophetic one, that 'the market place should be paved with smooth, rounded cobbles, the smaller the better . . .'. He would be disappointed. Yet this little touch he would exploit to great advantage later, and especially in Portmeirion, where visitors are now familiar with various cobbled surfaces of smooth glaciated granite pebbles. But Glasfryn was not without certain amenities to appeal to an adventurous young boy. For a start, there is a lake where Clough learned to mess about with boats, that perennial occupation of an island race.

He also enjoyed other country pursuits, or rather, tried to care about fishing and shooting, more for their 'grown-upness' than anything. He came to genuinely enjoy hunting, yet again for the ulterior motive of exploration rather than for the chase or the kill.

As the name implies, there are several strong and separate elements in Clough's lineage. The 'Clough' is for his paternal grandmother, who was descended from Sir Richard Clough of Plas Clough in the Vale of Clwyd. Sir Richard had been a glover in Denbigh and finally Queen Elizabeth's agent in the Netherlands and concerned, with Sir Thomas Gresham, in the founding of London's Royal Exchange. Sir Richard prospered and was an ardent builder, a fact which endeared him to his architect descendant. In 1973 Clough referred to him when he wrote to a fellow architect, John Taylor, about conservation matters in the Vale of Clwyd 'where my ancestor Sir Richard Clough built mightily in the sixteenth Century, though little now remains'. John Taylor possesses a pencil drawing by Moses Griffith (1747-1819) of Richard Clough's home Bachegraig. Clough must have known either this drawing or a reproduction, for he describes it as 'in the Dutch style' with 'a cupola on its high-pitched roof from which he studied the stars through a telescope, but where local report insisted, to his embarrassment, that 'he was communing with the devil'. That may be the reason why its owner early in the nineteenth century, Hester Lynch Piozzi, had it demolished. It is a great pity because, in an odd way, some of its features — the tall chimney stacks, the cupola and the towered and arched stable block — are not unlike his illustrious descendant's canon.

There is also a connection with the Victorian poet Arthur Hugh Clough. Clough's Godmother was Arthur Hugh's sister Annie, who was first principal of Newnham College Oxford.

The Williams side of Clough is recorded as established as far back as the sixteenth century, at Plas Brondanw, 'where my forebears had the good sense to establish themselves', and which was to become Clough's home for life.

Clough's early education was private. He and his four brothers can't have been easy for a succession of governesses, one of whom, Miss Barker, they nicknamed 'the Carcass'. Their 'governess-in-chief', as Clough described her, was a Newnham graduate, Miss Skinner, reinforced by lessons from their father. A suspicion of all authority became deep-seated from the beginning in Clough, in contrast to his father, whose attitude to work was painfully impeccable. Clough yawned through morning prayers. He was typical of many a son of the rectory, rebelling against this imposition to become ardently rationalist. It must be said that Clough loathed the cloth: 'Sundays were clouded by fine raiment and religious observances,' he later wrote. He was forced to attend services, but 'attended to very few, and so far as I can tell, was affected by none'.

In addition Clough was a compulsive agoraphile. 'Oh those interminable leaden hours of half-learning! The bitter contrast between the dead alive, snuffy hush or drone of the dim schoolroom and the blithe bustle of out-of-doors'.

Contact with the local community was minimal. In spite of his long Welsh ancestry, it seemed to me Clough in a way remained very English right to the end. The local boys would appear to him a slow and benighted lot, especially because of the language barrier. (It is quite probable that the local lads knew more English than he knew Welsh.) In his various publications it is quite remarkable that he hardly ever spells a Welsh place-name correctly. Even the original name of Portmeirion, Aber-Iâ, is spelt consistently by him as Aberia, which looks more Spanish than Welsh.

In the last century, Welsh speakers were very much on the defensive, despite the fact that practically everybody in North Wales, Mid Wales, and even the valleys in the south, spoke Welsh as their natural and native tongue. English was a foreign language. The local boys would have only broken English and the Williams-Ellis boys had only what Clough called 'mangled Welsh'. At that stage there was a crisis of confidence among Welsh speakers, dictated by the education authorities in London. Many teachers imposed the 'Welsh Not', a wooden label hung round the neck of the latest child to be heard speaking Welsh at school.

It took the appointment of a great Welshman, Sir Owen Morgan Edwards, as H.M.I. to correct this crisis, and the preservation and revivification of the Welsh language may be said to date from his appointment. But Clough belonged very much to the earlier dispensation, despite his fierce pride in his Welsh pedigree. None of this was Clough's fault, of course, and things have changed nowadays. Portmeirion is now run by his grandson Robin Llywelyn, twice winner of the Royal National Eisteddfod Gold Medal for prose.

The move to Glasfryn would prove not only a climatic shock to a young boy from deepest Northamptonshire, but also a culture shock. Yet it was a return to roots, for the Ellis part of Clough's name derives from Glasfryn. It was from Glasfryn that John Ellis in 1721 married the Williams heiress of Plas Brondanw, hence the double-barrelled surname.

Clough's father's parsimonious nature left its mark on Clough. He accused his parent of 'oratorical workhouse flourishes'. 'We shall end up in the workhouse, depend upon it!' was one favourite. Clough would forever afterwards measure the cost of a good meal and wine against the wages of a mason or a ton of bricks. In Clough it made for an odd contradiction, for certain enterprises, a boat or the raising of a new building at Portmeirion primarily to admire its pleasing elevation, would proceed regardless of cost, while he could never hire a taxi without a twinge of conscience.

In all, it was an interesting childhood, not only for its locations, but in its psychology. It was a Victorian childhood, with all that that implies: a blend of imposed discipline and piety, and of individual enterprise. It made for personal conflict, but the enterprise far outstripped the discipline. Individual enterprise would figure in his life so strongly that he remained forever outside the mainstream, the target of occasional condescension and grudging admiration among his profession, and beloved of the media and the public. In work, it would become a matter not so much of what his clients wanted as of what he himself wanted. Whatever the project, be it alterations at Attingham Park, say, or a village street at Cornwell, it was in a way a personal indulgence which the client came to love.

Clough's retrospective view of his childhood in general is touching. In his autobiography *Architect Errant* he wrote: 'I began to see how crushingly the odds are tilted against the child . . . . Everything is so inconsiderately big and heavy, everywhere is so far from everywhere else, the intractability of matter is a staggering obstacle to almost every enterprise, yet the child is not daunted.' He speculates that perhaps the great men of this world are just those who contrive to keep 'the sublime colour of their childhood'. It would have irritated his wife Amabel, child of Victoria's reign, yet most modern of women, that he omitted 'great women'. I can hear her saying: 'If we'd waited for men . . .'.

All told, Clough learned to be happy, and he is surely right to aver that happiness is not a gift but must be learned, as a bulwark against life's inevitable knocks, a lubricant that makes life more bearable. That is the picture he conveyed of childhood: 'to take disappointment easily . . . and quickly to forget what is not pleasant to remember'. In contrast to the prudent, even puritanical constraint of his parents and indeed of society in general around Glasfryn, he would hanker after the spectacular and theatrical, what he called 'gorgeous celebration'. Self-reliance was infused into the fabric of his life from early childhood onwards. He could live without people quite comfortably for long periods and preferred that contact to be kept brief and at reasonable intervals.

I came to know two of Clough's brothers, both as tall as he. Rupert inherited Glasfryn and made it into a flourishing tree nursery. He wore a beard and seemed to me the nearest thing to a Victorian gent. He was quiet, somewhat austere, or perhaps just shy and studious. Trees were his passion, and the tradition persists with his son Roger carrying on. I remember Rupert grew tobacco, and in the distant past when I smoked a pipe, I thought his tobacco rather good, if not quite up to a working man's brand called Erinmore, a taste I shared with Clough. In the record of self-reliance and enterprise, there is no mention of when Rupert started to grow tobacco or Clough to smoke it. My guess is that Rupert started growing it late in life, and that Clough started smoking during war service, when nothing seemed so comforting as a quiet pipe. That for Clough it was an addiction is borne out by the story (probably apocryphal) of him stalking round the grounds of Portmeirion and feeling like a smoke, and, finding both his tobacco pouch and his pocket empty, at once starting to trawl the Dolphin Fountain for enough tourist wishing coins to buy an ounce of tobacco at the shop nearby.

Clough's other brother living locally in later life was Martyn, who owned and managed the Wern Estate between Cricieth and Porthmadog. He was my first landlord. I can't recall who briefed me about him, but when my wife and I were demobilised from the Army and house-hunting in the area, he was a last resort. Housing then was a desperate business and I was advised to see Martyn. But obeying the advice, I went in full fig: Army uniform, Red Beret, and medals. Sure enough, he was interested in me, if not in the least in my housing problem. His immediate interest was in my Army service. He wanted to talk about Palestine, my most recent posting, where he had been an engineer building railways. Only at the very end of the interview, I standing almost at attention, he seated behind an old estate desk, did he attend to my request. It was all rather like a court martial. I had seen an old battered ruin, a quondam farmhouse halfway up the hill nearby, Moel y Gest. I wondered if I might rent it, God help me, for it was in a dreadful state, had been abandoned over thirty years. The uniform did the trick, I am convinced — he agreed reluctantly, for he was worried our presence there would disturb the pheasants. If I saw to repairs myself, I could have it for twelve pounds per annum.

Meeting all three brothers left me with the impression that the mark of both parents on their upbringing was clear and undiminished. It was a parsonage upbringing, involving that extra constraint of acceptable if not necessarily good behaviour. But early on, it was not Victorian appearances that mattered to Clough, those that must be kept up, but rather the outward appearance of people and things and the environment. His father's crusty old academic colleagues would occasionally turn up and their appearance would be assessed by young Clough. A tangled beard, a skew-whiff bow-tie, crumpled wine-stained tweeds, anything that detracted from pomp and even a little circumstance, would meet with Clough's disapproval. A gaffe would ensue, a flat refusal, say, to walk round the lake with the offending guest.

That the feelings of others were not necessarily at the top of Clough's agenda would be generally agreed among his countless friends. It did not diminish his affection for them or theirs for him, but he would never have made a good diplomat, and he knew it. He records one of his earliest failures in tact. He was very fond of a hard-drinking sea-captain who courted his nurse. His mother disapproved of the liaison and described the captain as no more than a 'barrel on legs'. This seemed to Clough so perfect a description that he passed it on at once to nurse. Tears ensued, the affair was ended forthwith, and Clough left to rue, but not to cure, his want of tact.

Glasfryn therefore seems to have cramped his style somewhat, and style would matter to Clough throughout life. Local nonconformist society was anathema to him, and he speaks rather unfeelingly of visiting the village school near Glasfryn with his mother. 'All the children large and small sat with their slates on a sort of wide staircase chanting their lessons'. It was a social fabric, however, that could produce a Prime Minister, a Cabinet Secretary, numerous Dons, writers, scholars and lawyers of distinction. To Clough, for whom appearances mattered more than for most people, it seemed like death. He seemed unaware that the constraints were often no less fruitful than his rather different ones.

He would have preferred a father who was a prince in a Venetian palazzo, with negro pages, gorgeous mistress, monkeys, painted ceilings, masked balls, processions and fireworks, 'the lot'. This was very much a retrospective gloss, of course, since it would be many years before he would explore the decadent glory of Venice.

Yet his taste in buildings would develop here in this apparently unpropitious landscape. Glynllifon, a house a few miles to the north, impressed him, though he regretted the various accretions that marred its Palladian pretensions. It was built by Lord Newborough in the mid-nineteenth century. Newborough was a keen gardener and landscapist. Clough noticed the three-tiered fountain, whose waters now pour out of one side only, since an earthquake in the area tilted it slightly in 1984. Glynllifon is now open to the public, and its derelict landscape has been converted, quite admirably I think, by artists into a sort of theme park commemorating the Writers of Gwynedd. I think Clough would have approved.

If young Clough admired this or that house in the neighbourhood, he was pretty scathing about the philistine taste of the local grandees, which in his opinion was mostly execrable. Their libraries would not extend much beyond *Debrett* and Ruff's *Guide to the Turf*.

One house he did approve of was Tanrallt, built around 1810 by William Madocks, whose damming of Traeth Mawr otherwise offended Clough. Tanrallt was Madocks's own dwelling, built on a low rise just above what would have been high water mark before he built his barrage. At the time of Clough's childhood the house was occupied by his aunt Hilda Greaves. Clough admired Tanrallt's low Regency spread across the knoll, with an imposing backdrop of hanging beech woods and granite cliffs. It has barely altered since it was built. It is not difficult to imagine its appeal to a boy of Clough's taste. 'Collecting buildings', both in the mind and in actuality, was to become a lifelong pursuit, and Tanrallt was an early passion, rather like the first sight of the Flying Scotsman to a trainspotter, I imagine. The old house is now a Steiner School. Its deep south-facing verandah would appeal to Clough. Light, celebratory, elegant, it would set a trend in his mind, in contrast to so much that was dark and grim around him, as he saw the world. Furthermore, Tanrallt had a history of Romantic visitors — Shelley had finished *Queen Mab* there and one of my earliest commissions was to inscribe a plaque to commemorate this, if that is the right word, for Shelley was practically hounded out of the district by creditors and irate farmers. A touch of maggot in a sheep's hindquarters is routine for a farmer to deal with, but Shelley could not bear to witness their suffering and shot them to end their misery. In the end, he was shot at himself in mysterious circumstances and left the district precipitately.

Richard Brinsley Sheridan had stayed at Tanrallt too, and one of Clough's heroes, Thomas Love Peacock. Clough thought Jane Austen would have felt perfectly happy there, and he may be right, though I imagine she might have found the landscape rather threatening. Clough's mother Ellen Mabel was born, and died at Tanrallt, and altogether Clough maintained a love of the place throughout life, both as his mother's home and as an architectural gem.

Aunt Hilda seems to have been his only soul-mate as far as building was concerned. He heartily approved of her perfectionism in restoring Tanrallt to its original glory, for like many a fine house, it had suffered both neglect and philistine maintenance during the nineteenth century. He admired her search for the right shade of watered silk for the drawing room panels. She was also an ardent bibliophile, which while not quite a passion with Clough, was certainly a pursuit. I remember, for instance, his joy at finding a copy of Bickham's writing manual, *Universal Penman* (1743).

Technology was not among Clough's abiding interests (despite a subsequent brief career in electrical engineering) and it would be fair to describe his approach to building as primarily aesthetic. This seems strange, since his father, though basically a scholar, enjoyed a streak of solving physical problems of a technological nature. He planned and constructed a reservoir with a long mill-race to a distant overshot water-wheel. It ran all the machinery for the saws and planers, pumped domestic water, ran the farm machinery a quarter of a mile away, provided electricity for the house and was regarded generally in the neighbourhood as a sort of marvel.

This particular Williams-Ellis streak was channelled into brother Martyn, who became a trained engineer. Of eccentricity and odd talents among relations there was plenty. I recall Martyn describing to me his uncle Dick Greaves at Wern, who had a splendid machine shop and provided all sorts of weird and wonderful gadgetry, including a hydraulic railway which ran from kitchen to dining-room and carried the children. Uncle Dick was a steam man and built the engines for a small paddle-steamer at Caernarfon around 1870. He had enough confidence to sail in her as ship's engineer to Japan.

Another eccentric who enchanted the boy Clough was a neighbour, Fred Wynne, a scion of the Newborough family. The first Newborough had been ennobled for contribution to the defence of Britain in Napoleonic times by building Fort Belan at the western end of the Menai Straits. What it had to do with the defence of Britain is difficult to imagine, except that invasion via

Ireland was always considered possible, and the last invasion of Britain had indeed taken place in 1795 further down the Welsh coast. Fort Belan is still there, quite intact, and a delight to child visitors. My own children ran round its ramparts, 'fired' its canons and generally decimated 'the enemy' in their time.

One of Clough's earliest sea voyages was in Fred Wynne's launch *Firefly*. Fred Wynne was landlord of extensive estates in Caernarfonshire, among them Ynys Enlli (or Bardsey), 'island of 20,000 saints', where the King of Bardsey entertained them to tea and a speech in Welsh.

Clough's childhood impressions were to persist through life and to have an effect on his subsequent vocation and pursuits. There were all the makings of the eccentric, of the single-minded builder, of the sailor and of the agnostic. He would not be the easiest of pupils to teach, yet he would achieve his own ends in his own way.

# Schooldays

The domestic problems of Clough's parents must have been considerable. In those days the education of boys at a reputable public school was obligatory for people of their station. There was less compulsion to educate girls, and indeed university entrance was mostly denied them, especially at the male bastion of Oxbridge. Educating five boys must have appeared daunting, but there was no question, to school they must go, and to a good public school at that.

Clough's preparatory education had been dealt with by the redoubtable 'Carcass' and a succession of governesses. For him, always with an eye on the outside world, it had proved tedious. But worse was to follow. He was decidedly unhappy when, at fourteen, in 1897, he was dispatched to Oundle, back in Northamptonshire it was true, but now far from home and in an utterly alien atmosphere. He was the only new boy in the school. To a man who was later to enjoy the greatest freedom to do exactly what he wished to do with his life, Oundle must have seemed like a prison sentence. His education under governesses had always been tempered by the proximity of his mother, whose sound common sense provided a base, an anchorage against the threats of the outside world. Now he was thrust alone into the harsh world of public school. The comfortable country tweeds were displaced by bowler hat, black jacket and tie and pin-striped trousers.

It was all so alien that he remembered it always with a certain irony. Here, inevitably, the message was disseminated that these were to be the happiest days of his life. Of course many a boy would fail to accept it and Clough was not alone in this. But it does not help to assuage unhappiness. He questioned the whole business from the very first. The Clough of later years was already being firmly moulded, away from conformity and towards the questioning of all disciplines based on established ideas and assumptions. He recalls: 'From the point of view of happiness, it was not a very good plan'.

It might have helped had the headmaster been able to express himself better. Frederick Sanderson was in many ways a liberal and radical man, prepared himself to defy the hearty assumptions of the public school ethos. He had to take care not to offend parents and governors, of course, and his behaviour perhaps explains Clough's incomprehension and bewilderment. Clearly he did not understand this dichotomy of conventional rewards and punishments, and Sanderson's ill-expressed idealism. Sanderson did not believe in caste and privilege; rather he believed in equal opportunities for all, in cooperative effort as against the prevalent individual competitiveness, and in the brotherhood of man as against patriotism. Such views would be highly suspect to the late Victorian establishment, about to reach its apotheosis in the Empress's Jubilee.

Sanderson was no cold-hearted pedagogue. When boys transgressed then conventional corporal punishment was applied, but in this case reinforced by the passion of a man who felt betrayed. Perhaps he saw the transgressions as a denial of his innate liberalism, or perhaps the liberalism was a denial of his true nature (though from Clough's description of him this seems unlikely), but at any rate, when Sanderson was angry he was 'tremendously angry'.

Clough had been destined for a scientific and engineering career, no doubt in accord with his father's leanings, and he came to regard Sanderson's science lessons as 'pure joy'. The practicalities of Boyle and Dalton fascinated him and he was impatient of any departure from them which sought to explain, say, the Old Testament by scientific doctrine. All told, Clough later saw in F.W. Sanderson a kindred spirit, and 'exposer of all sham and pretensions'.

Certainly a code of values seems well-established in Clough at Oundle, partly from Sanderson's tuition and example, but partly by kicking against the pricks, by that rebellion against irksome restrictions and conformity, for Oundle, headed by a liberal-minded head, nevertheless perpetuated public school traditions. For Clough, for instance, cricket was an absolute waste of time, and he felt even more constricted. He might be out-of-doors, yes, but whiling away the tedium of out-fielding, imagining all sorts of exciting expeditions he might have made once out of the classroom. The M.C.C. would frown on such heresy, but he genuinely suffered from cricket: 'Yet another golden afternoon wasted in tedious lounging or meaningless running about, when, if the world were not mad, I reflected, I might be revelling in the same sunshine miles away exploring some fresh part of that enchanting countryside'.

Yet the rules were strictly enforced. It would be difficult for a born anarch like the young Clough to understand. He would be the last to imagine the anxiety of parents should he be discovered wandering loose in the countryside. However, he did once break out, to explore the Elizabethan ruin of Lyveden New Bild, and he was to remember it forever. To 'collect' buildings was his particular territorial imperative, not to be denied.

He liked wandering in the old market town of Oundle itself,

mostly built of a beautiful mellow limestone. He would do anything to get out, as though he suffered from claustrophobia, as
well he might, so strong was his dislike of confinement, either
mental or physical. So he joined the Photographic Society, and
even wangled himself a place in the choir because it involved
outings.

It irked him that the school never encouraged, much less
allowed them to write an essay on some private enthusiasm, as
though to depart from the stern curriculum would be an unpar-
donable lapse from scholarship. He longed to write about the
noble Elizabethan ruin of Kirby Hall under the romantic title 'On
seeing Kirby Hall for the first time'. Nobody seemed to understand. At French he believed he achieved a long-standing record
by getting one per cent. He seemed to think he was unique in Art
by being confronted with plaster casts from the Antique, but he
was not to know that even students in top art schools like the Slade
would suffer much the same in those days, before they would enjoy
the privilege of drawing from Life.

Altogether he confessed to finishing his Oundle days 'a rather
bigoted Philistine'. It may sound an appalling self-accusation
from the builder of Portmeirion, but I think I know what he meant.
It may be that in his frustration at not being able to pursue his
preferred avocation he closed his mind to much else. It is difficult
to imagine eliciting any opinion from Clough on, say, Flaubert,
Debussy or Rodin. I could be wrong, but that was my own
impression. He was so utterly single-minded: Architecture was his
domain and that was that. As somebody once said of Clough's
near contemporary Ford Madox Ford: 'He was a writer and that's
what he did'. Clough was an architect and that was what *he* did.
And his days at Oundle, however ill he thought of them in
retrospect, set the pattern. Of course he was biased. For instance,
despite his flight from education in its formal aspect, how did he
come to write so well, to draw so well, to grapple with the formal
requirements of building a house, where measurements are required and must be accurate?

Despite his conversion to 'philistinism' (like his claim in politics
to being 'congenitally deviationist', it was probably his way of
hedging his bets) he is quite poetic in his summary of his feelings
about his schooldays at Oundle:

> School, meals, games, chapel, roll-call, lock-up and
> bounds on the one hand; on the other, finger posts with
> enticing and melodious names upon them — Fotheringay,

Barnwell, Lilford, Kings Cliffe, Rockingham, Stoke Doyle, Warmington, Polebrook, Warton Waterville and the rest — the meandering yet navigable river, maps and guides, and the most poignant of all, woods, villages, and church steeples to be seen in the blue distance and on the horizons of that softly rolling country — but never, never to be visited.

At the other end of the spectrum of influences was his first steam voyage, right round the coast, across the Bristol Channel, round Land's End and up the English Channel to the Thames. It was an arduous and uncomfortable voyage by all accounts, and he was not well disposed to Barking Creek, where they finally tied up to discharge their cargo: 'about as disenchanting a landfall as one could well imagine — then a lonely jumble of grubby industrial squalor where London's East End petered out in a marshy waste'.

The view from the dirty train on its journey into the city lowered his spirits even more, and again, as with Kirby, the impression would later inform much of his writing on planning and urban development. That human beings should be condemned to live and work in such squalor seemed to him a dereliction of the human spirit, especially since in his view it was remediable, given the current wealth of society. All this feeling and indignation informed his subsequent work and writings on planning, environmental awareness and amenity.

Even as a youth he soon developed a critical faculty in architecture. He records his impression of a visit to another ruin or rather half-ruin, Brynkir Hall, for it seemed never to be complete nor ever fully demolished, but always in a state of flux. It lies still, now a complete ruin, a pile of rubble at the foot of Cwm Pennant on the road between Porthmadog and Caernarfon. Clough drove with a party for a picnic lunch, for one thing because the view up the Cwm from Brynkir is one of the most dramatic in North Wales. On arrival at Brynkir, he found 'a vast and sprawling pile of sombre early Victorian masonry that had monstrously overwhelmed the demure Regency villa which itself had replaced the original seventeenth-century manor-house — the former still surviving incongruously as part of the great house, the latter but a ruin in the garden'. What offended him even more, however, were the appalling additions then being built by a gang, all on top of the existing muddle, additions that 'could only have been designed, if designed at all, by one who has failed as a chapel architect, so unhappy were its feeble attempts at ornamentation in lugubrious cement'. He would never, like John Piper, develop any affection whatsoever for Welsh chapel architecture, and indeed, would invoke it as an example of what architecture ought *not* to be.

He came away from Oundle with an abiding image, one that was to be a major influence on his life and work. His frustration at not being asked to write his essay 'On first seeing Kirby Hall' may appear a little precious from a schoolboy, but in fact it was very real. Obviously he longed to convey to some kindred spirit the effect on him of first seeing

> that lovely shell, its long grey flank catching the golden light of a July evening, the diamonds of its leaded casements flashing and glowing, the great mullioned windows in the court shadowed and blank where the glass had fallen away. Ivy and nettles, elder and briar, roofless galleries and grass-grown parapets — yet there were those still alive who had dined and slept there, who remembered the tapestries, who had trod the marble stairs since burned for lime, who had heard the great clock chime in the gatehouse tower.

Writing that passage some seventy years later, he seems to be shaking off all the schoolboy frustration and at last setting down that first impression. In old age, he was to revisit the old pile with a scion of the family that had once lived there, Sir Osmond Williams, Bt., his first cousin once removed, who recalled the occasion with real warmth.

Certain elevations, certain details in Clough's work later echo this or that bit of Kirby Hall. Could he have designed Llangoed Hall without having first soaked up the amazing aspect and detail of Kirby Hall? Seeing, sketching it and generally falling for the sheer majesty and beauty of the place was the major element in his training. No course of training at a formal school could have matched its influence. Later he summed it up:

> Nothing certainly could have been more stickily romantic — this slow decline of a great house into ruinous decay through the negligence of its noble owners — midsummer evening glamour — the exhilaration of 'the year's outing', and, on top of all, what I still hold to be the most gracious example of Elizabethan building in the whole of England.

His opinion of Oundle School and the public school ethos in general may not be flattering, but he came away from it with that major influence to motivate him for ever after. Would he have seen Kirby Hall had be not attended Oundle? Would he perhaps have seen some other 'lovely shell'? The fact is that he and Kirby came together at that time and from then on he knew who and what he was, and pursued his aim with a singleness of mind that nothing could diminish — not wars, nor poverty, nor the normal exigencies of family life.

All told, his Oundle days and youth in general left him with those two fixations — or, to use a current portmanteau word 'mindsets' — the sheer, haunting beauty of Kirby Hall on the one hand, and on the other that appalling contrast of London's East End. Both were a shock to him, both galvanised him, the former in his design, the latter in his writings and propaganda throughout a long life. And if, by his own confession at the age of eighty, he was known 'much less as a practical architect, landscape designer, town planner or whatever than as propagandist of these ploys', it was because the East End experience moved him so deeply that he would indeed become one of the prime movers and constant goads against bad architecture and planning. He was to become an indefatigable propagandist and it was that which earned him the gratitude and recognition of his peers.

In the end, he repaid whatever debt he owed to his old school by designing the War Memorial to go in the Ambulatory of the Chapel in 1923. The initial design was for a grille screening off five tablets recording the names of the fallen. Only the tablets were adopted, possibly for reasons of cost.

Clough left Oundle in 1900. His next step was to prove no easier.

# University

As an experience, university was no more than ordinary for Clough. Again, it was not what he would consider to be 'the best years of his life'. First, as to choice of university, no alternative was offered. 'Cambridge in my family was as axiomatic as porridge for breakfast, eaten with salt, and any idea of Oxford would have seemed as perversely heretical as sweetened bread-and-milk.' Strange similes perhaps, but there it is — Oxford was not to be contemplated, and Cambridge it must be. For a man addicted to fine architecture it cannot have been too hard a choice. The choice of college was left to Clough and that was inevitably towards living and studying close to that which he loved, Great Court and Neville's, architecture he had already seen and fallen for. Trinity it must be therefore, with the added bonus that the gown would be blue and not funereal black.

He had somehow 'dodged' the first part of his 'little-go' examination. That seems typical. But there was no escaping the second part, Latin and Greek. The glorious long vac between school and university was ruined by paternal tuition. Clough thought this ordeal by Caesar and Xenophon 'not only mad but diabolical'. Nevertheless, he had to submit, if with an ill grace, and passed. He would always regard the whole exercise as useless, yet though he claimed later to recognise only a very few Greek letters, how is one to measure its efficacy or otherwise in the civilising and refinement of youth? Clough always appeared to me and I don't doubt to others, to be both civilised and educated, despite his frequent disclaimers. As far as he was concerned, he suffered this imposition with impatience and scepticism. It did not make for the most favourable father-son relationship.

It came as a surprise to Clough, when he visited an old friend of his father's at Cambridge and they reminisced over seed cake and madeira, to learn that old John had been awarded the Gold Medal of the Royal Humane Society, for diving into the flooded river on a dark and snowy winter's night to rescue a drowning man. His father had never once mentioned the exploit. Clough later inherited the presentation gold half-hunter with a wreath surrounding the citation designed by John Ruskin, 'now lost as also Ruskin's drawing and covering letter'.

In 1900, Clough started at Trinity, not too willingly, but surrounded by the utmost temptation in the form of superb architecture. There was the usual introductory full-dress dinner at the Master's Lodge and with his taste for colour and decoration,

Clough's memory was more of the Master's 'gala dress of some high ecclesiastical purplish frock coat and apron, breeches, silk stockings and buckled shoes, looking like a bland and benign version of Henry VIII'. When he wrote these words is not recorded, but they were published in his *Architect Errant* when he was eighty-eight and demonstrate his remarkable memory for decorative detail over some seventy years.

He was seated next to Horace de Vere Cole, a practical joker who was celebrated, or more likely notorious, in the balmy days of Edward VII after the Boer War, when much fun was had, and before the killing fields of World War I.

Clough made a desultory effort, more for appearances than any conviction, to learn to drink, and seems to have decided it was not for him. It was neither piety nor health considerations that decided him, but once again, it was the sheer waste of time, the hours of getting drunk and the days of recovering. The antics of Sebastian Flyte and his set would have left him cold. At a camp on the Norfolk coast he decided once to test his capacity, since all about him were becoming steadily maudlin and he as sober as a judge. However, he stayed sober and the best he could do was to lean over the pier railings and fling his precious dress shoes into the moon's reflection on the shimmering surface of the sea and watch the sparkle of exploding drops. That sounds drunk to me, but it is true to say that Clough was not a drinking man. Like cricket, and Greek and Latin, it was a waste of time, and much over-rated as a pursuit. Literally, drinking had no meaning for him. He had no need of the lubricant and tongue-loosening effects of alcohol.

Whenever I encountered Clough on the road in a vehicle, I tended to give him as wide a berth as possible. This is unfair, suggesting he was reckless. In fact he was one of the oldest and most practised drivers, a first generation motorist. As an undergraduate he was one of that group of pioneer drivers, owning a small and primitive belt-driven vehicle which had difficulty in exceeding one mile before breaking down. Cambridge was already on the way to creating its own traffic problems. Charles Rolls was there, with a rather superior car, and went on from Cambridge to found Rolls-Royce.

Years later in 1912, Clough stayed in the same country house with Rolls and had the pleasure of being driven by him in an early prototype. He never passed up a chance like that. Once, driving his absurd little vehicle along what is now called the A5, he ran out of petrol and sat reading at the roadside waiting for a passing motorist to lend him half a gallon to get to Shrewsbury. None came, so he stopped a passing waggoner and asked if he knew of a local car owner. The reply was favourable: only half a mile away, at Atcham House. That was Clough's first acquaintance with yet another charming house for his 'collection'. Long afterwards he bought it and converted it into the Mytton and Mermaid Hotel, a well-known hostelry on the old Watling Street highway.

But back at Cambridge, where he was supposed to be reading Science, the great addiction kept him too frequently from the lecture room and on to the streets of Cambridge, admiring and drawing buildings. He copied from architectural engravings, and once again, his education could be said to really take place during the intervals away from the lecture room. Even while attending lectures in Science, his notebooks would gradually fill up with sketches of architectural detail, a triumphal arch here, an Ionic volute there, a cornice on the verso, or a Baroque pediment on the recto. In short, university did not stand a chance and his stay there was short lived.

There would be anxious domestic debates about a career, what would, what would not earn a living. His obvious vocation, Architecture, was *not* considered suitable. His elder brother was already the director of a new electrical manufacturing company. Why not join him? It might well have happened. All that practical know-how derived from his father would point him in just such a direction. The pressures were there. If he was not to complete his Cambridge degree, then at least he must do something useful. As the third of five surviving sons it must have taken great force of character to resist those pressures.

Yet so clear in his mind was his vocation that he did resist. He must have been dragged by the heels towards electrical manufacturing, if only because he had no idea yet how to enter the profession of Architecture. At that date, after the excesses of Victorian building, the profession enjoyed an indifferent reputation, being largely in the hands of local art teachers and country auctioneers. Clough was persuaded that it was simply not a suitable career for him, yet there was dogged persistence on his part to somehow find his way into it. I have known few more single-minded persons than Clough, and it is easy to imagine a rather cussed resistance to various ideas thrown at him by anxious parents eager only to see the young man into a suitable profession where he might make his way (that is, earn a suitable salary or fees). Nothing would turn him. Cambridge had proved very quickly to be a blind alley. It was the lectures, about arcane subjects of no interest whatsoever to him, it was his claustrophobia, his need to get out and about, to explore, it was all sorts of things that added up to a thorough waste of time as far as he was concerned. *He* knew exactly what he wanted to do. Any advice he might require was simply on *how* to make a start, how to get *into* Architecture.

He even submitted to being shunted into electrical engineering as a laboratory assistant. It was a case of getting out into the world and away from institutions, hovever improving. He was quite clear in his mind that any financial rewards were to be channelled into architectural practice somehow. In those pioneering days of the electricity industry, it must have been quite easy to become rich — or to fail altogether. The market was wide open. As a source of energy, electricity promised to be clean, economical and efficient. The industry was expanding and almost doubling by the years. Clough might have enjoyed a career as millionaire director of some burgeoning GEC or Ferranti. At the same time, in such a fluid situation, firms could fail just as dramatically.

Clough was all too aware of its seductive powers. He might succeed, he might become an industrial mogul, given the various possibilities and a few contacts. Everything was in place, the growth, the dividends, the wide open market, the gamble. All he had to do was to apply himself, and perhaps enjoy the dazzling prizes of a new enterprise that could expand exponentially. But he was aware too of people who had been deflected from their dreams, as he saw it: 'people made rich and even famous by treachery to themselves, but nothing very reassuring about their being happy'. The phrase is significant in his life, for meeting and knowing him was to be aware of a man who had steered his own course throughout life against all the temptations of wealth or position.

It is clear that Clough at this crucial period of his life required happiness from life, and he knew where it lay for him. Parental blandishments, fraternal openings, financial considerations, all directed him away from that goal, and there must have been self-interest, even selfishness in him that prepared him to with-stand all the pressures. It all points to the assertion of true vocation over the world's requirements. Clough was well aware that dreams of wealth offered by the new industry could just as easily evapo-rate, and indeed, his brother's enterprise showed distinct signs of weakening. Clough wondered if he had sold his soul 'for an IOU that was not after all going to be honoured'.

He was engaged to work alongside an inventor in a sort of darkened garret in Victoria Street in London, trying desperately to tame an experiment into some sort of a meter. All it seemed to do was to satisfy Clough's sense of the ridiculous. He *must* get outside. He could not breathe. The experiment produced only the most hysterical performance.

He went down with influenza and never returned to his inventor. He had a conscience about it, but he knew that if he returned to collect his personal belongings, he might be persuaded to stay. Despite a hurt, pleading letter from the inventor, he stuck it out. He was now, so to speak, out on the streets, sitting on the grass under a plane tree near Marble Arch, writing a letter home.

'And anyhow,' he wrote, 'I would far, far sooner be poor as an architect than succeed as an engineer; after all, if that's how I feel, why should I fail?'

In the event, Clough's parents proved complaisant and understanding. Perhaps they had observed him more closely than he would give them credit for. They simply agreed, wished him luck and vouchsafed an allowance of £160 per annum, which in 1902 was enough to see him off the streets and back into decent drawing rooms.

At last he was free, to explore, to trace a path into his beloved profession. But how, precisely? He had 'collected' buildings since his schooldays, had drawn and doodled Orders and details, finials and architraves — but now that he was free to make an entrance into the actual profession, where was the door? He had searched about on his own, he had no acquaintance in the actual profession, had no knowledge of its criteria or entrance requirements, or indeed anything. All he knew was that he must be an architect and nothing else would do.

He looked up the word 'Architecture' in the London telephone directory and came upon a subscriber called *Architectural Association* in Tufton Street, Westminster. It sounded promising. At least they would have some of the answers to his various queries, not least how to *begin*.

# *Training*

Number 18 Tufton Street, at once, did not appeal to Clough. The building was a rather grim Gothic edifice, just the sort of building that would so offend him that even the word 'Gothic' would have to be tempered by a touch of Classical wherever possible, as for example in the Portmeirion colonnade, which he would delineate as 'a Classical Composition enriched with Gothick detail'.

Nevertheless he entered, presented his card and demanded to see the Principal. Nothing was easier. The Principal entertained this youth 'off the street' at once in an easy-going conversation neither patronising nor condescending. They got on without difficulty. Clough's informal training, or even lack of it, proved no impediment. He skipped out of the building in a high state of elation. The academic term was nearly at an end, but, come next term, he could enrol. First there would be the long vacation to endure.

Perhaps, in his training as an architect, that vacation, waiting for the following term, was to set the pattern for his eventual career. He had a number of relations, property owners, in a position to commission design for building or restoration, and especially a 'sort of second-cousin', A.H. Clough, apparently not to be confused with the poet Arthur Hugh Clough. This remote relation not only owned properties but was keen to develop them in an enlightened way, that is, rationally, well-proportioned and with informed taste. Furthermore, he had the eighteenth century habit of working directly with his builder, rather as the great magnates and contractors had consulted and worked together in building the London squares.

Clough was invited to tag along as a sort of aide-de-camp. It was exactly what he wanted and needed. It is one thing to develop the taste to admire a noble facade, quite another to put together bricks and mortar and windows and roof and hold the lot together. This was when he learned the actual requirements and specifications of building, where he really got mud on his boots and not only witnessed, but assisted at the ramming of concrete into foundation trenches, at setting window frames, laying joists, raising roof trusses, arranging guttering and down-spouts, and seeing the respective services properly and conveniently into the building.

With his rather eighteenth century tastes, this was probably how he had always imagined an introduction to the discipline of architecture, working directly with the builder on site and learning all the tricks first-hand. He had never taken kindly to the classroom, lecture room or office, so this introduction to *real* building out on site contributed most to his education. He kept a notebook (which later he regretted losing). He was encouraged in every way by both this very accommodating 'second-cousin' and his highly civilised builder. He was allowed to design a tiled and rough-cast porch for one small house on the estate, supervised its construction, and like any designer stood back to admire his own work, then, after a week or two of reflection, decided it was rather overblown given the small scale of the house.

His cousin also wished to restore a fine old manor-farm he owned, and yet another necessary unit in Clough's self-imposed curriculum was achieved — the surveying and measured drawing of the fabric. This task he came to value as an integral part of his training, as well he might, for what has measured up in the past in both utility and taste is surely a sound base from which to start. Even before he had enrolled at the Architectural Association, Clough was already absorbed in the actual discipline of building. He was lodged in a quiet Sussex village over the tap-room of the local inn, sleeping on a hard truckle bed, but happy as a lad after the frustrations so far in his life. The builder/contractor was a most likeable man who not only had a knack for solving all building problems in a practical (i.e. non-academic) way, but also for passing on his lore to this youngster who had jibbed at university. Myths fell away, mysteries dissipated in a day-to-day address to the various problems of actually *building* something. Even the contractor did not fit Clough's preconceived ideas — 'a large head with a mass of waving black hair, a wide high forehead over deep-set and very large blue eyes that looked like a girl's, a small sensitive mouth that a drooping moustache was being sedulously trained to hide, a slight, rather frail-looking body, always neatly clad in blue serge or sober black — that was my contractor'. How closely observed and remembered for one who always claimed to have a better memory for facades than faces. At any rate, this man was to be one of the most important influences in Clough's training.

Although he absorbed everything in the matter of building and was already quite able to see through certain projects without any assistance, he came to regret later in life his lack of formal training, a training that normally takes anything up to seven years at a recognised School. Yet despite his respect for the rigour and length of such a course, he stayed outside the mainstream and would stay outside throughout his long career. It was not so much a matter of impatience and eagerness to get on with things, but also the fact that jobs came his way at once, following that early connection with his accommodating cousin. If you are already busy, and successful it seems, why bother to take time out to train for all those years? He enjoyed the most extraordinary luck, and not a little quiet nepotism. He had hardly started his second term at the Architectural Association when a commission came his way. He did not say precisely how or why a young tyro like himself should have been entrusted with a public commission, except to say that it was 'family jobbery'. The actual project was to design a country home for a charity near Oxford, to house about twenty people. It had to be plain and cheap yet attractive. It was a challenge he accepted with alacrity, at a fee of ten guineas with expenses.

He took it on, and being Clough he visited the site more often than is usual, perhaps to make up for deficiencies in his detailing. Where his knowledge and experience seemed deficient he would bluff his way through on site. The drawings were done, ready to suffer the grit and cement of workers' fingers on site. That filled him with pride. Compared with sitting through lectures and grinding through theoretical projects in class, this was real life, real work. It was all a great gamble, of course. It might have gone disastrously wrong, and that would have ended a glorious career scarcely begun.

And that was how, for a Miss Venables, Clough came to tackle his own first commission, to build Cumnor Cottage in 1904 and later, Cumnor Rise, 'Home for feeble-minded girls', completed in 1914. (Clough was always cavalier about dates and facts, and in *Architect Errant* it is possible he confuses the dating of these two projects. If so, his first commission was *Cumnor Cottage*, and not what he called 'a charitable institution'.)

There was one problem, however, which he half anticipated. Perhaps there was just a little self-doubt in his approach to the project, and he found he really needed all those extra site visits, or even worse, visits by the site manager to him in the school. In order not to miss lectures, Clough would take him in with him and the two would sit together, then return to Clough's desk to thrash out the day's problems. Naturally this was severely disruptive to other students and he was carpeted by the principal and warned he must either cease using the school as his private office or resign. The decision was inevitable.

Later there was an interesting exchange of views on this with the great Lutyens, designer of New Delhi and the Cenotaph.

When Clough declared he had left the school after three months, Lutyens replied: 'What, you took three months! Why, I was through it all in three weeks'.

In his various writings (and they were considerable over the years), Clough rarely refers to other designers of his period of training. Yet his training, or learning period, coincided with an extraordinarily rich period in design. The general ethos must have rubbed off on him, though he hardly ever mentions it. After the nineteenth century's almost static obsession with Gothic, and its unfortunate links with the worst excesses of industrial development, there was a fresh movement in the air, in nearly all departments of design. Not only building, with people like Voysey and Norman Shaw, but interior design, graphic design and product design were being re-examined by individuals like W.R. Lethaby, C.R. Ashbee, Edward Johnston (responsible for that clear sans-serif letter used throughout the London Underground), all broadly following the precepts of William Morris and often associated, like him, with socialist views.

Nor was Wales without examples of exploratory design. W. Eden Nesfield (1835-88) built Kinmel Park in Denbighshire some ten years before Clough's birth. It is a version of what is generally known as the Queen Anne style and well within Clough's range of tastes. Perhaps he knew the house, but nowhere does he mention it in his writings.

Sir Percy Thomas, born the same year as Clough, designed the City Hall in Swansea (1930-34), an example of Classicism modified to twentieth century taste, with the usual Orders and mouldings left out. The striking Willans and Robinson factory at Queensferry in Flintshire (1901) had been even more stridently modern, with an extensive fortress-like elevation and central tower resembling an Egyptian pylon.

Most symptomatic of this period was Charles Rennie Mackintosh (1868-1928) the Glasgow architect and designer, whose masterpiece, the Glasgow School of Art, transformed a difficult sloping site into one of the seminal buildings of the Modern Movement. In Spain, Antoni Gaudi y Cornet (1852-1926) was building his Cathedral of the Sagrada Familia in Barcelona in his own particular version of Art Nouveau. The Viennese School's version of Art Nouveau flourished, with architects like Otto Wagner and Josef Hoffman. In France and Belgium, Hector Guimard and Victor Horta were at the height of their powers, while in the U.S.A. Frank Lloyd Wright was defying inherited colonial styles and developing what was to become known as the open 'Prairie' style of domestic building. Design moved away from the purely national dimension to a broader international style. Glasgow influenced Vienna and vice versa. The exotic influence of Japan was also having an effect, and yet in almost all cases the end product bore its own national mark.

The odd thing about Clough is that, on paper at least, he seemed quite unaware of all this extraordinary ferment in design, or at any rate he makes no mention of it, except in *Architecture Here and Now* (1934), which he wrote with John Summerson. It seems the main and most persistent influence on Clough's approach to design was that early period at Oundle, when, as a young boy escaping the confines of the classroom, he went exploring and 'collecting' buildings, and most especially, the beautiful ruin of Kirby Hall; open to the sky, but in an odd way all the more beautiful, as though showing off the essential nature of its bone structure. These buildings were, in the main, English country houses, and his sketches of their elevations, facades, details and ornament were surely the one great influence on his architectural design to the end of his life. He might have been described as the last of the Palladians, except that, despite Frank Lloyd Wright, a great deal of rather ostentatious Classical building was going on for the wealthy in the U.S.A. Long Island and Rhode Island were cluttered with millionaires' retreats in the Grand Manner.

In one sense, Clough sold himself short not only in ending his Architectural Association course prematurely, but also in his apparently blinkered view of his contemporaries. He was essentially an outdoor man and was often impatient of interior detailing. Mackintosh, for instance, was never content with only the plans and elevations of broad architectural design but was intent on the least detail in his buildings, such as the appropriate lampshades (designed by himself) in the lecture room of his School of Art. Even little touches like the double swing doors as you enter the School bear his mark. A little heart-shaped aperture in each door is filled with brilliant blue glass and the effect is at once warm and welcoming. Clough, by contrast, could be cavalier in his approach to interior detail. But like Mackintosh, when it came to exterior effects, he did absorb certain vernacular forms to good effect. Mackintosh was adept at exploiting a particular form of local fenestration of small panes. With Clough, the best example of his exploitation of vernacular forms is his refurbishment of the village of Cornwell in North Oxfordshire. The same is true of his earliest Portmeirion buildings like Angel, Neptune and Mermaid. In all these cases the use of small rustic slates is his particular mark.

In the end, although Clough's design over a very long career would embrace many styles and schools, vernacular to High Baroque, Palladian to Modernism, he could be said to be a beneficiary of the Arts and Crafts Movement which flourished in his childhood and youth. Yet on everything he did he imposed his own mark.

Having bid goodbye, or been expelled from the Architectural Association (he would accept either interpretation), he might have found himself once again out on the street. On the other hand, since he had a job in hand and the prospect of more, it was merely a matter of establishing an 'office' and proceeding from there. He had connections and always, it seemed, those endless 'remote cousins'. He was always resourceful, and poverty would never be an impediment to future adventures in the field of architecture, now that he had learned the rudiments.

He was sharing chambers with his elder brother Rupert in Cork Street in 1902. They had a private bathroom and valet, so it was no wonder they frequently found themselves in debt, with occasional recourse to the pawnshop. Indigence and gaps in knowledge embarrassed Clough at this stage in his life — his watch and ring were often in pawn. Home in both Gayton and Glasfryn may have been frugal in some ways, yet they had always provided life's necessities without question, and even occasional luxuries. Now Clough felt the lack deeply. He had had no experience of living on the breadline. Despite his customary good luck, there are odd lapses of a Victorian nature. He complained that he would some- times miss his train 'through not being able to afford a hansom'. Not a few just east of Cork Street would exclaim: 'I should be so lucky!' Having been brought up in comfortable security, he lacked the techniques of poverty. Furthermore, now that he was free of the nest, he demanded a taste of the high life, decoration, splen- dour, entertainment. He learned quickly that there were the 'gods' in the theatre, that there were certain dives in Soho where you could eat very well at little expense. Even more startling was the discovery that you could wear a starched shirt twice for a dance or dinner party. That his poverty and this social round were reconcilable pointed to a certain native cunning. Certainly he grasped life in both hands and as ever rode his luck: 'one should crowd one's luck while it lasts!' was his declared philosophy.

His first drawing office was a little cubby-hole at £5 a quarter, 'approached grandly from the sedate precincts of Gray's Inn'. With his visiting card pinned to the door, he was installed as an architect in practice. He had no formal qualifications, no letters after his name. His landlord was also an architect who was amiable enough and probably well enough aware of his tenant's profess-ional innocence to offer a word of advice now and again. When Clough's Oxford builder enquired rather tentatively one day: 'What about a little sugar for the canary? Can't sing without sugar, you know!' Clough had no idea what he was talking about. His landlord soon apprised him and so Clough was initiated into the custom and practice of the architect's certificate of work com-pleted satisfactorily, which the builder then presented with his bill to the client. But despite his acknowledged shortcomings, he enjoyed a string of useful small commissions, all grist to the mill, all contributing to his training.

Soon he moved his office in 1906 from Gray's Inn to Arundel House on the Embankment near the Temple. Three attic rooms up five flights of steps provided an eyrie with a grand view of the Thames and its traffic, and without interference from clients, who would baulk at the two hundred steps to his office. He had his view through dormer windows. Remembering the etchings of artists like Muirhead Bone and J.M. Whistler, the Thames was then a great deal more interesting (and dirtier) than it is now. It was from this grand-sounding address that many of Clough's early drawings emanate. Practically all the Llangoed drawings date from Arundel House. He occupied this office for eight years up to 1914.

If he failed to find enough work in architecture, he used his brains and what electrical knowledge he had to invent things; for example an electrical switch, and a chair which Sir Ambrose Heal accepted and developed. It even paid taxi fares and washing bills — 'no more — until the patent expired'. Luck, ingenuity, a capacity to make the most of whatever knowledge and training he had, with a way of exploiting connections — these were charac-teristic of Clough.

He confessed that such was his enthusiasm at the time that all else was neglected. The rest of his life, he declared, was 'as near as need be nil'. But not quite, and here, those who came to know him in later life may be surprised at his pride at that time in his prowess as 'a dancing man, a regular and not unaccomplished dancing man moreover'.

During these rather lean apprenticeship years in the first decade of the century, when he did not always have a nice fee rolling in, Clough lived very lean, and relied on his frequent invitations to London gatherings for a decent meal. As a highly eligible bachelor, he was never short of invitations. As King Edward's reign

progressed all seemed well with the world and it was well with
Clough too. His luck would carry him on and on, and he was in
the right place to exploit that luck. With his small architectural
practice established in London and showing every sign of developing rather than failing, he found he could enjoy something of
society. There were balls and dinner parties, with hostesses ever
on the lookout for eligible young bachelors, especially a loose one
like Clough, quite ready to fill some immediate gap at a dinner
table. 'I'm so sorry to telephone you at such short notice, but
would you, if free, care to attend . . . .' He mostly was and he did.
He made the most surprising connections, some of which led to
architectural commissions. At one party near Windsor he met the
Officer commanding the Coldstream Guards, who invited him to
view the barracks. Would they interest or horrify him? They did
both, but more importantly, he and the Officer talked sufficiently
to leave a mark, for after the war and an interval of five or six years,
the Officer, by now a General, asked him to build a country house
for him and his large family.

At another country house party he excelled at clay pigeon
shooting from the terrace. I find this difficult to imagine, but he
not only remembered it, but claimed he ended up champion,
largely because he had been rather temperate in his drinking
compared with his companions. All this was just part of Edwardian
high jinks, *la belle époque*. With Empire over one sixth of the globe
and no sign of its disintegration, it must have seemed it would
never end. Great Britain was a World power, if not *the* World
power, ready with gunboat diplomacy to quell any disturbance in
its many spheres of interest, much as the U.S.A. does now. A great
deal of wealth was floating around, national confidence would
never be higher, warships came off the slipways regularly, ocean
liners carried passengers to the distant corners of the far-flung
Empire, and a great deal of building was going on. There can't
have been a more propitious time for a young architect to set up
practice. Clough's social life engendered commissions. It was not
without its hazards of course. A dancing man is bound to attract
various attachments. He always had a commanding presence. I
did not know him until he was sixty-five, but even then he attracted
attention — tall, gangling, with an air of easy eccentricity.

It was in 1908, when Clough was twenty-five, that his father
decided it was time to hand over ownership of the old Williams
property of Plas Brondanw in Meirionnydd. Clough had always
understood that it would be his some day, as second surviving son,
but the casually informal transfer rather surprised him. Naturally

he was delighted. It was to be a liason for life, a love affair that would never fade. As well as the aesthete who collected buildings, Plas Brondanw also satisfied a rather dynastic antiquarian respect in him. Brondanw was a small romantic estate surrounded by an immemorial landscape of mountains and streams, with the sea just visible to the south. The old Carolean hall, which had been in the family for over four centuries, was to be an exciting prospect, not merely in ownership, but in restoration and landscaping.

The house had been abandoned for Glasfryn on his grandfather's death, but beyond suffering some internal alterations to provide tenements for the booming slate industry workers, it was in fairly good condition. There were sitting tenants, it was true, but that would not deter its new owner, who always had an eye on the main chance. One tenant, a salmon poacher who smoked his fish in the great chimney of the brew house, left suddenly (probably in flight from water bailiffs), and gave Clough just the foothold he needed. He restored the poacher's quarters into a decent flat, and as tenants died or were rehoused on the estate, he gradually asserted complete occupancy of Brondanw. From then on, he would never cease to improve it and, as we shall see, even though he lost it for a brief interval, having recovered it he carried on, adding this, improving that, planting a yew hedge here, placing an urn there, and building an orangery in the garden.

He was particularly proud of its situation in the landscape and made the most of it. Looking along the terrace on the west facade, he achieved a magnificent view of Cnicht, most perfect of mountain peaks, and framed it by judicious planting. He was so enchanted by the place that he likened his devotion to that of a 'much-in-love husband and a devoted father'. It is understandable. He had set his course, he knew exactly what he wished to do with his life: to design, restore, improve buildings and their environment. Here he was, suddenly owner of just such raw material as any artist could wish, all his to cherish, to keep up and improve.

The day he took possession was cold and wet; he remembered a scene that might have come out of George Borrow's *Wild Wales* half a century earlier. He met an old harpist and a boy fiddler and invited them in for a bite and, with very little persuasion, perhaps a song afterwards. Touchingly, he recalled that they played two old Welsh folk songs, 'Codiad-yr-Ehedydd' (The lark ascending) and 'Gwenith Gwyn'. Always a man for connections, he would recall later that 'Codiad-yr-Ehedydd' would be adopted as a quick march by his regiment, the Welsh Guards.

An important landmark in Clough's development as an architect
was his meeting with Lawrence Weaver, editor of *Country Life*,
who in 1910 promoted a competition for suburban houses.
Clough's design attracted enough attention to warrant building it
for £500 at the architect's expense. The house, Reed Pond House
at Gidea Park in Essex, still stands and is just one of countless
small houses that Clough built. From then on Weaver and Clough
became firm friends, with Weaver as a sort of mentor and patron
to the young architect.

Two years later came an important commission from the Bishop
of Bangor, to build a parsonage at Pentrefelin near Cricieth in
Caernarfonshire. This handsome house built of dressed granite
looks as fresh as ever today and is a tribute to the quarrymen who
worked the stone in Trefor Quarry on the north side of the Llŷn
peninsula.

The reign of Edward VII (1901-1910) covered Clough's twenties,
and it must have seemed very heaven, provided you steered clear
of complications. He was free and determined to stay so. Certainly
he enjoyed country house life. He marvelled at the food and the
wines, the sheer wealth and number of courses at dinner. Nothing
was left to chance. 'I even recall one country house,' he wrote,
'where the fear of that fate [night starvation] befalling a guest was
such that, on retiring, after a monumental dinner, a dance and a
generous supper, I found laid out in my bedroom all the materials
and utensils for a sort of self-service barbecue.'

Clough's eager acceptance of invitations to all sorts of parties,
dinners, balls, country house weekends, seemed based on three
criteria. The first was expediency, since he was living on a shoe
string and a party guaranteed a good meal. The second criterion
was more interesting. He was, it seems, very attractive to women
and most certainly to London hostesses, especially those with
daughters on their hands. He recounts certain temporary liaisons.
'I sat next to and thereafter assiduously cultivated a most delightful girl. Everything went swimmingly — we exchanged addresses
and actually made a plan to meet again.'

However it all faded as the girl was summoned back to Scotland.
'I should like her to know how immediate and deep an admiration
she could rouse in 1913 or thereabouts.' He is writing that nearly
sixty years later. Did she ever read it? Certainly she left a lasting
impression.

Beyond that he was ultra cautious, determined to keep his guard
against any serious entanglement. 'A light-hearted flirtation con-
ducted more or less in public, that was fine, but if a tête-à-tête

showed the slightest signs of becoming at all personal I would take fright and do all I could to bring things back to cool normality. I was just plain terrified of finding myself somehow "compromised", thinking that even the mildest sort of "love-making" must be assumed to be the prelude to a proposal of marriage.'

On another occasion, dining with friends in Belgrave Square and going on to a dance in Cheyne Walk as sole escort of their only daughter, he recalls that they both knew lots of people but mostly danced together. At length, he suggested dutifully that it was time to take her home, lest her parents should be anxious. Judging by her response it was *he* who was anxious. 'Oh no', she replied, 'I have kept the brougham and I should like to drive *you* home. It's a lovely moonlight night and it will be along the Embankment all the way with the shining river for company.'

Despite his protestations she insisted. Dawn was breaking as he finally alighted outside Arundel House, shook the girl's hand, thanked her, said goodnight and 'bolted for cover'. 'Gentleman or cad?' he reflected after sixty years and decided the latter.

As for the third criterion, he confessed that his acceptance of invitations was based on hard-headed professional grounds. Artists, writers and actors or Bohemians of any sort might indeed be more interesting and often much more fun than the county families and city magnates with elegant town houses in Mayfair or Belgravia, but it was the latter and never the former who had jobs to hand out.

He freely accepted invitations to luncheons, dinners, balls, theatres, weekend country house parties, and nothing was expected in return, only his presence. 'I could only just afford pretty spartan living for myself alone, though I seemed to thrive well enough on a mixed and irregular diet of alternating quails and kippers.'

His social life was so full and happy that in retrospect all fades into an 'agreeable dreamlike blur'. But sharp little images emerge, of Pavlova and Lopokova dancing round the fountain in Lady Kennet's garden. She was the widow of Captain Scott the Polar explorer, and mother of Peter, who was the subject of a boyhood statue by her in the garden too. She was an accomplished sculptor and was responsible for the splendid bust of David Lloyd George in Llanystumdwy. Clough met Mrs Patrick Campbell at a commemorative dinner, at which he helped to carry out Augustus John. And so on. It was all grand, gay and carefree, when a young man could sow his wild oats without thought for tomorrow, unaware of the impending horrors of the twentieth century.

Looking back from days when anything goes in matters of dress, he records the extraordinary conventions of the day. 'With this morning coat went a top hat, a stick-up collar, a tie or maybe a cravat with (sometimes) a white "slip" between it and the waistcoat which was either black or white'.

Clough remembered one appalling photograph of himself, sitting on a log on an open hillside with a client having a picnic. He is wearing a 'frogged fur-lined overcoat with an astrakhan collar, stick-up white collar with generous black silk bow-tie, spats and bowler hat'. He must have looked like Stravinsky on a visit to St Petersburg.

Eccentric he may have been, but Clough submitted to these rituals with good grace, as well he might, for it all made connections. But as well as this consideration, it satisfied his taste for decoration, carnival, colour. Edwardian society was having a ball, almost as though it knew the crash would come, and things would never be the same again. Clough was not going to be left out.

He confessed to being 'too timorous a nonconformist to deny all this convention', but he did for a short spell break out with a deep blue waistcoat with pearl buttons, which attracted so much attention and discreet advice 'not to dress so theatrically' that he desisted.

One dance, at Kent House, was sharply etched on his mind and his feelings. The decor of the place was beyond belief, all designed by Paul Sert. On the black walls were etched in gold full-sized elephants and apes, which all made 'as exciting and dazzling a background as you could well have to a party that was in itself anyhow pretty gay'. Clough was so exhilarated that he all but proposed to his chief dancing partner on the spot, and indeed later came to regret the delay. But despite his inherent caution, luck was with him and it seemed the girl was just as keen. She was Amabel Strachey, daughter of St Loe Strachey, editor and proprietor of *The Spectator*.

Clough's interest in this particular girl had begun in rather unusual circumstances. He had received a printed postcard in 1913 from The Rural Cooperative Housing and Land Society, of which he was a member. Members were invited to attend a meeting on Merrow Downs near Guildford where St Loe Strachey had bought some land and had built on it a weather-boarded, tile-roofed cottage costing £150. It was a ploy by Strachey to solve the shortage of housing for the rural poor. He laid down a challenge to any interested architect. 'If his cottage will stand the test of wind and rain for one year and thus show it is not merely a butterfly house, I will purchase it from him.'

It was just the sort of challenge Clough was looking for, and he took it up at once, not without an ulterior motive, for he had been struck by a girl weaving confidently among the crowd. He wrongly surmised she was connected with Lord Middleton's party, the County Lieutenant. It took some time before he discovered his mistake and that his ingratiating efforts had been misdirected. All he knew was that he must pursue this girl with the toppling pile of red hair and confidence of manner. Clough was among the first to accept the challenge from her father. The architectural competition was just the catalyst he needed.

That was how he first came to know Amabel. Miss Strachey and Mr Williams-Ellis met thereafter whenever they could, partly in the Strachey town house at Number 14 Queen Anne's Gate, and partly in their country house at Newlands Corner.

At Newlands Amabel had enjoyed a very particular and privileged upbringing. The great and the good frequented the house, and there was never any question that *The Spectator* represented a special voice of the nation. Press barons like Lords Northcliffe and Harmsworth visited. Andrew Carnegie was a frequent caller, and Rudyard Kipling held Amabel on his knee while he told her the *Just So Stories* before they were even published. Politicians came, of course, the Third Estate courting the Fourth, for *The Spectator* carried weight. 'The younger members of our family', wrote Amabel, 'applied the term "Spectatorial" to any particularly pompous and respectable pronouncement.' But of more particular interest to young Amabel were visitors like the Sitwells and other writers. Poetry became a passion and Amabel was to become literary editor of *The Spectator* on her own merit and to write her first book, *An Anatomy of Poetry*.

Not by any means did poetry represent the limits of Amabel's interests. She was an early prophet of the effects that Science and Technology would have on society in the twentieth century. At editorial board meetings of *The Spectator* she would advance her ideas about scientific journalism. Einstein's Theory of Relativity, Rutherford atom-splitting at the Cavendish ('The Cavendish Hotel?' asked a shocked voice), Mendel on genetics etc — all this she advanced, only to be shot down. 'Our readers wouldn't have it. Nobody ever has to vote on a scientific issue' they said.

In the end, Amabel and brother John rebelled altogether against what they saw as the Establishment view. 'For us the honest thing to do was to join the Labour Party . . . . To do so was likely to have most unpleasant consequences.'

These two apparently disparate souls, Clough the single-minded visual artist, Amabel the wide-ranging intellectual, continued to meet as Mr Williams-Ellis and Miss Strachey, in accordance with the manners of the time. But how to proceed further?

Clough did not win the competition but his design attracted attention and so eased a link with the Stracheys that involved more than professional interests. Still, he was coy beyond words when it came to any sort of commitment. He would shy away from any threat of entanglement. Happily this was to prove one of the great long-lasting liaisons of the twentieth century, a marriage of true minds which no impediment would hinder in its course. Clough and Miss Strachey met at all the balls and parties, each seeking out the other. This was different, even serious. What was the protocol? There seemed to be no instruction available.

Clough happened to be staying at the country house of the novelist Mrs Humphrey Ward at a large weekend party. There he met Lady Bell, 'a most splendid and cultivated old lady'. Lady Bell knew Amabel, was full of praise for her and in particular admired her intelligence. Clough needed no convincing. Lady Bell was to act as go-between in the rather stiff prevailing rules of etiquette.

Later, taking a walk with Lady Bell's son-in-law, Sir Charles Trevelyan, Clough sought his advice on the procedure for courting. Clough recalled that Sir Charles made it all sound rather like walking on egg shells. It would take the Great War to shake out such things. But in the end, the advice was clear: 'Go right ahead and win her if you can'. Clough would later record: 'And so it was, and so I did'.

This retrospective view of his apparent shyness may come as a surprise to those who remember the amiable and sociable squire of Portmeirion, but he is recalling what has become known as 'Victorian values', for they persisted well beyond that lady's reign and through her son's reign.

Clough's interest and attention was no less bewildering for Amabel. In her admirable memoir *All Stracheys are Cousins* she records how she and her fellow debs 'had been trained to make ourselves agreeable, to conform and to be pleasant in society, and most of us were willing enough . . . . As for me, I just played along awkwardly but as well as I could, though I wasn't as happy as I was expensively meant to be.'

At first she felt derisive as she was asked to ride her mare down from Newlands to show the young architect the way when he was invited to lunch at Newlands. What was she to make of this man 'with his rather rakish good looks, his tall gipsy figure and one of those suspect felt hats . . .?' But later, as they danced together at a ball, she was so much at ease with him, she felt anything but derisive.

At about this time too, Clough began to widen his work base, in the sense that ownership betokens power, power to preserve landscape from the depredations of greedy and thoughtless developers, but also to exemplify to others, to advise how to look after what is now called 'Heritage'. In those days, the fate of any property, however historic, lay in the hands of the owners, who often did not care what happened to it. But mostly 'Heritage' had been the prerogative of the great landowners, the landed gentry, who for the most part could be relied on to preserve, improve and generally cherish what was theirs, even if for private and selfish reasons. The Industrial Revolution had ploughed great swathes into the landscape, especially in coalfields and the industrial areas of the North and Midlands. Some estates would even be subsumed into bleak landscapes of factories, mines and terraced houses, like Renishaw Hall, the Sitwell estate in Derbyshire.

There was no state provision or interest in guarding what had been lost to the landscape in the nineteenth century. Only a few enlightened souls took up the challenge, and Clough would be an early exponent of the ideals later enshrined by the state in the National Parks, and by public subscription in the National Trust. To demonstrate his conviction, Clough bought two most significant properties within view of Brondanw, the pyramidal peak of Cnicht and the twin summits of the Moelwyns, to protect them from any unwelcome development.

Clough confessed to 'a social as well as an aesthetic conscience' in his address to architecture from now on, and in Brondanw he would never cease to practise the necessary virtues. He would attract allies and join others in a gradually growing national consciousness. One friend, Peter Thorp, talked eagerly and dazzlingly of a new Britain, an almost Blakean vision of a land cleared of the satanic grime and poverty in the landscape, along with access for the people to their precious heritage, their restored landscape.

Peter Thorp (or Joseph Thorp as he was known in London circles), was an idealist. He had trained as a priest in the Jesuit order, an education as rigorous in its way as any architectural course, and even longer. Thorp did not last the course and was defrocked as unsuitable. Ill-equipped for a rough world, he had to find his own way, which he did by charm and not a little ingenuity. In a long chequered life he had been in and out of the church, had married a Slade painter, Helen Syrett (sister of the romantic novelist Netta Syrett), and had been in and out of the bankruptcy court more than once.

Thorp's ideal was to share all beauty and the arts with the masses. Clough viewed as over-simple 'his prescription for achieving this by soaking the conspicuously rich by disguising himself as one of themselves and pleading his cause from within their own glittering ranks'. To this end, however, Thorp did indeed dress as a dandy (in spite of intermittent poverty!) — top hat, collars and cravats, boots and spats, ivory-topped malacca cane, all made by the most celebrated tradesmen. As Clough saw it: 'He wanted the best possible, not just for himself, but for everybody'.

Thorp was a fascinating man to meet. By the time I met him after World War II he was full of years but as lively as ever, an indefatigable talker and pusher of ideas. In his time he had been typographer, writer, theatre critic (as 'T' of Punch, taking over from A.A. Milne when he went off to the First War), publicist (in fact an early PR man) and general one-man arts council extracting funds from his rich acquaintance to help indigent artists. He was the founder of the Agenda Club, a sort of extra-mural Garrick Club for the exchange of ideas. It attracted government ministers, editors, intellectuals, columnists and so on. One prominent member was Dr Thomas Jones of Rhymney, cabinet secretary to Lloyd George, Ramsay MacDonald and Stanley Baldwin. Dr Jones was a professional *éminence grise* who initiated enterprises outside government, like the Pilgrim Trust, and advised others like the Gregynog Press. The Agenda Club, among many other things, discussed a sort of Welfare State long before Beveridge made his Report. Thorp was very much part of the cauldron of London life, but in his later years he elected to leave it all and with Clough's help built a house, White Cottage, near Portmeirion.

As far as Clough was concerned, Thorp was a very active member of the Design and Industries Association, founded shortly before World War I. Clough was a prominent member and when Lawrence Weaver its first chairman retired, Clough took over in the chair. Its aim was to record and foster good design and to put industry in touch with designers and vice versa. Like such movements it would gradually mutate and develop into legislation and a public body of some sort, in this case The Design Council. In his book, *Design in Modern Printing* (1928), Thorp selected twenty-four members of the D.I.A. who he believed made an important contribution to aspects of Design, and one of these was 'Clough Williams-Ellis, who can build for purpose'. It was a compliment, yet I doubt if fitness for purpose was top of Clough's approach to design. I recall Thorp late in life at White Cottage complaining good-humouredly as he swept the floor of its triangular kitchen, that 'only Clough could have designed a kitchen with eighteen returns to sweep out!'. Clough and Thorp remained in touch as campaigners and friends throughout the rest of Thorp's life.

This was the sort of company Clough enjoyed, so long as it helped to forward his ideas on conservation and amenity. While Thorp simply loved company and wide-ranging conversation and was a cheerful caller, Clough was rather detached and would resist entanglement in theory or philosophising which might deflect him from his own particular pursuit in practical building and conservation.

The D.I.A. was the sort of movement that would encourage public awareness of Design and would publish propaganda to that end. Clough grasped the opportunity to push his own ideas on Architecture and Conservation and he began to write his first thoughts on the subject.

The axis of Clough's life now extended between London and Brondanw in Meirionnydd. In *Architect Errant* he recalls the exact occasion that sparked off his writing. Shortly before World War I he was searching for an island sanctuary for his yacht, or perhaps for some precious unspoiled landscape, but he crossed on a small steamer from Glasgow to the island of Islay. As he passed through Glasgow he found it incredible that people could be condemned to live in such appalling squalor. He had personally endured a period of penury in his desperate search for his goal of an architectural training and for a moment, writing that letter home from the grass near Marble Arch, he had reached what for him was the lower depths. But nothing had prepared him for this squalor. He had just met Sir Patrick Geddes, archpriest of Planning and Amenity. From Sir Patrick's Outlook Tower near Edinburgh, they had gazed on the tremendous sweep of the Firth of Forth and the mountains beyond, and the contrast of Glasgow lowered his spirits so drastically that he simply had to write down his thoughts. There is no doubt that his Glasgow experience had a salutary effect on Clough little short of that of Kirby Hall. If Kirby was the great initial impetus — and example in his vocation as architect — this accidental view of Glasgow (and that earlier one of London's East End) was the spur behind his subsequent zeal as an apologist for national planning. Clough would become the writer of well over a dozen books and many articles, which in some ways is surprising in one so single-minded about his true vocation of architecture.

He found the cathartic effect of writing so soothing to his troubled sensibilities that from then on he would write copiously. At the beginning, then, it was a way of ordering his thoughts, particularly on *social* planning, which was a new discipline. Except for the great estates, both country and London, most building and planning for the masses had been thoughtless and unfeeling, for both the people and the environment.

He was determined to widen his horizons by examining housing, town-planning and 'amenity' (a word that would creep in increasingly from now on) in other countries. Around 1910 he travelled to Holland on a tight budget, and was so absorbed in his admiration for a fine Dutch gable that he was bumped by a tram. The next thing he knew he was on the ground being proffered a glass of water by an old Dutch lady. He was always rather accident-prone and, as ever, had the luck never to suffer serious injury except towards the very end. However, he had enough of Holland and travelled on, slightly concussed, to Berlin. Still innocent, he took the first recommendation and booked into the Adlon Hotel, and only after consuming breakfast ('beginning with a delicious iced quarter of a cantaloupe melon') and admiring the palatial decor did it dawn on him that this might be all rather expensive. He rushed to the desk. It was, and he paid for the night and fled, with just enough left in his pocket to scrape home.

In London, his tenure on the Victoria Embankment would be marked by an almost excess of energy. He prowled in the early morning in the Caledonian Market, learning to spot bargains in antiques, occasionally succeeding where the vendor was either ignorant or careless. He even passed certain pieces on to a West End dealer at vastly improved prices, thus making a badly needed addition to his architectural fees. He developed quite an eye, though by no means a perfect one. He was eclectic in his acquisitions and would later fill Brondanw and Portmeirion with an intriguing welter of antiques, sometimes disparate objects, which somehow went together in his own chosen environment.

But he also tried two very odd pastimes, which I find it difficult to imagine in him. Even in my own youth I remember the newspaper advertisements of a chap by the name of Eugene Sandow, the Arnold Schwarzenegger of his day. Sandow was always pictured in a leopard-skin mini outfit, with muscles bulging: 'A body like mine in ten days or your money back'. The temptations for the normal weedy youth were enormous. Here we were, pectorals barely visible, biceps like elastic bands, and ten days would see us on the way to *real* manhood. Clough actually enrolled in Sandow's School, which I find hilarious. What is more easily imaginable is his quick disillusion and his precipitate departure, 'one of the Institute's gutless failures'.

More in his line, surely, was his attempt to become an accomplished ice-skater. Its graceful and elegant possibilities would satisfy the dancing man. But again, the sheer boredom of learning would set in and he would fail. Exercise as such was not for him, and indeed, he hardly needed it. Constitutionally he was not prone to fat, indeed would always be thin, tall, even gangling. But he moved well, strode rather than walked and at this crucial stage in his twenties on the Embankment, the two-hundred steps to his eyrie must have done wonders to keep him in trim.

Yet another very odd trait he confessed to at this time was a compulsion to trespass — albeit in a good cause, Architecture. Security and Big Brother were a good deal less evident then than now, when the merest breech of a fence round a vast estate can send alarm bells ringing. Not to put too fine a point on it, he was guilty of 'breaking and entering' certain properties that to him seemed abandoned and attracted his attention. Not that he broke anything, but the law is the law and it seems that by definition you cannot enter unless you first break something.

He had gone cycling in the King's Lynn area, no bad place for a collector of buildings. It was a fine Sunday and he wished to see Raynham Hall, an Inigo Jones house. He had no introduction, knew nothing of its owners, which is understandable, since he found it deserted and locked up. There wasn't a soul about, nobody to whom he might address his questions. But having gone so far, he was not easily deterred. He would not leave without first exploring. He hid his bicycle under a bush and climbed into the grounds. Approaching the house he noticed a basement window open. He was *in*.

He found the whole place in a state of restoration, with scaffolding and ladders in every room. This even furthered his cause, for he could climb up a ladder and sketch a cornice or a detail at close quarters. He was in his heaven, when suddenly he heard footsteps in the next room. He slid down the ladder (a lifelong habit) and by stealth kept just ahead of the patrolling guard. He was worried the guard might find his bicycle. How would he get back to base at King's Lynn? But he was safe. He kept one room ahead, found the basement window agape, left it as he had found it, dashed for his bicycle and was off! He had trespassed and got away with it, just. His usual luck! But the embarrassment of possible capture? The experience must have stayed with him over the years, because he recorded it some fifty years later with retrospective conscience. Yet it demonstrates the thoroughness of his researches and his sheer enthusiasm. He admired his compatriot Inigo Jones greatly and this was the sort of length he would go to to satisfy his needs.

This was not his only trespass by any means. Any house that particularly interested him would constitute a temptation. He actually confessed to 'breaking and entering' dozens of times, always with the same view in mind — to sketch elevations and details. There can't have been a better education for a young man keen to develop the architectural practice he had built already out of almost nothing. Despite the nineteenth century's overlay of industrial sprawl and the rather more straitened circumstances of certain of the landed gentry, there was still a great demand, both in building *ab initio* and in restoration, for the elegance of seventeenth and eighteenth century styles of building. Clough, by means both legal and illegal, was steadily gathering the right sort of detailed information he needed to complement his natural tastes.

On another trespass he found a beautiful old manor house, part seventeenth century, part Regency, absolutely abandoned, its lumber rooms full of past relics, a brass-buttoned old dress coat, a 'John Bull' top-hat still in its leather case, and old weaponry like blunderbusses. He felt something must be done to rescue this old gem, but found its owner was a drunk, who unfortunately just did not answer letters. This was particularly irksome, because Clough knew one of his numerous cousins was looking for just such a place in the country. To try to marry the two, Clough did his utmost, but to no avail. The owner's sole wish in life was to drink, and any approaches about his dilapidated house just drew a blank. It was all too sad to contemplate. He could only wait and hope it would not be too long before the dipsomaniac drank himself to death.

Many years later, it was taken up when the owner finally found his sober peace and his heirs were amenable. The family negotiated its purchase and knowing of Clough's interest in the place, engaged him to see to its restoration. Yet later, it reverted to the National Trust, so its future was assured, thanks largely to Clough's early interest and his engagement to restore it. All this earnest trespassing complemented Clough's practical work. It may seem an odd way to learn, but learn he did.

Odd, too, was the way his social life and his work went together. They were not the separate compartments that go for many people. Clough would attend this or that social function and somehow or other, he would be just the man somebody was looking for.

He always regarded 1912 as pivotal in this sense. From tentative commissions while he was training came the first large and important commission in his career, the completion of which he would always regard with affection and pride. 'The building remains', he wrote some sixty years later, 'to testify to my then architectural outlook and orientation. I have recently revisited this work and can recall all my bubbling excitement over every detail of what I still think a pretty good job.'

He was travelling back by train to London from a hunt ball in the West Country. He felt unwell (and contrary to the most ready assumption, it would not be from over-imbibing) and at Swindon Station he tottered out to see if a brandy at the Refreshment Room might help revive him: 'a remedy never sought before or since'. Creeping back to his compartment, he was hailed by a friend. One can imagine Clough in his present state, thinking 'For God's sake, just go away!' But no, that was not Clough's way. They talked. His friend informed him that a man in his compartment was travelling up to London to find an architect to build him a new house. An old castle ruin on the site was being demolished and — well — wouldn't it be a good idea if Clough came along to meet him?

And so it was that Clough landed the commission to build Llangoed Hall (or Castle) for Mr Archibald Christie. Designing it and supervising its construction stretched Clough's faculties to the limit. One senses that at the time he would have been grateful for greater depth and duration to his academic training in architecture, but since their lack was due entirely to his own impatience and claustrophobia, the actual execution of Llangoed could be regarded as his sort of special Diploma project, the consummation of his training, such as it was, and the extension of his horizons.

It was no mean task. Llangoed is in many ways quite a complex structure. Nor is it typical of the largely Palladian style of so much of his later work. The rather severe mullioned windows somehow echo Glasfryn. The central tower echoes Brondanw's. The whole place has a Tudor flavour, with a pleasing asymmetry about its roof-line. There is obvious enjoyment in the detailing, the railed balcony over the main door, the tall chimneys and the piers as you enter the courtyard. The stonework of the fabric must be among the last large-scale examples of that labour-intensive craft. Henceforth, to achieve a building of that scale and pretensions, there would have to be compromises or substitutes, like reconstituted stone or rendered and colour-washed surfaces.

The drawings for Llangoed Hall survive and faithful copies are now framed and hung in the first floor corridor. They are all signed as designed at Arundel House, where he had quickly developed that inimitable style of drawing and in particular of bold capital letters which are unmistakably his. He was an accomplished water-colourist.

Clough incorporated a surviving south-facing wing, including the panelled library dating from 1632, into the new building. The whole fabric in its extent, its placing and its detailing, exhibits the confidence and even maturity of a master designer, yet it was Clough's first commission of major importance. It demonstrates how deeply affected he had been by that early experience of Kirby Hall and its like, and how deeply he had absorbed it all. What is interesting is that the designing had been achieved in those cramped rooms in Arundel House.

The actual construction of Llangoed Hall took place in 1913 and 1914 until war interrupted proceedings. The gate piers at the entrance were added in 1919. The main south-west front is a broad E-shaped plan, with hip-roofed blocks in the angles. The two outer blocks are broad, with mullioned windows. The central tower is built of Gwespyr stone, a superb honey-coloured sandstone from North Wales that takes fine detail. The whole air of the place exudes a sort of confidence, it is such a happy blend of Tudor/Jacobean and modern touches. Both Clough and his contemporary Lutyens really were masters of accommodating tradition to modern needs and appearance in their design.

Interestingly enough, the later Clough is revealed in the Stable Court. It is light-hearted, with a turreted cottage on the left and a splendid pedimented cupola.

Llangoed Hall is a superb building, yet although it is less than a century old (excepting the old library wing), it has endured many vicissitudes. At one stage in the late 1960s and early 1970s, its then owner sought its demolition. It had become a derelict hulk, in danger of letting in the weather and gradually falling away as buildings can, however stoutly built. Thieves steal the lead flashing, sills decay and let in the rain and in no time vandals take over. Certainly the Hall was in a sorry state. It was already taking on the aspect of a ruin, like Kirby Hall, four hundred years its senior. Weeds choked the grounds and encroached on the fabric itself. The County Council at one stage even sanctioned its demolition. But a groundswell of protest, not least from Clough himself, saved it from an ignominious end. Of course, any owner after World War II would be embarrassed by the sheer upkeep of the fabric, not to mention finding a worthwhile use for such a large number of rooms. Yet there it was — Llangoed was undoubtedly a masterpiece of twentieth century architecture. Built at the end of *la belle époque* when confidence, wealth and Empire knew no bounds, the austerities of post World War II rendered many such places redundant. Only recognised national and truly historical treasures like Hardwick Hall and Knole could justify the expense of upkeep, and only then under the aegis of a body like the National Trust, with tourist and other income behind it. Llangoed at that time did not qualify for that sort of attention, and it may be that only Clough's almost fanatic championship saved it, for by 1970 Clough was a national figure commanding respect. Llangoed had been so crucial in his early career, so make-or-break, that he would always cherish it. However it was saved by Sir Bernard Ashley and it now flourishes as a hotel under his beneficent ownership.

The drawings of Llangoed demonstrate one precious faculty that developed early in Clough and which was unique — his draughtsmanship. Sir Osmond Williams owns an early garden design for Deudraeth castle by Clough and dated 1911, roughly contemporary with Llangoed. It is simple, direct, and is at the same time an attractive watercolour. The line is firm and decisive, accompanied by the strong capital letters. He may have baulked at university, at the architectural course and at his brief life as an electrical engineer, but clearly something must have been absorbed, principally at Oundle, I suspect, despite his professed boredom at school. For this is the work of a man confident of his abilities and with a certain background. Emphatically it is not the work of some untutored oaf. So one must take his frequent disclaimers to any formal education with a pinch of salt.

If posed with some problem, however small, by some client, he would sit down and draft a perspective solution on the spot. He could visualize a site *in absentia* and draw it out from memory, then incorporate additions and emendations without hesitation, all in that strong, confident line of his. Even the briefest sketch bears some interest. There are one or two later drafts for this or that at Portmeirion which are quite breathtaking in their audacity and sheer facility.

# World War I

By the year 1914 Clough could be said to be established as an architect, with enough work in hand. His future seemed assured. He had been cautious in his social life and had reached the mature age of thirty-one without any serious entanglement. Only Miss Strachey presented any serious threat to his closely guarded bachelor independence.

And yet, having at last broken through into his treasured vocation against all the odds, and having achieved a masterpiece so early in his career, he was quickly to set it all aside in what appeared to be almost caprice.

Was it his age? If Llangoed represented the culmination of his training, or rather his self-education, it had taken some ten years to achieve, from 1904, when he had enrolled and then quickly left the Architectural Association, to 1914. It had taken so long. Was there some crisis of confidence? It is difficult to imagine it in Clough. Was he chary of commitment to Miss Strachey? Again, hardly likely. Perhaps he felt that despite his career so far, he had not yet proved himself. We do not know and he does not discuss it in his *Architect Errant*. What came next, in fact, seemed so natural, so simply one with the fate of his entire generation of young men, that he would regard it as merely a fact of life, a necessary parenthesis shared with millions of others.

It was the beginning of the end of an era of unbridled empire, of world power, and of a sort of national innocence and self-belief that this state of international affairs could last forever. Britain's cavalry regiments were more or less up to strength, its naval forces patrolled the world unchallenged, protecting coaling stations for the nation's mercantile fleet. A career in architecture would appear to stretch ahead with contracts growing in number and stature.

When war broke out in August 1914, Clough was staying at Wroxall Abbey, for which he would later design gates to go with Wren's piers. The party proceeded despite the ominous signs of frantic diplomacy turning into war. Yet nothing seemed to harden into actuality. Transport rumbled, manoeuvres impended, newspapers fulminated, but then they always did.

So nobody dreamt of cancelling a large weekend party like that at Wroxall. Trains still ran, cabs were about as usual, what need to worry? With his architectural practice well on the way to firm establishment, there seemed no reason why Clough should not enjoy yet another party in the country.

The guests assembled, and all went swimmingly until Sunday,

when things seemed rather *too* ominous for further levity. The guests dispersed suddenly. Clough was offered a lift by car back to London. His driver was a Yeomanry officer and on the way they called at the officer's depot in Buckinghamshire where they saw the mobilisation and general mustering of men and mounts. The initial engagements with the enemy might involve a bit of infantry skirmishing, and a cavalry charge or two would soon see things tidied up.

Clough was already thirty-two. Amid general speculation and the bustle of mobilisation, his sense of duty impelled him towards the recruiting office, only to be dismissed as too old. That proved no deterrent. Walking towards the Horse Guards, he met one of the Asquiths and together they presented themselves for enlistment in the Household Cavalry, just like that. It promised riding rather than foot-slogging, and yet more of Clough's innumerable cousins were already posted in senior ranks. Organised chaos was always a favourite epithet among the ranks in the Army, and the Household Cavalry proved no exception. Clough and Asquith could not be sure whether they had been enrolled.

It is surprising that a man as single-minded as Clough should be so ready to throw away all and try so precipitately to enlist. Yet in the few short weeks in July and August of 1914, war fever so gripped the nation that it swept all before it. Mobilisation would be quiet if chaotic. The Army would be across the Channel in no time, protected by the Royal Navy, and the whole affair, it was said, would be over by Christmas. Who could question it? What man could resist the call? Indeed, men were worried it might be all over before they could play their part. Who could imagine the future stalemate, the Battle of Loos, the Somme, the holocausts of Ypres and Paschendaele? As usual, the general view was that things would be somewhat like the most recent war — cavalry charges across the veldt against the Boers in South Africa.

Clough was no exception. Unconvinced that the Horse Guards had enrolled him, he bluffed his way into the War Office with an introduction of sorts and was heard out. The War Office promised to see what could be done.

He opted for the Ninth Lancers, once again because of family connections. Within a month he had been gazetted to what he described as 'that elegant and gallant regiment'. Elegance would always move him, whether it be a ballroom, a pediment or a regiment of cavalry.

He had been 'gazetted' but not yet actually called to arms. In his impatience he found himself assigned to Kitchener's Army

Infantry Battalion with the rank of Lieutenant, when the call came
to the Lancers. Confusion? What to do? Where was he? Rumours
that the Ninth Lancers might become simply a remount depot
decided him to stay on his feet in the Infantry, especially since he
was not, after all, a particularly horsy man. Yet again his life
seemed to be run more by chance than choice.

One day he travelled on the train to lunch with the Stracheys,
for the liaison with Amabel was well advanced by now. As usual,
there was company in the compartment and inevitably the
conversation turned to war. His interlocutor was an adjutant in
the Imperial Light Horse. He advised Clough, if he was still
undecided, to turn up at a parade of the outfit at Hyde Park the
following Sunday and to join them as a full lieutenant.

Could it be all that easy? Who was this man in mufti handing out
commissions to a pukka regiment? But upon checking, the adjutant
proved to be pukka too, and Clough was almost there, a cavalry
officer ready for action in his newly acquired general service uniform.
Once again, he was swung back and forth like a shuttlecock. General
Bindon Blood (surely straight out of Kipling) made a speech in
Surrey, informing them that Kitchener required no more fancy
cavalry outfits etc, etc, but if they cared to disband themselves and
become infantry, they could stay together, in very much the same
spirit as the Pals Regiments that were mustering all over the country.

So, having joined a cavalry regiment which promptly disbanded
itself as cavalry and dismounted, so to speak, to become another
foot regiment, Clough found himself in Kitchener's infantry army
after all.

In fact, the Imperial Light Horse mutated overnight into yet
another battalion of the Royal Fusiliers in Kitchener's Army.
Clough was now a properly enlisted soldier, leaving uncompleted
Llangoed Hall, his most important building project to date, but,
even more important to him, leaving behind that important liaison
with Miss Strachey. Luck would have it, of course, that his
particular section of Kitchener's Army would be stationed near
the Stracheys, and come Christmas, when the war was supposed
to have been over, he and Amabel became engaged. The Strachey
home had been transformed into an Army hospital and Amabel
into a Red Cross nurse. She was a girl with views, and informed
Clough that when they married, she would continue with her
career as a writer, which suited Clough well enough, since he
professed to have no idea what to do with a 'full time wife'. Once
again he was a shuttlecock, since his leave and his beloved's
seemed never to coincide.

He mustered at a camp in Surrey, under canvas, with the usual mud and confusion; no uniforms, and for arms, only a few swords among the officers. In short, 'organised chaos' again. Their Commanding Officer, moreover, was a member of Parliament, who much preferred the comforts of London and was always absent.

Clough was never one for inaction, and his thoughts turned soon to news that The Welsh Guards had formed. He applied, was accepted, and joined them at Sandown Racecourse, and by good luck, even nearer to the Strachey household.

He had not entirely forgotten his architectural practice, however, for in a letter from Sandown dated 18 May 1915, he thanked John Bonnor (1876-1917, architect and model-maker among other things) for making a model of a cottage for him.

So far, it had been all rather fun, excepting the general tedium of camp life. Clough's prospective father-in-law was an ardent 'defence' man, and had organised his own 'Dads Army', the Surrey Guards, all mounted, and clad in bottle-green uniforms. Clough was persuaded to assess their performance in a night field exercise. After a perfect night's ride, a bath and breakfast at Newlands, he drove back sharply to Wellington Barracks just in time to take up his duties as weekend picket officer. His first duty was to parade the Welsh Guards and march them to chapel.

Perhaps he had overdone things on the night exercise, for in chapel, the next thing he knew was being awakened by the clatter of his sword against the wooden pew. He had dropped off to sleep, keeled over and worst of all, had done this in front of five old Generals who, apoplectic, trundled off at once to the Adjutant demanding the severest punishment for the miscreant. As it turned out, the punishment was no more than four extra weekend picket duties, mild by any standards, but extremely irksome to a young officer with a special interest in nearby Newlands. He would have some explaining to do if the liason was not to suffer. The Army, with its keen phraseology, has a special formula for a soldier who may faint on parade (thus disobeying orders) — he 'may faint in anticipation of sanction', but apparently this did not extend to dropping off to sleep in chapel. It was all so tiresome for Clough that he always remembered it, and at the time he debated in his mind whether or not to accept the alternative indignity of flogging. He accepted the four lost weekends with an ill grace.

On the other hand, the Army is quick to forgive. Clough formally sought permission to marry, which was granted, and was promptly asked what he would like as a wedding present from his fellow officers — a silver salver, suitably engraved perhaps, a silver teapot, what? Clough astounded them by asking for 'a ruin'. In other words, given the offer, he decided to 'collect' another building, albeit a modern ruin, built from funds collected by his fellow officers to commemorate his marriage to Amabel Strachey. And that is why, on a knoll behind Brondanw, there is a 'ruin' adding a certain cachet to the immediate environs of an already ancient house.

The marriage ceremony was planned to be in secret. It was to be held at the unearthly hour of 8 a.m. in the little chapel of St Martha's on the Pilgrims' Way above Merrow in Surrey. The early hour was chosen for two reasons: first to escape attention, second to leave enough time to travel the same day back to Wales and Brondanw. On the first score, the happy couple were proved innocents, for even the press was there. There had been a rumour that the marriage was actually an elopement, which could not be further from the truth, since Amabel's parents and brother John (a future Chancellor) and Clough's three serving brothers were all present.

The ceremony over, and the tiny porch and a guard of honour safely negotiated on the way out, there would be a quick change into travelling clothes and off at once on the journey to Meirion-nydd. I believe most partners in a long marriage as the years pass develop slightly different memories of the early days. While Clough makes no mention of the long train journey, Amabel gives a clear and touching picture of two young things setting out into the unknown:

> We caught the train, and settled down — in a first class carriage for once — and soon realized that, among all our manifold more serious and romantic feelings, hunger was now insistent. But again the absurd had not done with us. There was a luncheon car on the train, but through numerous confusions no one had booked places for us. There were war shortages and it was a full train. So now? In a suitcase of mine that wasn't in the distant guard's van but had mercifully come with us into the carriage, there turned out to be lurking an unlikely thing — a small plum cake in a box, also a small tin of potted meat and, less unlikely, a button-hook.
>
> Somehow Clough opened the tin and, taking turns with the button-hook, we scraped out and ate every scrap of the potted meat and then finished up the cake to the last crumb. Being young and slightly delirious with happiness, we found ourselves delighted with this curious gastronomic combination. I felt that for me, as a young housekeeper,

an unbeatable and satisfactory standard of unlikely meals
had been promptly set.
(*All Stracheys are Cousins*)

There was a warm welcome awaiting them at Brondanw. The
Lodge arch was decorated with a huge wreath with the legend
'Welcome to Lt Clough Williams-Ellis and his grateful bride'. I
never learned what Amabel made of the 'grateful', but perhaps it
was explained away as meant for 'graceful'. Speeches followed in
Welsh, with Clough responding in English.

In this way Amabel was introduced to Brondanw. This quin-
tessential English girl from Surrey, a bit of a blue-stocking by
nature, must have found it all very strange. There may be doubts
sometimes these days, with universal transportation and blurring
of boundaries of districts and class, but in those days Meirionnydd
was another country. Welsh was the first language (and still is),
and despite the fulminations of educationalists like Matthew
Arnold ('if a Welshman has anything of importance to say, he
must say it in English') English was a foreign tongue, spoken with
some difficulty by many. I know of only one record of Amabel's
reaction to her introduction to Meirionnydd, but there is no doubt
she came to be very much part of its life and spent her remaining
seventy years at Brondanw as its faithful chatelaine. Yet I can't
help feeling that that first acquaintance must have come as rather
a culture shock. To a young woman reared in the warmth, comfort
and privilege of life in Surrey, Meirionnydd and its people may
have appeared like a benighted peasantry. Yet gradually she would
learn to respect this Welsh-speaking community. Once, when
asked how she liked country life, she replied: 'Country life would
be quite unendurable were it not for its animosities'.

However, in *All Stracheys are Cousins*, she does record her
ultimate gratitude to her adopted country: 'living in Wales is better
than living in most places' — 'most' but not *all* places. There must
always have been a place in her heart for Newlands Corner, for a
woman of such intelligence had enjoyed that mix of illustrious
visitors and had learned very early to distinguish the truly life-
enhancing from the 'Spectatorial'. There is no doubt, too, that
the London years had been rich in that diversity that only life in
a capital city can afford.

For the honeymooners, the fortnight's leave would prove
desperately short. Together they set about tree planting, one of
the greatest demonstrations of faith in the future, for those 1915
saplings would become part of the avenue leading up to the tower.

On the second day a telegram arrived recalling Clough to Battalion
Headquarters. The First Battalion of the Welsh Guards in Northern
France had suffered heavy casualties at the battle of Loos.
Reinforcements were desperately needed. At once, the fortnight
was reduced to four days and much of that was taken up with
travelling.

With unusual dispatch, Clough found himself in the front line
at the Hohenzollern Redoubt. If the Army in general was a matter
of 'organised chaos', this was confusion worse confounded. The
front line was difficult to define or even to find, and the Germans
seemed to occupy most of the ground. Each side flung bombs at
the other, and likewise spent most of the time dodging them.
Clough's company commander went sick so he had to take
command.

It was a battle of attrition, a complete stalemate, but none the
less highly dangerous for all ranks. A cross rather than Blighty
seemed the more likely end for most. Each side was exhausted
after the Loos battle. They seemed to have fought one another to
a standstill and there was no movement. There are soldiers who
serve with complete unquestioning dedication, whose life is ful-
filled by service. The situation on the Western Front, however,
sometimes aroused critical comments and especially among writers
like Siegfried Sassoon, Robert Graves, Wilfred Owen, David
Jones, and Ford Madox Ford, or painters like Paul Nash and
C.W.R. Nevinson, who would later record their feelings about it.

The sheer horror of it all is quite explicit in their art, and Clough,
torn away from the peace of Brondanw, from his wife and his
work, was no exception. 'I seem all through,' he wrote later, 'to
have contrived to take a curiously detached view of the whole war
so far as my part in it went and — in my own view — to have
disclaimed responsibility for it or its conduct or its conclusion,
and generally to have reserved the right to remain fatalistically
critical.'

He would do his duty, was keenly aware that he owed at least
that to his comrades first, and then to his country. But he was not
one to endure with ease the inevitable boredom and appalling
absence of creativity. 'I have known no tedium so utterly blistering
as that of routine trench warfare,' he wrote. He devised all sorts
of ways to relieve the mind-numbing boredom. He wrote home
for his watercolours and made sketches of trench and billet life,
and such architecture as was left standing in the appalling satura-
tion shelling of the surrounding countryside. Dreaming, against
all the odds, of a life ahead at Brondanw, he found a Welsh-speaking

ex-schoolmaster among the ranks to give him lessons in the old but very much living tongue. And as ever, when at all free, he would go off exploring. On one occasion he borrowed a horse and explored the little Flemish town of Casell. He drew its windmills and its First Empire chateau, then hitched back by lorry and car and forgot all about the poor nag. It would not be the first time an artist in his absorption forgot to return a mount to its rightful owner, for a century earlier the painter Turner had borrowed a horse from a friend in Bristol and after an extensive sketching tour throughout Wales (passing by Brondanw) had failed to return the overworked beast. Clough's mount was recovered ultimately, and in a creative respite he wrote two articles, later published, about his adventures.

He would steal any time he could to explore, and even the Prince of Wales, attached to the Guards Division Headquarters, lent him a horse. Clough wrote reviews of books, sent to him by his father-in-law, for *The Spectator*. He sketched plans for houses, anything to relieve the monotony of trench life and to placate the constant need to create, plan, to 'think positive'. He was the consummate optimist in all things. He rode his luck with an enlightened self-interest. Late in the war he heard the good news that Amabel had borne a daughter, named Susan.

His activities and escapades did not go unnoticed. Divisional Headquarters took note. He was taken off routine trench duties and set to surveying and sketching enemy positions from any vantage point he could find. He scrambled up trees, occasionally ascended in a captive balloon; anything to get a panoramic view of enemy lines. Once, in a basket suspended beneath the balloon, he was shot at. As things became too hot for comfort, Clough telephoned to ground crew to haul him down. No response. It began to be so dangerous that Clough climbed to the edge of the basket ready to parachute, when he felt the tug of the cable and was brought safely to earth. The officer-in-charge commended him — 'Jolly good show, sticking it out like that!'. But it was not quite like that. An N.C.O. turned up quickly to report that the reason Clough got no response to his telephone call must have been because the telephone cable had been severed by enemy fire.

Clough made no great claims about his activities at the front. Men may talk of Army life as a joke but not of war itself, and he was no exception. Despite his commission, his own account of service sounds more like the Good Soldier Schweik. Naturally he would wangle any means to explore and literally widen his horizons. He approached Lord Cavan to allow him to survey the German

lines by aeroplane and at once received permission — anything to
sharpen intelligence. He went to the nearby airfield, eased himself
with some difficulty into the tiny cockpit (no easy task given the
length of his legs), and was handed a Lewis gun. Clough had never
handled a Lewis gun and asked what he was supposed to do with
it. One can imagine the answer. Fortunately, as they patrolled the
sky between the lines, no German plane challenged them, so the
Lewis gun lay idle by his knee as Clough sketched away. Clough
remarked to his pilot on landing back at the airfield that he had
not realized one got so bumped about in flight. The pilot acidly
retorted that one was bound to get bumped on a day like that, for
both German and Allied air forces were grounded because of
rough weather, and only that direct order from Lord Cavan had
induced him to fly. Clough did speculate later on how he would
have coped had an enemy plane turned up. As it was, his work of
observing from the plane was commended by the top brass, and
it most certainly rescued him from the blistering tedium of trench
life.

   This new aspect of officially sponsored exploring and reconnaissance did bring a few perks: billets at Brigade Headquarters, and
greater opportunity to rove the countryside, where he sketched
the moated Chateau Esquilbec. Clough was a canny twister of
Army regulations to his own advantage. In bomb-damaged Ypres
(still to suffer its complete devastation) he began to collect various
architectural items and wrought-iron work and store them in
Headquarters cellar. When he was reminded that this amounted
to looting, Clough replied that it was salvage, which was officially
encouraged. In the Second World War, the word 'commandeer'
mutated into 'borrow' or 'liberate' in much the same way.

   From all this exploring and reconnaissance Clough later com-
piled his first written work *Reconnography* (1918). He was very
keen that all this awareness of landscape and its features, and
above all the methods of remembering and recording them should
be codified and made into a sort of textbook. He visualised it as
the sort of things Boy Scouts would enjoy and use. He was
enterprising enough to write to the Chief Scout Robert Baden-
Powell for an Introduction. He submitted the manuscript to the
Pelman Institute, which specialised in this sort of memory exercise,
and they accepted at once, offering a £100 fee, and in no time
proofs came back. He corrected them but soon found himself
hauled before a tribunal to explain himself. The censor had
noticed the landscape features in his maps for the book, and
thought them some sort of code for reality in the trenches.

Obviously Clough's notions of landscape and memorising were too reminiscent of actual trench dispositions. When Clough explained that one feature named 'Susan Wood' was not the cover for some real feature, but rather a sort of celebration of the birth of his firstborn, whom he had not yet seen, the authorities accepted his case and the book was finally published, his first of many, and perhaps his least successful.

At Brigade Headquarters he was ordered to collate and duplicate all this intelligence for the benefit of neighbouring units in the line. This meant a certain amount of desk work. During the Battle of the Somme when morale was low and suspicion of G.H.Q. high, he often drew tail-pieces to the more bizarre communications from G.H.Q. and on one occasion when looking through a glass partition he saw the back of the General's neck go purple with rage at one of his more irreverent drawings. He was hauled in, practically hung, drawn and quartered, and dismissed. Only Clough could have got away with it, and this generally agnostic, irreverent view of anything pompous and mandarin was characteristic throughout life, part of his self-styled 'philistinism'. However, he remained in post, and it was the General who was moved, much to Clough's relief.

Life was so awful for all the troops on the Western Front that many broke down and were ill. Clough confessed to feeling constantly impending illness and only infrequent leave made the whole thing barely endurable. It was just as difficult on the home front. There is a touching letter from Clough's father-in-law St Loe Strachey, to his old friend Theodore Roosevelt, President of the United States:

> My daughter's husband went to the front last Wednesday ... I am glad to say that my daughter has a really stout heart and though she is only twenty-one and has been married a bare three months, she is facing the music splendidly. I was with her at the station to see her husband and a small group of officers off and I was really proud of her. Of course she did not break down.

There would always be a day or two in London either end of leave and Clough kept alight the flame of his ideas of conservation. If Britain was to be 'a land fit for heroes to live in', then he would express forcibly his views on that. He met up with, and kept in correspondence with his friend and mentor Sir Lawrence Weaver. Clough's view of Britain at the time was pretty jaundiced, as might be expected, for much of the country was despoiled, some of it beyond redemption it seemed, by nineteenth century industrial expansion. In a *Manchester Guardian* article, he regarded Britain in its use of land as a 'frump and a slattern'. He would fight to the end, but alas, things have not changed all that much.

So, even in the trenches, Clough was already fighting the good fight, writing to newspapers and magazines, hectoring those in power, ever ready to exploit a connection, and corresponding with people like Weaver. Sometimes they would meet and conduct what amounted to seminars on the subject, and as a result of one of these round tables Clough published in the *Manchester Guardian* article:

> Anyone who cares for England must be interested in national planning, the provision of a comprehensive co-ordinated and compulsory development and conservation scheme for the country as a whole, urban and rural, public and private. The economic case for an orderly and far-sightedly man-aged national estate is so overwhelming that one really need not speak of national pride or the need for beauty.

From one such leave, he was recalled prematurely. He could only fume, especially since the reason was not the exigence of military operations at the Front, but merely the completion of a G.H.Q. course. He was so incensed that he attributed a bad bout of influenza to the protestation of the unconscious. He used the period of convalescence to explore the region of St Omer in a car cheekily borrowed (or 'liberated').

Sometimes there would be long spells without leave, which is particularly galling for a newly married couple. On one occasion, the authorities, out of compassion for those who had been deprived of leave over a long period, granted Clough a special four-day Paris leave, allowing two days and three nights in the city. Clough had sufficient notice to advise Amabel to arrange leave for herself from her VAD duties and come over to Paris to join him in good time at an agreed hotel. Clough endured the rickety train journey from the front to civilisation in Paris in high spirits, and raced to the hotel to meet Amabel. Alas there was no sign of her, nor had the *patron* any news for him. Clough's French was practically nil, in contrast to Amabel, who had fluent French. But he managed to find out about train arrivals from all the Channel ports. He spent two days shuttling back and forth from station to station, back and forth, meeting every train from the Channel. But there was no sign of Amabel. He was sick with anxiety and frustration. Eventually he was forced to return to the Front in a state of deepening gloom. Whatever could have happened?

When finally he received a letter of explanation from Amabel, the reason seemed sensible enough, if perhaps a little too cautious. A young husband locked away in trench warfare would not have been impressed by either sense or caution. Apparently the authorities were so concerned about U-boat activity in the Channel that non-military personnel were forbidden to embark. It was small consolation to Clough, and to Amabel, but at least she knew the explanation. *Her* agony must have lain in her inability to get the news to him in time and thus spare him the agony of waiting and waiting.

He became interested in a recent innovation he had heard about, tanks, and one day he walked, unannounced, to see Sir Hugh Elles, the officer commanding the new tank outfit. There was an element in Clough, planted early in his childhood and his brief electrical engineering days, which enjoyed the act of invention and he was always ready to design some new dodge or gadget that involved a bit of lateral thinking. The tank struck him as the device of future military ground warfare, so it aroused his curiosity.

It did not take him long to be persuaded that he must join this new arm in some capacity or other and in due course he wangled a transfer to Third Tank Brigade, just before the Battle of Arras. His immediate superior in tank reconnaissance had the urgent name of Major 'Boots' Hotblack.

That was Clough's last posting in a chequered Army career. It was all an interim existence at the best of times, which he would never grace with the name of 'life'. Hotblack was severely wounded in one skirmish and Clough had to take over command. Thus he ended the war as a Staff Officer, with access to strings to pull where it mattered, for instance in the matter of demobilisation once hostilities ceased, if not before. The tanks swept on from the crucial second Battle of Cambrai to ultimate victory. In recognition of his courage and gallantry in tank warfare, Clough was awarded the Military Cross. He had fully earned it, but by now he had only one thing on his mind — to get back to wife, child, home and work as quickly as possibly.

Never one for holding back, he was keenly aware he could be retained for some Army of Occupation, so he began lobbying for release at once. His writings on Intelligence for the Army had convinced his superiors that here they had the author of a history of the newly formed Tank Corps. He had fought in all its battles, so why not let him go to get on with it? Lawrence Weaver also sought his services to advise on architecture at the Ministry of Agriculture, to build homes fit for the returning heroes.

Yet again, a sharp bit of lateral thinking was needed. Since his wife was a professional writer, Clough pleaded, would he not be better placed to write this history at home under her guidance? Two weeks after the Armistice he was back at home for good.

He was as good as his word, and Amabel no less, despite the fact that she was pregnant with their second child. The book involved a race with time, with the impending birth of Charlotte. The minute the proofs had been read and dispatched she was born. It was published in *Country Life*, with the proceeds earmarked for the Tanks Corps Benevolent Fund. The book was well received and became the standard reference work. In summing up the authors wrote: 'a superior force of Tanks can always tip the scales of the military balance of power'. Alas, British governments between the wars took no heed and at the outbreak of war only twenty years after the Armistice, the German Army was much better equipped in tanks, and even at the end of that Second War.

The book was topical enough to be serialised in the *Daily Telegraph*. When finally at peace in his beloved Meirionnydd, Clough came to reflect on the war, and in many ways his conclusions were much the same as those of other disillusioned souls like Siegfried Sassoon and Wilfred Owen. Clough's ultimate pacifism, if that is not too strong a word for his position, was built on memory of the colossal damage involved in modern war. War by definition is destructive, and victims of, say, the Thirty Years' War would have agreed. But it was the sheer scale of modern war, the efficiency of modern weaponry in its capacity to pulverise all before it, all the waste of human beings and their resources, all this appalled Clough; 'the fabulous destruction of life, wealth and beauty'. He was by no means alone, of course, but his particular conviction about the environment was further reinforced by his war experience.

'I was confirmed in my original conviction,' he later wrote in *Architect Errant*, 'that war is the most disastrous madness for all concerned, and my abhorrence of it inevitably led me to take an interest and even some small part in politics. Incidentally it left me greatly questioning much that in the old days I had innocently accepted as right, or at any rate inevitable.'

# Between Two Wars

Clough's disillusion was not easily assuaged in the peace that followed. The colossal individual and communal effort so evident in Britain during the war itself could surely be sustained in an almighty initiative in post-war reconstruction: plans for ex-servicemen's small-holdings, model settlements, new housing and even the beginnings of some sort of welfare state.

Whatever patriotic zeal and self-sacrifice had impelled the British war effort, the ensuing peace would soon see the return of the old enemies: greed, corruption, weak government, lack of central will. After three months as a civil servant under Weaver, Clough resigned, preferring the freedom and insecurity of private practice. His brief to design homes for the returning heroes proved altogether illusory and he was not the most patient of men. It is difficult to imagine him in a secure post for long, with an assured salary, security of tenure, paid holiday leave, sick leave and a pension at the end of it all.

Yet freedom was no easy option. Llangoed Hall was to be completed, so there was work in the office. In the event, he soon found commissions but the volatility of the market, the rise in the cost of building materials, and the inconsistencies of building legislation all meant constant headaches. Fixed price contracts were almost impossible to agree with contractors. Yet the architect is in overall charge of a contract, he or she is ultimately responsible, and Clough was well aware of all this when he resigned.

He refused to let it cramp his style. When it came to a work base, he and Amabel chose a stucco-fronted house in South Eaton Place, in which they could live 'over the shop'. For its decor, Clough had been very much impressed by the stage design and broadsheets of Claude Lovat Fraser, full of subtle colour, bright and cheerful. Lovat Fraser was the epitome of of Twenties taste, with his posters for the Underground, book jackets and illustrations and stage design. *Vogue, Country Life*, and later the *Radio Times*, all sought his work, which infiltrated into fashion design, textiles and interior design. He was the graphic part of what became known in retrospect as Art Deco. Clough took note, approved of the gaiety and uninhibited use of colour. The office and home must have been such sweet relief after the squalor of the four years of war. With the birth of Christopher in 1921, Clough and Amabel now had three children, and he spared no thought or ingenuity in fitting up the place to the highest specification, from ground floor offices to a balconied nursery and pillared roof garden.

The practice flourished. Here Clough could widen his horizons and, with luck and good connections, could exercise his influence in contributing to the reconstruction of a New Britain, and to town and country planning. For him it was no mere politician's slogan, something to gloss over the painful inertia of government. National planning was virtually a new movement. Clough was in constant touch with what he called his 'seven knights errant' of Planning and Amenity: Sir Patrick Geddes, Sir Raymond Irwin, Sir Charles Reilly, Sir Guy Dauber, Sir Lawrence Weaver, Sir Patrick Abercrombie and Sir Herbert Griffin. He continued his writings and publications, became an active and prominent member of the new Council for the Preservation of Rural England, but after the virtual collapse of response through municipal and governmental inertia, he tended more and more towards direct action and to see that words alone would not achieve reconstruction.

Throughout the 1920s Clough, now Chairman of the Design and Industries Association, would use all his powers of persuasion, and would extend the parameters of the association to include Architecture. His message was clear. It was little use monitoring Industrial and Craft design if the resulting objects were to be housed in ill-designed buildings.

It amounted to missionary work in the wilderness. The lethargy of local government, the entrenchment of respective political parties and the general inclination of the British to let things be, all had to be faced head on. Representatives of the Association would travel to a town, say, Oxford, Carlisle or St Alban's, and would photograph environmental monstrosities, of which there was no shortage, to demonstrate the residual awfulness of so much past British urban development. The town fathers would then be confronted with the evidence, and depending on the relative hard nose of the local great and the good, it might make an impression — or it might not.

Clough had been inured to wars of attrition and this would be a hard fought and continuing one. Regardless of the degree of the monstrosity or the practicality of the proposed solution, the most immediate response would be 'Can't afford it'. The fight continues to the present and if it were not for the zeal and enthusiasm of old warriors like Clough, I have little doubt our environment would soon decline again into the thoughtless and unfeeling squalor of so much of the nineteenth century townscape.

Clough would use any means to convey the message. He had been used to collating intelligence in the Army. Now he would do likewise in this war against ugly and thoughtless development. So he wrote the text of the D.I.A. publications as they went out to local authorities, not without a characteristic note of humour and, especially, rude captions under the more appalling atrocities. No doubt he ruffled a few municipal feathers, but that would be the least of his worries, given his nature. Yet the message often got through, sometimes as late as the Second World War and the New Town movement. Occasionally local zeal would be misplaced, creating even worse monstrosities, as in Newcastle-on-Tyne in the Poulson/Smith era in the Sixties.

But the countryside, if anything, concerned Clough even more, for despite the smart address of his London office, and his easy access to society there, he was basically a countryman, born and bred in Northamptonshire and Caernarfonshire, and deeply attached to his patrimony at Brondanw.

It was not simply defending one's country from an external foe that concerned Clough. It was a matter of having a country really worth defending. His book, *England and the Octopus* begins poignantly: 'I dedicate this book to the beauty of my country, natural and other, in gratitude and grief. This grief is for all the destruction of lovely buildings and for the spoiling by war of beautiful places almost throughout the world'. He goes on to list a few of the treasures that have suffered the hammer blow of modern shelling and bombing: 'the [loss of the] pastel tinted walls and bubble domes of some provincial Kremlin would leave Russia that much poorer, whilst some gilt and fretted temple in Mandalay would be pounded to dust. Next, a mellow little Tuscan town of touching beauty would be rent and crumbled, or a great Baroque church, a Touraine cathedral, some fortified Norman farm, a Dutch Town Hall, or a mediaeval quarter of some famous old German city . . .'.

A few have levelled criticism at Clough, that his first thought should always be buildings and not people, and it is noticeable that in the above litany of destruction he does not mention the innocent civilians (now known as 'collateral damage') who perished in the process. But it was his persistent thought, that people were not living their lives to full potential if they were denied the rightful heritage of a decent and beautiful environment. If he had a single crusade in life, it was to provide, or design, or advise or write about the proper environment in which people might live, and to deplore its absence.

The war had represented the most appalling hiatus in his life and work, and its lessons, if any, would never leave him. It was not that he came to recall the war in some form of art like David Jones or Siegfried Sassoon, but rather the gap, the break in progress, the waste of time, in reaching the new world of a restored and reformed environment for which he hoped. Still, he would see a certain amount of progress. People's indifference to environment would always irritate him, but he was pleased to see the foundation of civic societies here and there, eager to eradicate the more unsightly advertisement hoardings and dumps, to plant trees and generally to take note of the D.I.A.'s criticisms.

Then, out of the blue, and perhaps as a result of this higher profile he had adopted in order to fight the good fight, he received one of the major commissions of his career in 1923. Stowe and its estate is one of the eighteenth century's great masterpieces. Once the residence of the Dukes of Buckingham, the house and its environs had become empty and it was proposed to turn it into a public school. Clough was delighted and honoured, for Stowe represented exactly what he believed: that not only building, but also its context mattered in adding quality to life. Follies, grottoes, temples and monuments, designed by distinguished names like Vanburgh and William Kent, were scattered throughout the grounds, each rich in architectural detail. There was a monument to Congreve crowned by a monkey, and the grounds had been laid out by Capability Brown.

There had been a public announcement of the sale of Stowe, and St Loe Strachey asked Clough to contribute to *The Spectator* an article about its place in British architectural history and its possible future.

Clough went to Stowe and explored it in a state of exaltation, for here was all he cherished: enlightened patronage of architects, artists, landscapists and gardeners to a single end. Of course, the article was read by those intimately concerned with Stowe's fate, and soon a Reverend Percy Warrington was calling on him. Clough later described him as 'reminiscent of Chesterton's Father Brown, but entirely lacking his touching humility'. Nevertheless, Clough learned that Warrington was the driving financial force behind a decision to adapt Stowe as a public school, the latest in a whole chain of schools he was in the process of establishing. Clough's article had interested him, and though the Board of Governors was already appointed and in place, he had no doubt they would accept his proposal that the writer of the article should be the architect of whatever alterations and additions might be deemed necessary to make Stowe suitable for its new purpose.

The fabric of the great house and its four hundred rooms was intact but not its services — no water, no drains, no heating system, no schedule of maintenance. It would prove a vast enterprise to adapt all this to the twentieth century requirements of a public school. It would take years of work all told, though the initial phase to have all ready for the first intake of two hundred boys was up to schedule. Examining drawings for Stowe, it is evident that Clough's office was working overtime and over several years. One can detect the different hands at work, but ultimately the master's overall control is evident. There were additions to plan: two classroom blocks, laboratories, a sanatorium, a boarding house, a gymnasium, squash courts and all the facilities that a school needs and which differed from the residence that had been Stowe's function formerly.

J.F. Roxburgh, the newly appointed headmaster (who had been persuaded by Clough to apply for the post in the first place) was a staunch ally and support, though the Reverend Warrington proved rather a slippery character, especially on finance. This is Clough's recorded opinion, so one must take it with a pinch of salt, for Clough and financial constraint never mixed easily on a project. From time to time on the conversion, funds would run low. Certain things were lost. The great ornamental lions from the south terrace were sold off at auction. Some fine bronze urns had to go. Clough employed a sculptor, John Bickerdyke, to model in concrete some substitute lions to adorn the plinths vacated by the originals. One precious figure of Freya, the Scandinavian goddess of love, was purchased by Clough and now stands below Dolphin at Portmeirion.

In his pursuit of environmental goals, Clough was prone to quite quixotic deals. The Stowe governors were so strapped for cash that they had to realise further assets. They proposed that the Grand Avenue, a mile and a half long in a straight line stretching from the triumphal arch looking towards the house across the lake to the twin lodges at the far end, must be put up for auction. Clough's fervid protest at this proposed desecration and philistinism fell on deaf ears. Were they not aware of what they were proposing? But funds had truly run out, a point Clough simply could not accept as a reason for selling off the avenue. Funds *must* be found somewhere, they replied, or nothing could proceed. Clough was horrified that the sale might lead to ribbon development right across this precious site, and in days before there were planning restrictions or any thought of 'heritage', it could well have happened. So he foolishly attended the auction, determined to sabotage this proposal. He eventually had to bid himself to ward off the land-dealers, and found himself the embarrassed mortgagee owner of the avenue, with no use for it but to leave it well alone.

Of course, it was a millstone, however intact and beautiful, and he soon had to plead for some interested benefactor to take it off his hands at a loss. Eventually it was taken on by Old Etonians in an act of generosity to this new member of the public school system.

Clough's work at Stowe does not meet with universal approval. The artist John Piper thought Stowe 'rather wrecked' by Clough's twentieth century additions. I believe this to be an extreme view from an artist worthy of the greatest respect on environmental matters. I think A.R. Powys, in *The Architect's Journal* of April 28th 1926, puts it more fairly and objectively: '. . . it is in these circumstances [finance] almost inevitable that the casual visitor will remark the change in scale of the new buildings, and may condemn without thought or belittle with superficial knowledge, the really sound effort that Mr Williams-Ellis has made to meet the requirements of his clients. The architect, ruled by these conditions, has designed the new buildings so that any idea that they were intended to compete in grandeur with the old house may not ever be presumed. Where he has added to the house or altered it he has done so as an artist and as a straightforward builder.'

It is certainly a daunting project for any architect to add to an existing eighteenth century fabric in the twentieth century. To match the original labour-intensive work is impossible, and any dilution in design or execution is bound to appear to fall short of the original. The same has been said by some of the recent Venturi addition to the National Gallery, regardless of the retreat from what Prince Charles condemned as 'a carbuncle on the face of a well-loved friend'. There may be, however, aesthetic reservations about Clough's work at Stowe, that there is a lightness of touch about it that does not accord well with the sheer weight of the incumbent High Baroque.

The grounds of Stowe are now open to the public (with the usual and understandable restrictions) under the care of the National Trust. A first sight of the noble pile of Stowe reveals the extent of the task facing Clough and his patrons. Stowe is no less than a palace, in appropriate scale and High Baroque style. The sheer volume of the arced colonnade leading to the North door is surely among the gems of British architecture. Entering the doors and crossing the reception area, one enters a vast rotunda with glazed dome flooding the room with light. Straight across from this a second door leads into another magnificent room, initially a banqueting hall. Finally, a door at the far side opens on to one of the finest contrived landscapes in Britain, rivalling Stourhead and Blenheim. The ground falls away majestically to the lakes, with a superb Palladian bridge to the left, and further left a Gothic temple. The architect John Taylor of Taylor Chapman, an old Stoic, declared 'Is it any wonder a young lad, faced with all that and living in its midst, should want to be an architect?'

This was all so majestic it was a case where angels fear to tread. Yet tread they must, or the whole place would have come under the hammer, whether of auctioneer or of demolition workers, or even of both. Clough was never easily daunted, and he seems to have had no difficulty convincing the governors that he could meet their requirements.

There can be little doubt that in the haste of providing another public school to cope with the baby boom that would ensue after the Great War, a master plan seems to have been missing at Stowe. First, there was too little time. The whole project was regarded as urgent. Secondly there was finance, which was necessarily finite. In the event, there is a certain piecemeal air to the ground plan — things not aligned as they might have been, fenestration varying too much for comfort to the eye, internal details like staircases sometimes treated in cavalier style. Clough's own characteristic version of Palladian occasionally obtrudes, sometimes with a sort of gaiety that contrasts too forcibly with the sober grandeur of the original. Yet what was a man to do? Had a purer architect like Lutyens been engaged, it is doubtful if the conversion to a public school would ever have been achieved. It is one thing to have the resources of Empire behind you to build a New Delhi, quite another to convert a Stowe to the requirements of a school on private funds. Personally I found myself moved by Clough's work at Stowe, for it has enabled the place to become a living organism again, with boys and girls, teaching and domestic staff, bringing the place to life. Stowe lives and will live, and Clough is largely responsible for this.

My own personal favourite is his addition of the laboratory to the west wing, the Orangery. There was no way he could have continued the magnificent march of the Hornton-stone arched windows. Instead he simply interrupted the elevation with a new two-storey block of Palladian symmetry, with his own characteristic fenestration. A.R. Powys regards the laboratory, and the new buildings in the East Court as 'simple and unaffected, while the planning is direct and sometimes adroit'. The word 'adroit' could be applied often to Clough, and can cover a multitude of sins. To achieve the right scale and elevation he sometimes created what can only be described as lethal staircases. Merely to look at one steep concrete staircase with inadequate treads is enough to make one blench. Yet the laboratory takes its place as an addition, honest, elegant in its own right, and all crowned with a brilliant cupola. Messrs Parnell of Rugby were the general contractors for the laboratory and its classrooms at a cost of £6,621.

The other major addition, set apart on its own tree-girt site to the south-west from the main buildings is the boarders' house, Chatham House. Its elevation is one of Clough's finest, severely Palladian, with characteristic ornament. The columns supporting the portico are magnificent. Where, I wonder, would one be able these days to obtain unjointed columns of such height and proportions? They are truly magnificent. The urns at each corner are so apt that it would be regrettable had economy expunged them from the design. It is apparent the governors were very patient. It is typical of Clough that whatever the financial constraints, he would not compromise on such a detail. One criticism has been made regarding Chatham's siting. Certainly it interrupts rather rudely the view from the doors of the chapel set above it on a rise, and in this respect must be regarded as infelicitous. But the chapel was built *after* Chatham House and by another architect altogether, Sir Robert Lorimer. However, Clough is not blameless, it appears, for a comprehensive master-plan undoubtedly from Clough's office though not lettered in his inimitable hand, shows Chatham House in place and the site above and behind it marked 'Site of future chapel'. So now, one emerges from the chapel in a state of spiritual uplift, to be confronted at once by a view of the *rear* of Chatham House. In fact, Clough had designed a chapel (1925) but it was rejected (perhaps as being too ornate against the general severity all round) and the chosen architect incorporated sixteen peristyle columns from the Temple of Concord in a more severe design.

Chatham House, and the Stowe additions in general, display one individual quirk of design that is very much Clough's — the sort that led to people coining the term 'to Clough-up' a building, meaning introducing a certain amount of fun into the elevation of an otherwise dull building: 'such and such could do with being Cloughed-up'. The particular Stowe quirk, seen for instance in the entrance doors to Chatham House, is the odd fenestration here and there, panes divided into what A.R. Powys called 'union-jack bars', diagonal bars, which must have irked the joiners and glaziers and can disturb the eye somewhat. 'It is easy to poke fun at such things,' writes A.R. Powys rather generously, 'noting

likenesses that make them appear incongruous, but it is often
unfair and sometimes malicious.'

Nevertheless, while this union-jack treatment does convey
Clough's sense of fun and decoration in the Palladian front to the
Gymnasium (otherwise an Army hut!), its use in the main doors
of Chatham House was possibly enough to raise John Piper's
hackles for once. One has to admit in the end that it is quite
unnecessary and does nothing for an otherwise superb building.

Clough was not only concerned with site-plans and elevations,
but also with certain precious and characteristic details. One
example is the bells, hung at either end of the great north portico.
Again he commissioned John Bickerdyke to deal with this and
the result, incorporating the school's Arms in the bell yoke, is
charming.

There was one major problem in dealing with Stowe, and that
was the proportion of fenestration. In the original fabric, the
proportion of window space to wall is perfect but alas, well below
present-day educational requirements. Classrooms must now be
designed with a certain high minimum of light falling over the
pupil's shoulder so that he or she may read and write in comfort.
No wonder then that Clough, or indeed any architect, would find
it difficult to make any sort of accord with the original fenestration,
for when the original fabric of Stowe had been built, educational
requirements would have been the last of considerations.

All told, it must be said that the successful adaptation of Stowe
from duke's palace to public school owes as much to Clough and
his work there as to the original house. The school thought
sufficiently highly of him to have a bronze portrait bust by Hans
Feibusch, with laurel wreath denoting honour for his noble work,
and with an inscription beside it.

With such a project behind him, Clough was now at the enviable
stage in a freelance career when one job leads to another. Once
he had finished with Stowe (and he would be concerned with it
intermittently for some time afterwards) he was commissioned in
1928 to undertake a similar exercise, if rather less for his part, at
Ashridge Park, near Berkhamstead. He had known the house
when it had belonged to Lord Brownlow. Like many a country
house after the First World War, and increasingly after the Second,
it was impossible for a private owner to maintain it intact, and it
came on to the market and was snapped up by a property
speculator. Again, like Stowe, it was a great house in magnificent
grounds which might have been sold off piecemeal as an invest-
ment, so there was anxiety about its fate. In the event, an American

millionaire engineer, Urban Hanlon Broughton, provided funds for its conversion into the Bonar Law College for the study and propagation of Conservative principles. Key areas of the grounds were acquired for the National Trust, with help from George Trevelyan and Miss Courtauld.

Ashridge is enormous. The site dates back to 1283 when Edward Earl of Cornwall, a nephew of Henry III, first occupied it and built there. By 1604 it had passed on to Sir Thomas Egerton. In 1803 a descendant commissioned James Wyatt to create the existing structure. It is the largest Gothic palace near London, sited in a vast park on a ridge of the Chilterns. Wyatt's nephew, Sir J. Wyatville completed the project.

The palace sprawls along the ridge, a vast edifice that reputedly had only two bathrooms originally! If ever one needed an example of the difference between nineteenth and twentieth century life-styles of the aristocracy, Ashridge is a superb demonstration. It would take whole armies to service and maintain it. The gardens, as with Stowe, were laid out by Capability Brown with Humphry Repton, but in this case were of less concern to Clough, in the sense that he was not required to change the ground plan in any way, or to add additional items, as with Chatham House. His remit was once again to adapt a redundant palace to its projected use as a college. The twentieth century is ill adapted to the use of these sprawling edifices from the past.

However impossible the whole thing looked, it is indicative of Clough's career at this stage that he should be chosen to see it through. In fact, in the Twenties and Thirties, conversions great and small were a staple in his office. Ashridge was crying out to be 'Cloughed-up'.

The main work was to adapt the interior to modern needs and to convert the conservatory (a long cloister in fact) into a dining hall with eighteen bedrooms above fitted into a mansard roof (a device he would often use). Compared with Stowe, Ashridge was far from ideal in Clough's book. The fabric was early nineteenth century Gothic, which might have signified Strawberry Hill but didn't. Gothic was a style that would always offend Clough's sensibilities. 'If, for an early nineteenth century house,' he once wrote, 'you can accept a Gothic Revival Abbey — "an apt mixture of Castle and Cathedral styles" — complete with cloisters, vast central tower, chapel steeple and all the rest, then Ashridge is well enough'. Upon completion a year or two later, it was ceremonially opened by the serving Prime Minister Stanley Baldwin at a grand Conservative garden party, no doubt with a view to fund-raising.

Clough worked on and throughout the Twenties and Thirties had a thriving practice. Drawings of this period reveal the hand of numerous assistants. 'Cloughing up' was by now a staple, as though a number of buildings, embarrassed by their redundancy, were waiting for his tender ministrations before embarking on a new life.

At Bolesworth Castle in Cheshire, built in 1830 by William Cole, he changed the interior for the Barbour family in 1921-1922, removing the Gothic frippery and replacing it with a grand classical style. The central hall has pilasters in two tiers and a balcony, and he devised a new entrance hall with columns. On the estate he built a pair of semi-detached cottages linked by a typical tetrastyle Palladian portico and divided by an arched access to the rear, in 1927.

At Oare House in Wiltshire, built in 1740 by Henry Deacon, a London wine merchant, Clough in 1921 and 1925 added two symmetrical wings, with another facing the front garden, incorporating a blank Venetian window. Above it all a tall chimney emerges, embraced by two volutes, one of Clough's happiest conceits. The library, pillared and pilastered, is a superb room.

To build additions to a two-hundred-year-old house is sometimes to introduce a jarring note to the fabric. Brick production, even different clay, over the years produces different shades and surfaces. It is not possible to 'distress' brickwork artificially. At Oare House Clough used bricks from an old chapel that was being demolished on top of the down close by. This was a typical Clough ploy. The effect at Oare is so beautiful that Oare House and its twentieth century additions by Clough make it one of England's finest examples of domestic architecture.

But Clough's contribution, working with the then owner Sir Geoffrey Fry, to the 'revivifying' of Oare House is not confined to the house. The garden is a perfect English example, and Clough introduced many features to make it one of the grandest. Indeed, Clough's garden designing deserves wider recognition. While he made no great claims for himself as a horticulturist as such, he was adept at planning a garden that the horticulturist could exploit to the greatest advantage, rather as Lutyens did for Miss Jekyll. Clough was a great opener-up of views and prospects, to which end he would break down obstacles and enhance the new prospect with a new yew-hedge or a belvedere, along with walls and urns, echoing those on the house. He would introduce or enhance various axes and had a genius for extending a house into the garden, as though the respective areas, closed off with shrubs or hedges, were rooms off the house, as indeed they are. Seats, flagged terraces, avenues between pleached limes, all help to make the most magnificent views from Oare House across to the Marlborough Downs. Clough's sheer enjoyment in this sort of exercise is no more evident than at Oare. As at his own ancestral home at Brondanw, columnar Irish yews direct the gaze along paths, and a certain intermittent wildness is all calculated.

Every gate, every seat, is a characteristic Clough design and it is this comprehensive approach to design that places Oare House firmly among Clough's most satisfying projects. Even as late as 1960, at the age of seventy-seven, he returned to design a belvedere and seat at the end of the terrace.

In 1922, Clough built Cold Blow at Oare, just over a field from the House. A bold example of Clough's vernacular style, it is a two-storeyed thatched building with, placed centrally, a bow on columns, providing welcome shade or shelter over the entrance, and a fine projecting room with a view above. The original green shade of the shutters has been beautifully maintained by the present owner.

At the southern end of the village, Clough built a terrace of cottages (1926), finished with white stucco (now pink, alas) and provided a Palladian break in the form of a central archway. Unfortunately, now that individual occupiers own the separate cottages, the overall appearance is somewhat run down, with gutters, soffits etc all in need of attention. The general paintwork is shabby. When, like Council houses, a corporate building is sold off to its individual occupiers, it is important that a Residents' Association be formed to raise funds for general maintenance, otherwise each individual property may be devalued, not to mention the environment.

Sir Geoffrey Fry had such trust in Clough's capacity to solve building and environmental problems without any compromise in taste that he commissioned all sorts of projects: the Power House (1924) for instance; additions to Oare Pennings; the Apple and Garden House; and even a Parsonage (which, though designed, was not built for some reason).

Deep in Cotswold country, hidden in a little valley somewhere between Chipping Norton and Stow-on-the-Wold is another beautiful example of Clough's work at its very best. In late life, in a fit of self assessment, he would write that he had 'an instinct for responding to a site or a building's requirements appropriately, and to have a judgement of proportions, that is unerring'. Cornwell Manor demonstrates this instinct perfectly. It sits above its little valley overlooking a lovely formal pool contrived by Clough, and shielded from the world by two pairs of gates with appropriate piers. The whole aspect of the place is idyllic and kept strictly private in a world where that state is ever more difficult to preserve. Hard by, the village centre of Cornwell was also improved at the behest of its enlightened patron Mrs Gillson (later Marquise de la Fregonnière). The Village Hall (1939) in particular exemplifies Clough in his half-vernacular-half-Classical style, with a superb chimney and bell tower to top it off.

Working with Lionel Brett (later Viscount Brett), Clough designed six cottages for visitors at Tennyson's House at Farringford on the Isle of Wight. At Tattenhall in Cheshire, he built Rose Corner, again a fine example of his domestic style, with its Palladian facade and tetrastyle portico and pediment.

Although Clough designed comparatively little work for London from his various London offices, his practice flourished both there and in Wales. In Wales he remodelled Garthewin, a rather distinguished house near Llanelidan in Clwyd, in 1930. He removed its Victorian excesses, simplified the whole place and remodelled the service tower. For a number of years Garthewin provided a stage for drama, mostly in Welsh, and made its own unique contribution to Welsh culture. None of this would have been possible without Clough's drastic alterations.

In 1931, Clough was responsible for a rather arcane bit of history, when he built the first ever Youth Hostel, at Maeshafn in Clwyd. It is a neo-Georgian structure with pediment and shutters, typical of Clough's style, adding a certain grace to an otherwise humdrum building as far as function went. He never saw the point of lowering his sights to plebeian rawness just because a building had an ordinary function. The merest toll-booth or toilet would always receive that extra bit of attention to design and detail, even if it meant just a little more thought over its decoration. Beauty was always the main criterion, however humble the function. Even when designing a roadside restaurant on the A5 at Conwy Falls near Betws-y-Coed, he would provide it with pediment in the Georgian style and an open loggia on the upper level. It is a pity this loggia has been filled in with plate glass windows, completely out of kilter with the sash windows gracing the rest of the facade. It is the sort of interference with his design that caused him extreme irritation. Perhaps an earlier proposed treatment of 1938 in a modernist manner might have avoided this fate.

However, with an office in London, Clough was responsible for a number of projects in the metropolis: conversions, alterations, remodellings, and general 'Cloughing-up'. In Farm Street in 1923 he converted a mews building into the Georgian style, and at 32a Ovington Square in Kensington he was responsible for another fine London residence.

Lord Cushendun in particular engaged Clough's services, in County Antrim in Northern Ireland. All told, Clough was responsible for quite a number of schemes there; a Memorial Hall and School at The Giant's Causeway (1961); a new Lodge for Glen Mona at Cushendun; and a row of cottages with a stylish Mansard roof allowing dormer windows. A central archway there completes a typical Clough elevation.

Earlier, in the late Thirties, he had exploited the same sort of Mansard roof with dormer windows for Romney Bay House in Kent. Right on the edge of Romney Marsh and almost at the sea's edge overlooking the Channel, this is a unique elevation, with the usual high Palladian portico on the three-storeyed front and at either end a two-storeyed wing. It was built for one of the early Portmeirion habitués, the actress and journalist Hedda Hopper, and Romney Bay House in its brochure makes the most of its creator and Portmeirion, a distant rival in the hotel business. Evidently Clough's is a name to drop when it comes to attracting business.

With commissions rolling in like Ashridge and fine town and country houses it must have appeared to many that Clough was the official architect to the Conservative Party, which was far from matching his vaguely leftish political convictions. But commissions simply implied connections, and out of the Ashridge project other jobs emerged from the Conservative Party Chairman, John Davidson. The Ladies' Carlton Club needed alteration and enlargements, and Lord Carson, Bonar Law, Sir Geoffrey Fry, and other Tory grandees all sought Clough's services at various times.

The driving force in politics in the family was, of course, Amabel. Her father had always declared himself a Whig, which would probably be described these days as vaguely Centre. While being an old-fashioned Conservative, he and *The Spectator* espoused many social causes, such as the environment, the National Trust, and proper building for the poor, since the rich could look after themselves. But when his son John took up the socialist cause, he was shocked. Amabel was no less zealous in her Leftish views. Her picture of politics in the Thirties in her autobiography is lively and evocative, 'Maxton and Jennie Lee were among those who particularly stick in my mind'. Aneurin Bevan, brother John, Sir Stafford Cripps, H.G. Wells and countless luminaries of the Left were friends of the Williams-Ellises in the London years, and even *The Spectator* began to move leftwards.

Clough served whoever commissioned him, of whatever political persuasion. Politics, especially in those days when there were hardly any women at all in Parliament, was largely a men's club and word got around, of course. He converted an old manor house for Sir Oswald Mosley (then still a Labour Member), and he designed Richard Crossman's Oxfordshire garden. He was even more involved with David Lloyd George who, after all, was a near neighbour in North Wales, a few miles along the road from Brondanw. Clough converted the fine old house of Tŷ Newydd in Llanystumdwy, Lloyd George's boyhood village, and would be glad to know his work is intact and that the house is now a retreat for writers and students, with the Arts Council of Wales as its guardian. As usual, Clough was as interested in designing the garden as the house, and his interest in cobbled paving is nowhere better exemplified than in the path leading up to the front door, where an old millstone is laid down and surrounded by granite setts in a radial pattern. Lloyd George died in Tŷ Newydd and Clough was consulted by Lady Lloyd George, his second wife, about the burial place for the old statesman. A spot was chosen on the banks of Lloyd George's beloved Afon Dwyfor, and Clough designed a simple oval enclosure, with a huge boulder in the centre, resting, again, on cobblestones. I was asked to carve Lloyd George's name and dates on the two oval slate plaques either side of the wrought iron gate on the roadside. The gate is an excellent example of Clough's design for wrought iron, and he would make much use throughout his North Wales years of the Glaslyn Foundry in Porthmadog. The other side of the grave is open to the river bank and the purling waters below. It must be one of the most beautiful burial places, and thousands of people visit it every year. The great man's memorabilia are collected in the nearby Lloyd George Museum, also designed by Clough. Lewis Mumford wrote about the grave in *The New Yorker*:

> The point of the design is that the pilgrim who visits this grave can pass around it, while getting a full view of the interior of the enclosure, without being tempted to trespass. In fact, no sign is needed to warn him against intruding, since the spiral walk was contrived to keep him far enough above or below the grave to prevent access. Apart from the simple inscription and the serene enclosure, nothing disturbs the landscape that Lloyd George saw and only a small sign by the roadside reminds the tripper that this is consecrated

ground. To the honour of the tourist there was, when I
visited it, not a sign of his presence in so much as an empty
cigarette packet or a scrap of paper. The restraint of the
monument only emphasizes the perfect combination of
pure form, delicate textural contrasts and sensitive siting . . . .

Later Clough and I would combine on the placing of a flagstone
Memorial to Lloyd George in Westminster Abbey. Clough designed,
and I carved it in Penrhyn Conifer Green Slate, and the dedication
was unforgettable. All the political leaders of the time were
present, with Jeremy Thorpe, always the best of company at
Brondanw, Portmeirion or Tŷ Newydd, giving a moving address
to the grand old man's memory.

It might be supposed from his numerous commissions in mid-
career that Clough was the Tory Party's tame architect. He was
not, however, a particularly political animal, though he would
never hide his leftish inclinations. In his zeal for environmental
reform, perhaps he most resembled Robert Owen (1771-1858),
that early Welsh reformer who preached that Man's character is
affected by environment, and built factories, houses and schools
for his workforce and their families in accordance with his convictions at places like New Lanark, New Harmony in Indiana,
U.S.A., and his native Newtown in Montgomeryshire.

Politics affected neither Clough's architectural practice nor his
social company. He consorted with ease with anybody of any
political persuasion. He was such good company in any case that
it would never be a barrier (and why should it?), and since politics
was never a great motivating force, he would rarely advance his
political opinions. In the event, they would be concerned with
environment if he did.

There would be occasions when politics as such angered him,
not because of any particular party but because the very practice
of adversarial politics could actually obscure, even obstruct some
environmental issue. Politicians are interested in votes. That is the
one great weakness in democracy, and by definition cannot be
altered. But there are times when, listening to Clough or reading
some plea by him, one could imagine him wishing for a benevolent
dictator to enact some environmental measure over the heads of
people and politicians. He could not accept the workings, the
eternal rantings of adversarial politics, when all too often some
environmental problem was being swept under the carpet in
favour of more vote-catching issues. He confessed in the end that
he joined his old friend E.M. Forster in awarding two cheers for

democracy. When it came to actual voting, he stated that by and large he voted Labour.

At one stage, Clough even joined the Independent Labour Party, which in the years between the wars and for a short while after the Second World War was a strong ginger group to the Left of the Labour Party. Perhaps Clough saw it as a sort of Owenite (one must be so careful — *Robert* Owenite would be more accurate!) environment-friendly grouping. The polarisation of politics, especially in the Thirties, was affected by the dire state of Britain then, with the Depression in deep contrast to the apparent success of Communism in Soviet Russia, where various Five Year Plans seemed to be achieving miracles of progress in hydro-electric dams, collective farming, and full employment. Only later did the world come to know the full truth and the cost of all this in terms of human misery. But at the time the contrast seemed too great for complacency, and further polarity came about with the rise of Fascism in Europe.

So Clough would vote Labour and even speak publicly on environmental issues at seminars and summer schools, meeting figures like Ramsey MacDonald, James Maxton (leader of the ILP), Oswald Mosley (then a Labour MP before he deviated sharp Right), H.G. Wells, brother-in-law John Strachey and other notables of the Left in the Fabian mould.

There was nothing unusual about all this. The Left Book Club flourished, as did the Left-wing publisher Victor Gollancz. If there were to be any hope for Britain, they proclaimed, it lay in this general Left and Radical polarity. And for Clough, part of the better Britain would involve environmental legislation.

British politics in the Thirties was particularly *laisser faire* and the Conservative Government represented an establishment bias which seemed to ignore the appalling social problems of the time. Only after World War II did the Labour Party enjoy power with a massive majority and a mandate for change. For Clough (the 'congenital deviationist') and Amabel, that post-war victory for Labour represented the reward of years of campaigning, writing, speaking to a largely indifferent society in the Thirties.

Clough, however, while believing the political shift might help expedite some of his environmental concerns, would gradually take a more critical view of post-war politics. Various plans like the New Town legislation, and Sir Patrick Abercrombie's plans for our cities and roads, Green Belt legislation, all helped towards a new Britain, but it would never altogether satisfy Clough. It is possible that, with hindsight, he might have come to applaud what

*was* done now that the world has been able to witness the appalling
industrial chaos left behind by the collapse of the Soviet Empire.
It is an extremely difficult problem to eradicate the awful and ugly
and replace it with the right and beautiful.

Mankind has a propensity for mess, and it was something
Clough could never tolerate. Most of us come to accept in the end
a sort of collective desperation over the human condition. He
would walk around with a litter picker in hand, always fighting the
good fight and always failing to comprehend that Man, basically,
is a thoroughly messy animal.

While it may seem hard to reconcile the architect of fine
Palladian houses for the rich and privileged, with the Socialist and
his concern for the hungry masses of the Thirties, it was quite
evident that Clough believed the alleviation of mass misery was
possible with a concerted attack on the slum legacy of the nineteenth century. From his various writings on environment, he
advocated much that has since been enacted in this area at a time
when it was not regarded as a top political priority. For much has
been achieved. Nobody who has lived through the appalling
wasteland of Thirties industrial Britain has any illusions that all
the social problems of the present do not for one moment add up
to the misery of the Thirties.

Much of the improvement is owed, first, to the demolition of
vast areas of Victorian streetscape, and secondly to the preservation of 'green lungs' in cities, and to the designation of National
Parks and the development of New Towns. It may not yet be ideal,
but it has meant alleviation of much needless misery, and it is due
largely to those seers of planning and amenity like Clough who
wrote, lectured, generally lobbied and sometimes even worked for
government.

The Victorian slums did come down eventually; New Towns
were built, motorway systems were planned and implemented,
causing their own environmental problems. Inner cities got their
tower blocks, to avoid further ribbon development. But they too
would prove a doubtful solution. Nevertheless this was all part of
the reforming programme to eradicate the nineteenth century's
awful legacy.

There was much to show for Clough's kind of reforming zeal.
But human nature, with its capacity for error, nearly always gets
things wrong. The railways, which had done so much to spread
and develop industrial Britain, brought their own stigma in time
and gave way gradually to motorways, just another form of ribbon
development. Now we begin to regret the loss of the railways. The

Beeching Plan, which decimated them, may eventually be seen as the worst planning decision of the twentieth century.

Clough was a missionary, a proselytizer — religious terms he would eschew, but which are best suited to describe his general zeal for environmental improvement. One thing he *never* was, and that was a bore. In the end Clough best summed up his political stance when he said: 'Though a congenital deviationist, I have generally voted Labour, but not without flirtatious glances to the right and left'.

One thing moved him greatly: that human beings should be condemned to live and work in nineteenth century squalor seemed to him a dereliction of the human spirit, especially since, in a wealthy society, it was remediable. All this informed his politics (such as they were) and his subsequent work and writings on Planning, Amenity and Environmental awareness.

He was quoted by the Webbs in their book on Soviet Russia for his published views on Russia's heroic efforts of reconstruction, yet at the same time he was urged by Conservative Central Office to stand as a candidate (in fact his understudy stood and won!).

Such heightened professional activity and domestic considerations meant that 'living over the shop' became increasingly fraught in South Eaton Place by 1927 and Clough moved office premises to Ebury Street. Over the stucco Doric portico it bore a classical inscription: 'The arts, sciences and letters may the Holy Ghost prosper', a sentiment he could only applaud and enter thereunder to help implement.

He enjoyed working in the finely proportioned great room, and it spoiled him forever for working in the usual architect's office conditions. With the sheer scale of the room he was able (or cajoled) to offer hospitality to the oddest assortment of guests. The Everest explorer Sir Francis Younghusband once brought along a group of Tibetan lamas, all flowing robes and exotic head-gear, booming on their strange bass horns. They were nearly immured there for a time by the descent of one of London's notorious 'pea-soupers' which still afflicted London before Clean Air legislation forbade the burning of solid fuel.

Another booming guest was the American poet Vachel Lindsay, whose daughter later married (for a time) one of Bertrand Russell's sons, John. The Georgian poets also came frequently, since Amabel's first book had been *An Anatomy of Poetry* and she had been poetry and literary critic of *The Spectator*. Poets came not merely as guests, but also as performers.

On the domestic front, with the children growing up, South Eaton Place was abandoned and the family moved to Royal Avenue, not far from Wren's noble frontage to Chelsea Hospital. Already the free upbringing of the children was in marked contrast to the norm. They would play among the trees in the avenue, braving the gravel in bare feet, and generally setting the Williams-Ellis trend of complete freedom and sometimes unorthodox, if harmless behaviour. Anything stuffy was anathema, recalling Clough's own childhood dislike of his father's starchy visitors to Glasfryn.

Later, this free and happy-go-lucky way of rearing children so impressed scientist Solly Zuckerman that he asked if he might introduce one of his research baboons into their midst. He was currently researching for his book *The Sexual Life of Primates*, which seems a doubtful reason for introducing a baboon into a nest of children, however free their life style. Betsy had her quarters on the flat roof in Hampstead for several months. Of course, Betsy proved not nearly as amenable and easily accommodated as Zuckerman had imagined, (or had he?). Betsy was dirty, did not respond in the least, and if Betsy benefited, the children most markedly did not. But it was an indicator of the free, unfussy way of rearing children that Clough and Amabel assumed, that the experiment should have been thinkable in the first place. Perhaps they thought Betsy would have acted as a sort of *au pair* girl who might help relieve parents of certain duties to entertain. That both parents were deeply preoccupied by their respective vocations was never in question, and it seems to have done no harm whatsoever to the children. Indeed the choice was as much the children's as the parents'.

One friend whom Clough valued particularly was Humbert Wolfe. He had been a Jewish refugee long before Hitler came on the scene, and when he did, Wolfe was instrumental in helping a number of Jews escape from his clutches. Clough took in a couple of Austrian architects, which was not the easiest of matters, since the office was already fully staffed, and finding sufficient work to satisfy their professional standard was difficult. Yet it was typical of Clough that he took them in and would always help where he could.

One further move was necessary, this time to Hampstead in 1930, where Clough took George Romney's house, a Georgian gem with a superb interior. Clough renovated and improved the house. The fresh air of Hampstead, a garden, and a good school for the children were all guiding factors and the family would remain there until the outbreak of World War II.

Hampstead in the Thirties was described by Herbert Read, the archpriest of Modernism who himself lived there, as 'a nest of gentle artists' (taking a cue from Turgenev). John Summerson lived there, his sister-in-law Barbara Hepworth, architects like Walter Gropius and Eric Mendelsohn, the Bauhaus designer Marcel Breuer, and in 1938 Mondrian settled there. With figures like these Hampstead could just as well be described as a 'nest of gentle Modernists', except that Modernism, by definition is radical, defiant of tradition and ready to overturn the past even if it be ungentle to do so. Clough seems to have been quite unaffected by all this, except that his *Architecture Here and Now* (1934) was written with John Summerson and can be said to be a layman's guide to Modern Architecture. But as far as actual building went, Wells Coates may have designed Lawn Road flats, but Clough either did not see them, or chose to ignore such a revolutionary approach. So although Clough was flourishing at the time, it is difficult to place him in the narrative sequence of Architecture. He was not of his own time — or was he? He studiously ignored what might be called contemporaneity. It was not ignorance, since no man had more wide open eyes. It was choice, not defiant choice, but simply natural choice. He had been deeply moved by Palladian ideals of proportion and elegance and he felt no urge whatsoever to stray beyond these ideals.

By now, with a fair body of work behind him and having made extensive explorations, Clough's taste could be said to be formed and summed up in that word: 'Palladian'. He was quite versatile as an architect, was fond of a certain, broadly Cotswold vernacular style, but by and large, when it came to his subsequent large commissions, he could be described as 'the last of the Palladians'. And that is what he stands for in his own time, the champion of a sort of Palladianism that stood up well to the twentieth century and its turmoil — a calm, still point in a turning world.

Andrea Palladio (1508-80) was first among the Italian Renaissance architects, quite a large claim when one recalls the depth of talent then: Brunelleschi, Bramante, Michelangelo, Alberti. Palladio was born in Padua and in a way his training, like Clough's, was anything but academic, for he began as a stone-mason. But he became an ardent student of classical Roman architecture, twice travelling to Rome to explore and draw the ruins in the Forum and other sites. His great work *I Quattro Libri dell'Architettura* (1570) was to influence architects for generations, not least Inigo Jones (1573-1652). Palladio built extensively in Venice, Vicenza and the Veneto. Sometimes his buildings aroused such admiration for their grace and perfection of design that they were more or less copied directly, for example by Lord Burlington at Chiswick House or William Kent at Mereworth Castle. Both were versions of Palladio's Villa Capra at Vicenza.

Palladio was really at the basis of much of Clough's work: Chatham House; the First Church of Christ Scientist in Belfast (1925); Bishop's Stortford College Chapel (1921); Dalton Hall (1963); Dunwood House and Cornwell Manor. Symmetry and order prevail. Four columns support a central pediment, often with urns adorning each end.

But there was more to Clough than the label 'Palladian'. He was very much his own man and refused to be pigeon-holed. He produced designs that come well within the general concept of Modernism, most notably the 'Fishponds' restaurant at Cobham in Kent (1933), a timber structure which projected grandly over water like a pier or ship-deck. It was alas demolished in 1960.

The natural countryman in Clough craved a rural retreat within easy reach of London and when the Duke of Northumberland in 1933 offered some woodland and a couple of farms at Stapledown on top of the North Downs, Clough took the lot and there built a sort of tree house, based actually round the tree trunk with lead flashing directly off the bole on to the roof, and the oddest method of water collection. But it worked as a house and became for a time the home of those two old Bohemian friends Charles Laughton and Elsa Lanchester, who only left it when it became difficult to maintain (a tree trunk, after all, is a living, growing organism) and took another two-storey house next door, built by Clough in 1935.

The London years were busy ones for Amabel too. As well as rearing three children, she wrote voluminously. First came her *Anatomy of Poetry* (1922), then a string of novels: *Noah's Ark* (1926), *To Tell the Truth* (1933), *The Big Firm* (1933) and *Learn to Love First* (1939). Combining with Clough, she wrote *The Pleasures of Architecture* (1923) — and after World War II they combined in writing *Headlong Down the Years* (1951), which was very much part of the campaign denigrating the Central Electricity Board's plans to dam certain North Wales mountain valleys for hydro-electricity.

Amabel was also a prestigious collector of fairy tales and folk tales. All told she kept her vow when they became engaged, that she would pursue her own career as a writer independent of Clough, and she was also a firm champion of women's rights in a world where they had still to fight for the vote. Amabel, in short, was formidable, and rightly so, for with a character as strong as

Clough for a partner, she could well have been overshadowed by him.

Clough never stopped writing, either, having found it such a good tool in his fight against thoughtless development. He had ascertained from legal experts that you cannot libel a place and he took every opportunity to hit where it would hurt most, anything so long as it stirred people's conscience and precipitated action towards eradication of some monstrosity, and its replacement with appropriate taste. But he did once fall foul of the libel laws, by naming a contractor, and he was obliged to apologise publicly. Nevertheless, he would still be right in his original assessment and it did not deter him in the least from naming environmental atrocities. It still goes on, and we need to remember Clough's zeal in this regard, for he never held his tongue should this or that development offend him. And he often found the right readers. Sir Arnold Wilson M.P. commissioned a couple of long articles from him for his journal *The Nineteenth Century*. This gave Clough ample opportunity to air his views. When some appalling development had taken place, it was nearly always possible to name names, since many were the background of court cases concerning fraudulent conversions, corruption of all shapes among councillors and contractors. With recorded convictions to back his case, Clough would quote names with confidence, and would have no compunction to name the perpetrators where some atrocity had been built.

He called all this his 'Squalid Towns reconnaissance' and he would employ researchers to winkle out the more unsavoury acts of speculation, nepotism, bribery and perjury. He surprised himself at the extent of the corruption. Touchingly he observed later: 'Maybe there is now no need for the sort of exposure that I then felt called for, which, owing to the outbreak of the Second World War was a somewhat stifled cry. Or is there?' Alas, there is.

There was a strange aside to this memory of the environmental fight in the Thirties. Sir Arnold was a secret admirer of the European dictators. After all, Hitler and Mussolini *got things done*. When war finally broke out, Sir Arnold was sufficiently penitent to offer himself for the more dangerous military duties. Although over age, he was eventually recruited for the arduous duty of rear gunner in a bomber, and was killed shortly afterwards. 'And our cleansing campaign was forgotten,' Clough wrote 'in the welter of greater issues that soon engulfed us.'

These London years, from his mid-thirties to his late fifties, were the busiest and most fruitful in Clough's life, though much would lie ahead in the years following Hitler's war. By now, he was well-known and he had a number of major building projects to his name, as well as a growing number of publications, some of which would carry weight when environmental legislation was being considered.

He and Amabel enjoyed a large acquaintance, ranging from the Bloomsbury Group to the aristocracy: Maynard Keynes and his wife Lopokova; Harold Laski of the London School of Economics and doyen of the Left in London; Baroness Budberg, former wife of the Russian writer Gorki; Miles Malleson the actor; both Julian and Aldous Huxley and their wives; Rose Macaulay; and even Charlie Chaplin. The catalysts in forming these various friendship were Jane and H.G. Wells. All this generally Leftish circle would now be apostrophised as 'champagne socialists', except that in Clough's case food and drink did not figure all that high on the agenda, and as a 'congenital deviationist' he would keep his options too wide open for the more convinced party faithful. It was not his scene, as they say, but friendship *was*, so long as it did not get in the way of Architecture, always top of his agenda.

Sir Oswald Birley the Royal Academy portrait painter was another host who gladly garnered the Williams-Ellises, and there they would meet figures like Serge Diaghilev and other ballet folk.

All told, the Hampstead years were rich in both friendships and building commissions, and might have gone on indefinitely if Hitler's War had not intervened. Among the commissions there was even one important one from China for the British firm of Butterfield and Swire in 1924, all of which was managed by remote control, the site surveys being made locally on Clough's behalf and dispatched to him. Everything was expedited to his drawn or written specifications. Plaster mouldings were achieved by preparing the moulds in Britain and sending them out for casting on site. The clients were so pleased with the result that they offered Clough free passage in one of their ships to see how it had all turned out, along with other work of his at Tientsin. He felt he could not accept, being too busy, but he came to regret it later, especially when his appetite was further whetted when he met Dr Joseph Needham, the great Sinologist and expert in Chinese technology through the ages.

Clough was so amiable with even the most tiresome and eccentric clients that on occasion his precious time was wasted by prospective clients exercising their supposed right to alter designs indefinitely, and on a few occasions he reached completion of the design stage when the whole scheme was abandoned, as though design was but an hour's pencil drawing on a sketch pad. One client had him converting and embellishing his house and estate, then just abandoned the lot and went to live abroad; all this after dealing with house, gardens, terraces, pavilions, archways, bridges, gateways, monuments, waterworks and swimming pools. The sheer caprice of the 'beautiful people' between the wars was a sign, surely, of the last days of unbridled wealth among the landed gentry. Nowadays, death duties, various and almost punitive taxes, and the sheer cost of labour, have rendered them powerless to exercise such profligacy, and the state or the National Trust have to take over, and even then, not without a suitable endowment towards upkeep. In one way Clough could be said to be fouling his own nest, for while he seemed tied mainly to the rich and privileged for his commissions, his radical political views however lightly held and always open to deviation, could only have one conclusion: the ultimate demise of such wealth and privilege.

Whatever, Clough sailed blithely on, enjoying life, friendships, a growing family, and the axis of location between Hampstead and Meirionnydd could not be better. He was sufficiently successful, with some very desirable contracts, that he was considered well worth testing with the occasional 'sweetener' from contractors. In *Architect Errant* he wrote feelingly about what has become known as the 'sleaze factor' in public relations, no less prevalent in the building fraternity than in politics. Contractors angling for some prize contract would offer him various delights, 'dinner at the Savoy, a ringside seat at some crucial boxing match, a special champagne luncheon-car rail ride to Aintree and back for the Grand National'. Nothing could have appealed less to Clough. But he had no illusions about their purpose so he had printed for him an acknowledgement slip worded in his rather lofty Baroque style for just such occasions:

> Mr Clough Williams-Ellis, whilst fully appreciating the generosity that prompted the dispatch of the present received from your firm, has had to make it a rule not to accept gifts of any sort from any business with which he has or may have professional dealings. He has therefore passed on what he cannot enjoy himself to an institution where he knows it will be most fully appreciated, he hopes with your approval.

It seems to me the perfect riposte and should be used as a pattern by politicians, civil servants, architects, indeed anybody in a position to award favours. As with Clough, it would benefit the less privileged. One can imagine a Dr Barnardo bunfight over a Christmas hamper, or some nice old boy fallen on hard times, long retired from active working life, joining alpaca-coated contractor gents on a jaunt to Aintree. Yet inducement (for want of a more pejorative term) was quite prevalent, and Clough was once embarrassed by a contractor who sent cars to convey him to a distant site where they were working to his plans. When he protested, it transpired it was not a bribe but a touching gesture in appreciation of Clough's *not* asking for a *pour boire* from them, which apparently they regarded as normal practice.

He was always very conscious of the patron-architect relationship, and he tried always to maintain the correct balance of professional detachment and personal friendship, since many clients were, or became, personal friends. He records in *Architect Errant* one occasion when a woman friend left him in charge of the refurbishment of her large country house while she went off on a year-long world trip. The builder had hardly started when he found extensive dry rot, which required urgent treatment at great expense. Clough had no means of getting in touch with his client. All he could do when she returned was present her with the greatly enlarged bill and explain its reason. Such was her trust in Clough's integrity she murmured not a word.

He was constantly aware of, and often depressed by, the indifference, even blindness of the British in general to the visually aesthetic. Before World War I lack of any planning legislation meant that individuals and, even worse, local and central government, could build anywhere and anyhow. His contribution towards rectifying this must have been considerable. He did his best to set an example, designing what he regarded as appropriate to a given setting. The response to this considered approach could be quite negative, however, and obviously it irked him sometimes. He might take pleasure in some felicitous solution to an environmental problem, or design and erect some satisfying elevation and be greeted with utter indifference. So he did quote, with such obvious relish, one of the 'heartening little yelps of pleasure' from one grateful client:

> It seems a waste not to tell you — and in writing, so that
> no one can interrupt — that your building had given me
> more kick and pleasure than anything that has happened
> for years. The outside is wonderful and satisfying, and the
> upstairs passage gave me a lump in my throat and for 2d.
> I could have burst into tears. Ordinarily I have only felt like
> this for music, and once, when I first saw Westminster

> Hall. So really this is to say thank you. I just feel thankful
> and delighted and rich because it has been built and I'm
> glad it was you that built it.

Such marks of appreciation helped Clough 'to think less doom-fully of my countrymen's visual unawareness'. But his anger over philistine development could be savage, and no more explicitly than in his *England and the Octopus* which he wrote in 1928.

Clough's life in the years between the wars mark his middle life from the age of thirty-five to fifty-six. They were occupied creatively in numerous commissions large and small, but also by what might be called the polemical side of his nature, his need to drum home to any who would listen the virtues of good architecture and planning, and the vices of ignoring their need. His London office was kept busy, but he worked too in Brondanw, where he was near enough to his future demesne of Portmeirion to practise what he preached and where increasingly he would preach what he practised, in books, articles and radio and ultimately television broadcasts.

# Travels

Although he designed many public buildings in his career, Clough's prime interest was domestic architecture. Yet his ideas and propaganda in the Twenties and Thirties might have brought him many tempting offers of large scale developments. Why he did not take this leap is difficult to fathom unless you knew him. To be a famous architect of international renown must be a tempting prospect and there seems little doubt that Clough could have achieved it. For instance, he might have changed the face of Russia of all places. His general desire that a benevolent dictator would implement his environmental ideas on a country-wide scale can never be realised, if only because benevolence for one is malevolence for another. But he did admit to a curious admiration for what had been achieved by central government in Italy and in Russia; that is, not to put too fine a point on it, by Mussolini and Stalin.

Clough's propaganda work with the Design and Industries Association and Civic Trusts was beginning to attract allies from the entire political and social spectra, like Lloyd George, Stafford Cripps, J.B. Priestley and Julian Huxley. They were keen to see how other countries were dealing with what came to be termed 'amenity'. The Revolution of Soviet Russia from a benighted peasantry to a modern industrial state was bound to attract attention.

In the middle of the first Five Year Plan (1928-33) Clough and Amabel sailed to Leningrad on the Soviet ship *Smolny*. They were accompanied by the Commissar for Physical Planning and Reconstruction, and were taken on an extended tour by rail, road and air to Moscow, Leningrad, the new town of Kharkov, the Dnieprostrov Dam and other developments. Clough was impressed, but also had reservations, which he did not hesitate to air. The overall drabness of design, the uniform pattern of fenestration in great blocks, the tendency to build them in long rows, all offended his sensibility. He had seen the sort of squalor they had replaced, yet still it all seemed to him an opportunity lost.

Back in Moscow, Clough felt a distinct chill as his guide reminded him he had been so critical, now he must be good enough to repeat his words of wisdom in front of the Central Committee. Clough faced the Committee and soon forgot about secret police, for he realised this was a technical committee rather than a political tribunal. In other words he was speaking to colleagues in his own profession. He spoke at length, adding some afterthoughts for good measure. They heard him out politely.

They were curious, asked questions, answered his own. It was a healthy exchange of views between professionals. He awaited the outcome, which took him completely by surprise. He was presented with a pile of books, plans and portfolios, and then invited to take up the job of architectural commissar, so to speak. His brief would be to select sites throughout the Soviet Union, to provide outline planning of New Towns and generally to oversee all that he had so recently criticised. He would have his own train to house him and his surveying and drawing staff.

He was sorely tempted, and accepted in principle. But it proved impossible to proceed, for in reality it meant exile from his own country for extended periods without financial reward, since his fee (which in theory was very generous) would be in unexportable roubles.

Politics meant so little to him that there may have been things he ought to have noticed but did not. He wrote long articles on national planning and the environment there for *The Manchester Guardian* and *The Daily Telegraph*, and when he returned to Russia later to see how the Committee had proceeded he was very impressed, and in particular by the Moscow Underground. In retrospect, one might wonder how he would have measured Stalin's terror (about which the West knew little or nothing at the time) against the classical orders, marble, carving, gilding and chandeliers of the Metro.

Clough's interest in Russia was sustained and on one occasion a visit coincided with that of another delegation, Lady Astor, Lord Lothian and Bernard Shaw. Shaw was viewed in Russia as an apologist for the achievements of Communism, and he enjoyed his popularity there. Ever the old popinjay, he explained that the presence of his two companions, the Aristocracy, the 'Enemy', was a chance for them to see what had been achieved by Communism.

On this visit, Clough had just taken his seat in the dining car of the Moscow Express when the attendant brought along two English-speaking passengers to join him. They proved to be American. Clough explained his own mission, and that he was an architect.

'You are an architect then?' said the stranger. 'So am I.'

'Your name?' Clough asked.

'Frank Lloyd Wright.'

'Ah, how kind of chance thus to turn a legend into present reality.'

But world fame can present problems sometimes. Lloyd Wright presumed that Clough's ready recognition of his name would also go for the Customs people at the frontier. Lloyd Wright flatly refused to unlock his baggage for inspection, and the more they insisted the more Lloyd Wright dug in his heels. Matters got so heated, with invidious comparisons of United States freedom with Soviet repression that Clough had to take Lloyd Wright aside and tactfully explain that he must either open up, or be turned back, and so lose American representation at the Architectural Congress they were both due to attend.

All this Soviet-British interchange of ideas was prompted by interest in what the Five Year Plans were achieving. There was a great deal of propaganda both ways, and Clough made no bones about 'propagandising' — but about what? He never really explained. My impression was that since so much was being done in Russia, while things were almost stagnant in the West, where we were coping with the Depression, architects and others were curious to see what was going on in the Soviet Union.

Clough was not alone in being curious and even seduced by Russia. Oxbridge in particular was affected by Russia to the extent that it influenced debate and new writing. In the Thirties, Clough's old college at Cambridge was not unknown for extreme Left-wing sympathies. Subsequent events and politics have overtaken that view, and the impression now prevails that there was quite as much bad as good development in the years of Communist rule, and the appalling cost in human terms is now seen for what it was.

It was understandable that Clough should have been as impressed as he was. His politics, such as they were, would be quite simple. It was not enough merely to build and landscape for the select and wealthy few, but to enlarge one's horizons, to think of the greatest good for the greatest number in his concern for landscape and its buildings and conservation. Clough was so very determined to build for whomsoever would allow him that, however much it seemed to turn out to be only for the rich, and so little for the community in general, he probably had few qualms, like William Morris when he declared that he seemed only to be 'ministering to the swinish luxury of the rich'.

Russia, however, was only one destination among many in his travels. Clough travelled a great deal with Amabel on her attendance at International PEN conferences, and on one occasion in Stockholm he met, for the second time and without recognising him, a member of the Swedish Royal family; 'such is my memory for people, even when really interesting as well as princely'. Which may sound rather high and mighty, but it should also be recorded that when the local Primary School at Croesor near Brondanw

1. John Williams-Ellis and his sons, from left to right Martyn, Clough, Rupert, John and Edric, *c.* 1893

2. The wedding to Amabel Strachey, 1915

3. Portrait by Sir Oswald Birley

4. Llangoed Hall, the first commission

5. Plas Brondanw, the family home

6. Bishop's Stortford College Chapel

7. First Church of Christ Scientist, Belfast

8. Chatham House, Stowe

9. The Laboratory, Stowe

10. The Long Row, Stowe, purchased by Clough Williams-Ellis to prevent development

11. Nantclwyd Hall, in the Vale of Clwyd

12. The Fishponds Restaurant at Cobham in Kent, an example of Clough
Williams-Ellis' modernist capability

13. The Youth Hostel at Maeshafn

14. Cold Blow, Oare, showing a vernacular style

15. Dalton Hall

16. Cornwell Manor

17. The ornate tall chimney at Cornwell village now lacks the original figures for the plinths on either side.

was doing a project on Clough and Portmeirion, he entertained the children as though they were visiting royalty, speaking at length into their tape-recorder and showing them drawings and explaining at length, all without condescension, as though they were compiling some prestigious broadcast.

In Sweden he also met the sculptor Carl Milles and so admired his mermaid that he asked if he might adapt it as Portmeirion's symbol. Permission was gladly given, yet Clough never got the sculptor's name right, anglicising it as Miles. One can only say that as far as people went he meant well.

The PEN conferences would take them far and wide, enabling Clough to collect buildings he might otherwise have known only from photographs. Stockholm, Prague, Vienna, Venice and Dublin, each had distinguished architecture and he would store them in his memory as he so often failed to do with human faces. He always recalled most warmly his visit to Melk, the great Baroque monastic church set high on a bluff at a bend of the Danube. At the Austrian PEN conference in 1930, delegates were being conveyed to Melk by special train, perhaps at Clough's special instigation, for he was really keen to collect this particular masterpiece. On the way, the train stopped at a station for luncheon, which Clough declined so that he might explore the charming little town and examine its architecture. He got so absorbed that when he returned to the station he found the train had left ten minutes earlier. He was furious with himself — only twenty-five or so miles more and he had missed Melk through his own stupidity.

He had no German, but the local signalman soon sensed the source of his distress and immediately drew Clough towards a shed where he uncovered a high-powered motor-cycle. There followed a hair-raising trip, Clough's first attempt at pillion-riding. They tore round the Danube bends, clinging to cliff sides and it seemed to Clough, escaping death plunges only by inches. He only just managed to hang on, but they got there and Clough was delighted to be acquainted with Melk in the flesh. He claimed that if he was going to die, 'Melk was better worth dying for than quite a lot of other causes'. I never thought to ask Clough who manned the signals in his chauffeur's absence, nor what Amabel was doing during all this.

He might have landed a most desirable commission, to plan a hotel somewhat along the lines of Portmeirion, on the island of Korcula off the coast of Dalmatia. This he could enjoy, for the environment promised all the delights he enjoyed in the little dell of Portmeirion. He applied for a Yugoslav visa to visit the island,

but to his consternation, he learned he was *persona non grata*.
Puzzled and annoyed at this ignorance — what was he to Yugoslavia
or Yugoslavia to him? — he went to the top at the Foreign Office,
but they too drew a blank. Furthermore they told him a country
could refuse without giving any reason, and there was nothing one
could do about it. He could discover no reason for being *non grata*
— he had committed no indiscretion that he could remember,
indeed, had never had any truck hitherto with Yugoslavia and its
authorities. It transpired later that Amabel, along with other
luminaries like H.G. Wells and Bernard Shaw, had protested to
Yugoslavia earlier about its imprisonment of dissidents. Most
governments are like elephants.

# The Pleasures of Architecture

In trying to assess Clough's place in the scheme of things, and especially in the opinion of his peers, it is probable he would be satisfied and proud enough to be remembered simply as 'architect' — or, as he entitled his great autobiography, *Architect Errant*. A great party of homage late in life would confirm this, for Portmeirion on that occasion would gather in what Clough called a 'colloquy' of his peers to pay due homage. Yet the odd thing is that, surrounded as they were by what I have called this *jeu d'esprit*, they would not be overly impressed. Even Clough himself on that occasion would ruefully admit: 'no great work of mine stands out against the sky in splendour to excite men's wonder. I shall never appear in Banister Fletcher . . .'. All of which is undeniably true. Yet he was indeed held in high regard by his profession and was elected by them Fellow of the RIBA. I believe their regard grew because Clough fought for architectural and environmental concerns with an energy and fervour that few of his peers could match. Perhaps they were too busy at their drawing boards with their own 'great work standing against the sky in splendour . . .'.

At any rate, Clough stood apart and ahead as warrior against the forces of endemic British Philistinism. Whatever methods were required, frontal attack or guerrilla tactics, Clough would be there when others hid in the safe bunkers of architects' offices. He not only felt passionately about his causes, but was intent on conveying this passion to anybody who would read and listen. His great achievement, aside from his buildings (and let us not diminish his contribution there) was his writings. And no treatment of Clough's life and work would be complete without a consideration of his written works.

Certainly he seemed to work to Bakunin's dictum: 'I shall continue to be impossible so long as those who are now possible remain possible'. Despite the unpropitious political climate of the inter-war years, Clough could view both his architectural practice and his extended connections with pleasure. He might have sat back withself satisfaction. But that 'visual-unawareness' of the British never ceased to irk, however much he accomplished. The Design and Industries Association had infiltrated certain corners of the community, and had recruited worthwhile names to its ranks. Civic Societies had been established in various towns and cities, and a dining club known as The Architecture Club had a distinguished membership, including practised propagandists like

G.K. Chesterton and J.B. Priestley. But how to get to the masses? — that was what concerned Clough. He would never cease to be the missionary, the proselytiser and the scourge of the Philistines, whose ranks were filled with those who were indifferent to their environment. He had earlier confessed to being himself a Philistine in other areas, but to be fair, the art of writing was not among them. He wrote beautifully, in an inimitable style, best described as light Baroque, or even Rococo. With Amabel's help and sometimes with her co-authorship, he would never cease to write throughout his career, right into extreme old age.

*The Pleasures of Architecture* was their joint attempt to get at the masses they felt had been missed so far in the propaganda war against the ravages of environmental indifference. First published in 1924 by Jonathan Cape, it reached a second impression the same year, another in 1929 and in 1930, and then a revised edition after the war in 1954. Its jacket is an immediate pleasure, the lettering overlying a reproduction of an architectural section of the superb Rex Whistler mural at Plas Newydd in Anglesey.

While Clough was the ardent practitioner in architecture, Amabel was quite as adamant as educationist. They wrote separate introductions. Clough thought the book would 'offer a better picture of the world around us; it has certainly brought things into fresh and truer focus for ourselves'. Amabel thought that 'in most ages and places the art of architecture flourished where it had critical and knowledgeable patrons, and wilted where and when it had not'.

The text opened with a general treatise on the failure to look critically at architecture around the middle of the nineteenth century. While a new novel or musical composition or play, or a Tennyson ode, would command aesthetic consideration, architecture and architects received at best indifference. Only towards the end of the century did sons of wealthy families dare to suggest that architecture might be their chosen profession, so low was the general opinion of it among the well-to-do. Otherwise public indifference persisted.

There is little doubt that the Williams-Ellises, children of Victoria's reign, should bring a certain amount of its baggage to bear in their writing. It is not only the dark, prevailing Gothic of the century that appalled them and made them look with hope and gladness at the twentieth century. 'For instance,' they write, 'women unquestionably dress both themselves and their children better than they did . . . . Men also have largely ceased to insist in their clubs, smoking rooms and offices upon what we may perhaps be allowed to call the "Spittoon style" of furnishing, with its brown leather chairs, fumed oak, golfing prints, tantalus and red turkey carpet.'

They nominated the period 1660 to 1780 as the great and exemplary period of architecture. 'What were the dominant social and intellectual ideas of this great architectural period? In the first place, we cannot point to another century and a half so homogeneous. It was notoriously a reasonable, realistic and settled age. It substituted for a religious conviction the conviction that it could be independent of religion. It was witty, it delighted in beautiful workmanship, and in learning. Above all, it studied the art of life in all its branches, and its architecture reminds us that the age of Nell Gwynn was also the age of Newton. Its voluptuousness and hardiness were matched by its fine passion for knowledge.'

In all this, compared with other works by Clough, one detects the pen and mind of Amabel. 'The world as it is and human nature as it is, makes a bitter pill to swallow. But in the reaction to Puritanism, we in England during that age followed the French and swallowed it. This is, we believe, testified no less by Greenwich Hospital than by the sudden development of both the Royal Society and the novel.' Amabel, (for surely this is she), brings comparative studies to bear on Clough's normally single-minded approach to architecture. Amabel had opinions and would be the last either to regret or to apologise for them in any way. And why should she? 'Puritans, Romantics, and Escapists never are, or even desire to be, at home in the world, and if to these two classes of professed nomads we add the entire race of Celts, we can perhaps account for a good many of the dark and light places on the architectural map and time-scale.' One cannot help wondering at the whole sweep of poor Celts and whatever they had done to deserve this.

As for poor old Britain, well, Baedeker would guide the visitor to the various salient features of its towns, but they were barely visible for want of design and planning. One could not see past this hoarding, or that offending excrescence, nor could one negotiate with any ease this or that winding street in order to see the great structure, whatever it might be. There was, both literally and figuratively, no vision.

Then the nineteenth century comes in for their especial treatment. 'In England from the time when the young Disraeli first entered Parliament and wrote his flaming *Sybil*, till an octogenarian Gladstone resigned on his Home Rule Bill, they never ceased building. Britain, as we now know it, rose from the fields and the

moors . . . . Leaving aside for a minute then the thin red line of
Mr Street's, Mr Webb's, or Mr Norman Shaw's activities, we can
agree that the nineteenth century produced a larger proportion of
solid and inconvenient eyesores than any other century of which
we have records . . . .'

The entire Gothic Romance earns this treatment. '. . . Lakes,
mountains, Mr Ruskin, Italy, Dr Pusey, the Middle Ages, Norman
castles and Arthurian cycles, such were the objects which engaged
the attention of the sensitive, just as admiration of the beautiful
workings of the laws of supply and demand employed the money
makers.'

Ruskin had said 'power in the dominion of art is regrettable.
Blessed with the keenest sensibility and a rare gift of expression
with pen and pencil, he judged buildings much as one supposes
candidates for Anglican ordination were judged at the same
period.' But, the authors declare, after all this and the hiatus of
the Great War, architecture is lifting its head again. A younger
generation is building on the pioneering work of Street and Webb
and Shaw and the rest of the brave few. This is the twentieth
century and now is our chance.

Well, at the end of the twentieth century we know the rest, and
now we plan waywardly for the twenty-first century and the new
millennium. Reading *The Pleasures of Architecture* one wonders if
anything has been learnt. Perhaps it is time to place architectural
studies on the National Curriculum.

At any rate, the Williams-Ellises direct us towards figures like
Maxwell Fry and Walter Gropius, and to movements like the New
Towns. And so, having doled out both praise and blame, they
declare that it 'ought to be possible to derive pleasure from the
forms of a Malay, a Tuscan, or a Cotswold village, to be exhilarated by the romantic towering storeys of the Rockefeller Centre,
to be awed by the mighty ruins of Anuradhapura or of Rome and
to derive sharp intellectual enjoyment from the layout of Pekin,
Bath or Siemenstadt.' Then follows a chapter on how to look at
buildings, how to drink in, enjoy, assess this or that structure. And
again, the advice is offered: to draw is to concentrate, to concentrate is to appreciate and enjoy aspect, detail and context.

In these more cynical times, it may all sound rather tedious,
even pious, to a generation whose attention span has been put at
three minutes. But the loss would be theirs, for the whole book is
really a treatise on Pleasure, and especially the pleasure of architecture and how to achieve it. Clough, throughout his writings,
constantly reminds us of the ubiquitous presence of buildings,

good, bad and indifferent. We cannot escape from them, as we can close a book, or leave a play or a concert. Buildings are *there*, apparently for all time, and all round us in their commanding presence.

Having adjured the reader towards an appreciation of architecture, the book outlines the broad criteria of a critical faculty:

1. That beauty should be unadorned. Therefore a plain building will be preferable to one covered with ornament.
2. That a building should be expressive
     (a) of its construction,
     (b) of its purpose,
     (c) of its architect or period.
3. That sham materials are an abomination.
4. That the style of a building must be pure.
5. That styles have a biological life-history and can be divided into infancy, youth, full vigour, and senility.
6. That buildings whose main lines are horizontal ought to be built in hilly country. Conversely, buildings with many vertical lines are suitable for flat country.
7. That architects ought to invent a wholly new style and, on pain of being declared bankrupt of ideas, must not make use of traditional, Classic, Gothic, or Oriental detail and general effects.
8. That the object of studying any art is to form a pure and exclusive taste.

These are stern criteria, and I am not sure that Clough himself stands up well in numbers 1, 3 and 7.

The book cites the good, the bad and the downright ugly in building, the latter with almost a relish. We are instructed how we may positively enjoy architecture. Enjoyments are shared: the sheer panache and fun of the Festival of Britain and Battersea Pleasure Garden, some New Towns, and, not to be left out of it, Portmeirion, with Mr Christopher Hussey's encomium from *Country Life*.

In some ways, the book is enjoyable for its incidental prejudices. Poor old Ruskin, for instance, seems to have offended the authors. They seem to miss, or to ignore, his contribution to the salvation of Venice from the depredations of rich Europeans and Americans who were buying crumbling Venetian palazzi for a song and restoring them disastrously. It took the writings of Ruskin to halt this, and conscientious and responsible restoration took over. Ruskin's worship of the Gothic blinded the authors to his many qualities.

It has to be said however that a great deal of rather tedious and outdated philosophising dulls the impact of the book. It lacks the directness of Clough's normal approach. That is a pity, for the book otherwise hits hard and true. The authors, in their plea for recognition of the rightful place of architecture in the human psyche, find the 1923 edition of *The Encyclopaedia Britannica* devotes more space to an obscure Austrian general than to, say, Bernini. Claude Perrault, builder of the great facade of the Louvre, is not mentioned at all.

One chapter is devoted to a survey of twenty-two architects, among whom appear the great and the good: Inigo Jones, Wren, Le Notre, Soane, Vanburgh, Hawksmoor, Adam, Brunelleschi, and so on, ending in a profile of the qualities required to achieve success in the profession:

> If we see an architect as a man fulfilled, we may be able partly to account for the apparent absence in the profession of lyricism and mysticism. There never was an architect like Blake or Coleridge. Yet of a different sort of 'inspiration' there is plenty of evidence. Nothing but 'inspiration' will account for the 'five small designs on paper' from whose merely reminding evidence Bernini could certainly have carried out his grand design, or even for Vanburgh's Castle Howard.

Alas, it is not the sort of book, or the sort of pleading, that would move many today. It is not that anything the authors say is in the least irrelevant or untrue or even dull — it is perhaps the great changes in presentation, in information technology, and perhaps it must all be gone over again, in another way. Clough, by the quite frequent television presentations towards the end of his career, instinctively saw this. But the general thrust of *The Pleasures of Architecture*, its barbs and commendations, is as true, as necessary and as urgent as ever, given society's perennial Gadarene flight towards chaos, barbarity and sheer tastelessness.

# England and the Octopus

While *The Pleasures of Architecture* is meant to provide pleasure, or to introduce the reader to the subject as a source of enjoyment, the next volume was by Clough alone and is by contrast an angry book. *England and the Octopus* is a seminal work in twentieth century environmental studies. It was published first in 1928 by Geoffrey Bles, was reprinted the following year, and seemed to survive so well in the canon of works on planning that a new edition appeared in 1975, when Clough was ninety-one. Upon its first appearance it received favourable attention from writers as diverse as G.K. Chesterton and D.H. Lawrence.

Writing an introduction to the 1974 edition, Lewis Mumford suggested that 'part of it has become the flying banner of the ecological movement that is now sweeping the planet'. That may seem rather high-sounding, but there *is* a sense in which the ecology movement is sweeping the planet in a way that was not evident in the Twenties when Clough first wrote *England and the Octopus*. Clough was a pioneer and visionary, one of the early pilgrims whose example and publications have engendered movements like Greenpeace, UNESCO, the Woodland Trust and so on, all bodies whose object is to conserve and improve the environment, whether natural or manmade.

Sometimes the very earnestness of these various bodies tends to kill interest in the subject and one returns to that state of quiet desperation that seems the only retreat from a world gone mad. Clough is never guilty of that. As Mumford says, Clough 'is never more serious than when he is at play, never more playful than when he is serious'. Mumford firmly places Clough in the ranks of the prophets who have railed against the 'Octopus' of industrial expansion — Blake, Ruskin, Morris and others who have seen the ills of this malevolent development, not only on the environment but even on the basic health of the pawns of industry, the workers. Ruskin said to a gathering of city fathers in Bradford: 'Purify the water of your town, keep a girdle of open land around it, and clear the air of the smoke before you dare to talk of beauty'.

Clough in 1928 was the latest in this succession of prophets who had preached against the greed, thoughtlessness and ruthlessness of so much urban and industrial planning (or rather lack of it).

Yet Clough was never simply nostalgic for the green and pleasant land of pre-industrial Britain and morris dancers. He was firmly a twentieth century man. What irritated him was the sheer ignorance, the lack of thought which typified most building

development. And he was not afraid to declare for Beauty. He was
not a member of the Functionalist School which would declare,
as Eric Gill had: 'Look after Goodness and Truth and Beauty will
look after itself'. On that he could be described as sceptical —
Beauty does not look after itself.

*England and the Octopus*, then, is a plea for that Beauty which
seemed to have been the least of considerations in nineteenth
century industrial expansion. Despite the book's publication in
1928, along with continuing concern from others like Mumford
himself, by the seventies there was even more to worry about, so
that Clough declares in the 1975 preface: 'This is an angry book,
written by an angry young man nearly half a century ago. Now I
am in my ninety-second year and still angry . . .'.

In despair he asked his friend Bertrand Russell, likewise a
nonagenarian with a millennial view of things, for suggestions in
the 1975 revision. Bertie replied with a blistering piece of doggerel:

> The Nuclear Boffins, God bless 'em all,
> Have fall-out assessed to a decimal.
> But my nephew and niece
> Have three legs apiece
> And their intellect's infinitesmal.

Alas, it is all too deserved, and it is fair comment on the twentieth
century's own sinister tentacle to the Octopus.

But of more precise concern to Clough was actual building;
bricks, mortar, concrete and steel, in thoughtless ribbon development. Of course, we now know it is not as easy as it might have
appeared then. In post-war planning, it was as though *England
and the Octopus* had been read, marked and inwardly digested —
no more ribbon development, let us build in a more concentrated
way inside our cities, in central tower blocks, and thus preserve
our precious green belts and the surrounding countryside. Many
of those Fifties and Sixties blocks have already been demolished
and the great prophet of twentieth century architecture, Le
Corbusier, stands condemned. As usual, it is selective indignation,
for Le Corbusier was responsible for some fine architecture, like
the chapel at Ronchamps. But he must stand responsible to some
degree for the tower block, that inhumane prison, eyesore to so
many of our towns and cities.

The arguments and the definitions must go on, that is really the
central message of *England and the Octopus*. It is interesting to
notice how wrong the author can be on occasion: 'I think the only

country left that I should like to have a look at now is China,
where, a generation ago, I did a considerable amount of building,
but all by remote control'. It was indeed 'remote'. It is possible at
this approach to the twenty-first century that China is among the
worst offenders in environmental devastation and now threatens
to join the Nuclear Club.

Clough preaches, of necessity. Had things been left too long for
redemption? 'The horse having been well and truly stolen we are
about to stage the great national ceremony of locking the stable
door — not quite fruitlessly, as we are fallen so low that even the
remaining straw and the halter have become precious to us as
emblems of our former wealth.' It is admonitory, couched sometimes in the terms of a Calvinist minister preaching to the non-
Elect. 'In the late war we were invited to fight to preserve England.
We believed, we fought. It may be well to preserve England, but
better to have an England worth preserving. We saved our country,
that we might ourselves destroy it.' That is the crux of the
argument of *England and the Octopus*. The tone is indeed angry.
The English *did* once have a green and pleasant land, a superb
landscape of towns and villages and grand estates, and indeed
great natural and man-made beauty. The largest town outside
London at the end of the eighteenth century was Norwich. Now,
despite the desperate struggle of war to protect all that heritage,
first in the Great War, then in the Second, they are guilty of fouling
it up, of averaging it all out in senseless sprawl, planting trees in
the town and bungalows in the country.

> We know well enough that decent, God-fearing, God-
> damning Englishmen live very contentedly in the pink
> asbestos bungalows; and if they chance to be on Salisbury
> Plain or Dartmoor or the South Downs or some command-
> ing hill in the Cotswolds or the Chilterns where they can
> be seen from miles around, they are the more content and
> very far from being ashamed.

He sorts out the sheep from the goats. 'Cultivated people of all
classes must deplore what is happening; the unseeing and un-
thinking (also of all classes) are no doubt more or less indifferent.'
The Elect and the non-Elect? Maybe, but he is so outraged and
angry that he has no qualms about the language. The little
parenthesis about class is also indicative. It is not about the rich
and the poor, the privileged and the un-privileged. Indeed, the
rich by their very wealth and capacity to build are the more likely
to offend. It is more a matter of the Enlightened (in the fullest

eighteenth century sense) and what he says is that the Enlightened ought to know better than to allow all the despoilation to happen.

*The Octopus* is certainly polemical in tone. Clough will use any means of propaganda to extend his message to an indifferent world. He is sarcastic, ironic, sardonic and even downright nasty if it helps to illustrate his thesis:

> You may ravish and defile the most divine landscape in the world, and your children (being your children) will rise and call you progressive. You are 'a lucky prospector' or 'a successful real estate operator', a 'live wire' and what local newspapers call 'a prominent and respected citizen'. By your exploitation of the land you have enriched yourself and your heirs. You have done very well. God's footstool!

He goes on to outline all sorts of horrors and crimes for which we are punished either by society or by Divine wrath. 'If we technically blaspheme — mere perishable words — we are threatened with hell fire *and / or* six months hard labour.' But an eyesore built on a precious site is not perishable, yet its perpetration goes unnoticed and unpunished.

He invites us to recall and consider our more distant past, when building took place round some craft or occupation — milling, fishing, weaving or ceramics, and was modest enough in scale to develop a village or small town or harbour round it without loss of amenity. Then he quotes the nineteenth century's rapid expansion from craft into industry:

> large factories, terraced housing for their workforce and all this done ruthlessly, with no thought whatsoever for either the environment, the future or the health of that workforce. Then, unforgivably, twentieth century emancipation of wealth and the enlargement of the middle classes meant the spread of further isolated, unplanned development away from the conurbations, so that a glance at a present-day Ordnance map reveals a sort of chicken pox of sites spread over the terrain. *Mon Abri* stares vacantly at the shameful hinder parts of *Loch Lomond*, which in turn is overlooked and put out of countenance by the baleful scowl of *Kia-ora* on its flank.

He knows the reasons, of course, and heads them: 1. A monstrously swollen population. 2. The drift from agriculture to industry. 3. Improved means of locomotion.

Put like that, it seems there is little we can do about it, short of some sort legislated birth control *à la Chine*; severe fuel rationing; and a rash of land-armies spread over the landscape. But there are examples of environments where all this is dealt with humanely and with aesthetic considerations in mind. He gives examples of enlightenment, quoting Germany (perhaps with the Bauhaus in mind?), as a country which, coming after Britain in the process of industrialisation, learned from its own mistakes and remedied them: 'there has been a definite move through all the country not only to apply decent architectural standards in the new factories erected, but as far as possible to humanise them by planting them with trees, grass and flowers'. All this not for philanthropic reasons, but because it promoted a more content and loyal workforce, thus obviating industrial unrest. That does sound rather rosier than the full truth, it must be said.

He pleads for smoke abatement. As for towns, he is an ardent apologist for New Towns, building from scratch on a green or cleared site, but in a sane, civilised way that has room for aesthetics as well as function. The old idea of mean dormitories for a docile and impoverished workforce is condemned as cynical, inhuman and uncivilised.

Writing before post-war legislation, Welwyn is cited as an example, and it must be said the town has stood the test well. He even cites Baku, the Russian New Town built at an oil terminal on the edge of the Caspian Sea:

> Even at Baku, one of the most remote industrial towns in all Russia, this is thoroughly understood and acted upon so far as the limited resources of the Soviets will allow. Here on the barren shores of the Caspian Sea and the farthest edge of Europe, among oil gushers, sledges, fire-worshippers, veiled women, and camels, the barbaric, common-sense Russians are doing as a matter of course very much what we are so proud of having accomplished at Letchworth, Welwyn and the Hampstead Garden Suburb.

Well, we may wonder, perhaps. But we know what he means. In his tour of the Soviet Union in about 1930, he had witnessed due consideration for the workers' needs when a new industry was being developed, and that it made for good sense and decent environment in spite of all the industrial development. It was what he came to call 'good manners' in architecture.

He then writes a fictitious example of what mostly happens, or seems to happen with our national heritage. He imagines an attractive site on the Ordnance map, a place we would surely wish to visit on a day trip, or even stay at, because it has such an attractive name and promises much — say, 'Castle Malory'.

It is true, he writes, that once there was a castle ruin on a rise at this seaside site. There was an attractive beech grove, and an interesting quayside with the masts against the sky, charming cottages, all a sort of Whitby. Alas, the ruin has gone, the mound has been built over, the railway has cut off the town from the quayside, the police station is absolutely hideous, the castellated Salvation Army building is likewise, housing is a mere unplanned mess, and the false demands of tourism have taken over, with the accent on trade rather than any thought or memory of the original attractive castle site and its historic framework.

> Then what is there to charm or beguile one in Castle Malory? A romantic past? An industrious if philistine present? It is not enough — we have already stayed over-long, and we will leave the unhappy place by the next train with the blinds drawn down — for ever.

Another chapter imagines some get-rich-quick-Johnnie-come-lately who arrives at a place, does well, builds, expands, and generally offends all the locals, but, as the Army says, 'bashes on regardless'. This fiction, of course, is all too often true, and Clough's imagination runs riot, as well it may:

> You knew that excellent building land was readily available elsewhere, but with a speculating builder as your accomplice you could not resist this perfectly legal opportunity of turning a dishonest penny . . . you ridiculed the council's nascent interest in town planning, with the result that in order to reach the open country it is now necessary to pass your calamitous villas for a weary mile of unrewarded walking whichever route be taken.

He then suggests various actions for those who, having been appalled by his horrible scenario, might wish to do something about it. He wonders about Education. What *is* taught — what is 'the aesthetic horizon' in the art schools for example? For a start, if we must have school prayers, could we not include a prayer for 'the apprehending, making and guarding of Beauty, and more especially for the state of England'. He, the kicker over the traces of religious belief, the 'congenital deviationist', actually writes out an entire prayer and his priestly paternity is so well-remembered that any self-respecting headmaster would be happy to intone it before the assembly:

> We pray that he that buildeth or that maketh a road or that
> planteth or felleth a tree or doth aught else to change the
> face of this our country, may have a right guidance in all
> things, lest haply the beauty and the glory of the land be
> utterly destroyed . . . .

The teachers must be taught, Clough warns us, and even the
educational authorities. Politicians, local and national, must be
badgered. He is contemptuous of all parties: the Conservative
Party conserves the wrong things; Liberals and Radicals are
neither; the Communists are all Marx and no Morris . . . none of
them really cares. He wonders why churches, with their concern
for spiritual values, do not have more to say.

Some of *England and the Octopus* reads rather sadly. He pleads
for schoolmasters to teach pupils that to throw litter is 'ill-
mannered, un-neighbourly and filthy'. Alas, we are worse than
ever and any journey abroad, especially to Germany and the
Scandinavian countries, demonstrates that the British are filthy
by comparison. No wonder he was still angry after nearly fifty
years of preaching the gospel. He ends in despair: 'unless you are
really rich, it is wise to be born an Italian or a Scandinavian'.

He devotes a chapter to what are now called 'listed buildings',
that is, sorting out the good from the bad and the ugly in our legacy
of redundant grand houses. This is one suggestion, of course, that
has been taken up, and considering he wrote it in about 1928, it
demonstrates the time-lag from published word to actual legislation.
He then develops certain environmental themes. For instance, a
local council can actually legislate for good lettering, decent shop
fascias and advertisements, well-painted signs, the use of white-
wash in appropriate cases. And as in a didactic work of his,
*Architecture Here and Now*, he advocates the 'collecting' of good
buildings for the layman, self-education in the assessment of local
architecture, so that gradually we shall become the enlightened
democracy. We shall come to love (and thus to preserve) this or
that precious item, a Georgian doorway, an avenue of pollarded
lime trees (we remember his own quixotic purchase of the mile-
and-a-half Stowe avenue to save it from speculative builders) or
a good shop front with fine lettering. Otherwise — and he goes on
to quote from Ruskin's *Fors Clavigera*:

> The sun has drawn landscapes for you . . . in green and
> blue and all imaginable colours, here in England. Not one
> of you ever looked at them then; not one of you cares for
> the loss of them now, when you have shut the sun out with

smoke. There was a rocky valley between Buxton and
Bakewell, once upon a time, divine as the vale of Tempe;
you might have seen the gods there morning and evening
— Apollo and all the sweet muses of the light, walking in
fair procession on the lawns of it, and to and fro among the
pinnacles of its crags. You cared neither for gods nor grass
but for the cash (which you did not know the way to get).
You thought you could get it by what *The Times* calls
'Railroad Enterprise'. You enterprised a railroad through
the valley, you blasted its rocks away, heaped thousands of
tons of shale into its lovely stream. The valley is gone, and
the gods with it; and now every fool in Buxton can be at
Bakewell in half an hour and every fool in Bakewell in
Buxton; which you think a lucrative process of exchange,
you Fools, everywhere!

Clough appends this with a despairing thought: 'Perhaps England
is in sober truth one of the "backward peoples"'. And he ends this
contentious book with 'A Devil's Dictionary containing Some
Specific Complaints, Warnings and Proposals'. It advises us on
everything from Advertisements and Aerodromes to respect for
Trees against Water, ending touchingly on a 'beautiful little village
. . . that is perhaps the most engagingly water-conscious place in
England . . .'.

Since writing this, I travelled one day to one of Clough's sites
that I had not seen before. It was a Sunday in August and the day
was bright and sunny. Suddenly I came across this heavenly place,
quite obviously 'the most engagingly water-conscious place in
England'. Clear rippling water ran through limestone pavements
parallel to the road, little bridges crossed it, willows shaded it, and
the houses were pure English at its best. It was all so idyllic I gasped
at its sheer beauty — and yes, it was indeed 'most engagingly
water-conscious'. Alas, Clough's secret is no longer. I crawled
through the snarled-up traffic, there was a fight for parking space,
people covered every square foot of the place's beautiful surface.
This is the perpetual dilemma for those who value beauty as
Clough did. It is right and natural to wish to share it, yet we do
so at its peril, for we lay it open to the one thing that can devalue
it, even destroy it — crowds of admirers.

There is one last touch to the book, an *Epistola Epilogica* or
Afterword by Sir Patrick Abercrombie, in which he reinforces
Clough's arguments, and ends with such admiration that 'I would
propose *You*, Clough, for a Knight Grand Cross; it would become
you well'.

Despite the National Parks Report of 1931, nothing was done

by Government to encourage recognition of its aims or to implement its recommendations. In the *Geographical Magazine* of May
1939, Clough wrote an article on Snowdonia, one of the areas
recommended for National Park status in the Report. He outlines
the history of the region and the odd opinion of it held by its rare
visitors in the past. John Leyland in 1536 complained that it 'is
horrible with the weight of bare stones' and the astronomer Halley
described it as 'this horrid spot of hills'.

Clough writes feelingly about the mountains, valleys and lakes
of Snowdonia. He regrets that the native Welsh revere its history,
folk-lore and legend rather than the place itself. 'Archaeology,
hagiography and ancestor worship are not enough. To sing our
national anthem, *Land of my Fathers*, is not enough.'

Snowdonia has survived thus far more by good luck than by
good management. Clough then weighs into the powers that be.
'The report of the Committee set up by the Government to
consider the whole question of National Parks is well known . . . .
That was eight years ago, and thus far nothing whatsoever has
been done about it — by the government . . . man cannot survive
in full bodily health and spiritual vigour if denied the healing
contact with unmanipulated Nature that the wild places of our
teeming country can still afford.'

This is a typical article of Clough the propagandist, and he never
lost any opportunity to press home his views to any who would
hear. He had always been good at exploiting connections and he
would do the same when it came to getting at Government. If
we had to wait till after the Second World War for the sort of
legislation Clough was looking for, it was largely due to him and
a few pioneers like him that National Parks came about at all. The
editor of the magazine headed Clough's article with the words:

> In the first issue of *The Geographical Magazine* (May 1933)
> attention was drawn to the Government's failure to imple-
> ment the National Parks Report of 1931, to which Mr
> Williams-Ellis again refers in the present article. While
> foreign 'crises' fluctuate, some of the loveliest parts of the
> Britain we are preparing to defend may be ruined; and
> nothing can excuse the Government's continued inaction
> and apparent indifference in a matter which, though per-
> haps insignificant from the standpoint of vote-catching, is
> of deep and permanent concern to the whole nation.

'*England and the Octopus*,' wrote Lewis Mumford in retrospect
some thirty years later, 'was the opening gun in a fresh campaign

to overcome the devastating ugliness that was spreading again in
the motor age, as it had spread in the earlier railroad age, over the
small historic towns and still verdant rural areas of Britain.
Williams-Ellis was resuming and following through the pioneering work done by William Morris two generations before; and as
a result of a sharpened public conscience about both the natural
landscape and historic buildings, a whole series of public trusts
and national foundations are now addressing themselves to this
task . . . .'

# Architecture Here and Now

In some ways Clough was a poor apologist for his own views on architectural history in general. In *Architect Errant* he portrays himself as an undiluted Classicist, despite his 'congenital deviationism', and gives the impression that little else interests him. But in a slim volume, written with John Summerson and published by Thomas Nelson in 1934, the views expressed are much more tolerant and catholic than one might expect from Clough. He was, it seems, more broad-minded than he allows in his autobiography. The Nelson volume is *Architecture Here and Now*. It is populist rather than professional in its approach. While it is a fairly didactic introduction to current architecture for the general public, it does not preach like *England and the Octopus*.

John Summerson (later knighted) was an architectural historian and for many years was Director of the Sir John Soane Museum in London. It is difficult, if not impossible, to know who wrote what but there are several passages which are vintage Clough. The introductory chapter, for example, recommends viewing buildings as a rewarding and pleasant pursuit: 'A knowledge of architecture is the best of travelling companions'. The authors believe this sort of viewing is enhanced if some sort of record, either photographs or sketches, is made of each building 'collected'. That is a very Cloughian term. He realised the instinctive human urge to collect, yet no one seemed to express any urge to 'collect' buildings. His instinct and habits from childhood onwards indicated that the use of a word like 'collecting', in relation to buildings, with its faint hint of eccentricity, might just break down this apparent inhibition.

He is surely right. I know of nobody who collects buildings in the sense he recommends, yet I know from my own experience that a visit to a city like Venice or Rome is heightened by recording their various architectural gems by pencil or camera.

*Architecture Here and Now* is a guide to any layman who may take up this suggestion of 'collecting' buildings. Although it is a very slim volume, a mere seventy-five pages, it packs in quite a lot, and its drawings and photographs are clear and comprehensive. It embraces Modernism and Functionalism too, since no volume of the twentieth century can honestly claim 'here and now' and ignore modern method, taste and materials. One hardly associates Clough with revolutionary modernists like Le Corbusier, but he is there in the book, along with others in the Modern movement, like Alvar Aalto and Serge Chemayeff. It is a charming book, in both its text and its illustrations. Even the captions are illuminating. Aalto's Paimio Sanatorium near Helsinki is familiar in style to us at the end of the twentieth century, a plain cantile-vered block, clean of line, uncompromising in its horizontal bias — 'eloquent of health and cleanliness; yet there are people who disparage such simplicity as "a vertical filing cabinet for sick human beings"'.

The strange thing about *Architecture Here and Now* is that it is precisely that, a guide to the principles of what we know as Modernism by two people who were basically Classicist in out-look, training and vocation. Of course, Classicists such as Lutyens figure in it, but the dominant message, after the introductory chapter on the basics of post and arch and beam, is that there is a logical and inevitable progression from a Greek temple, a Roman aqueduct or a Romanesque cathedral to twentieth century Modernism and Functionalism. For example, the light and space facilitated by reinforced concrete of the church of Notre Dame at Le Raincy near Paris, the authors declare, is something fifteenth century builders would have coveted.

There have always been regional variations in architecture and the same goes for Modernism. The materials may be much the same, but different countries offer different treatments. A Peter Behrens house in the Taunus mountains is admired not only for its uncompromising modern line but also for the way the horizon-tal bias of its structure harmonises with the terraces of the garden, which in turn grow out of the landscape.

Not everything modern is admirable. The authors come down heavily on some American architecture: 'many of the largest American skyscrapers are remarkable, apart from their size, only for the stupidity and vulgarity of their design'. Frank Lloyd Wright is admired, of course, and the great man later would meet Clough in Portmeirion.

Architecture is always changing, declare the authors, 'and if you are still alive to read this book in forty or fifty years' time you will find it strangely old fashioned'. Yes, indeed, and how right they were, for the book also goes into town planning, citing certain eighteenth century developments like the Adelphi as good, and others as lost opportunities. They castigate ribbon development and commend Le Corbusier's *Town of the Future* with its residential tower block. 'Why should we spread buildings all over the ground, when by building vertically we can have gardens on the ground and houses in the air?' Well, we now know, sixty years later, that it is not as simple as that. They were merely expressing a Thirties orthodoxy which ultimately led to a rash of tower blocks after the interval of war. For every Alton Estate at Roehampton, there were far too many Tower Hamlets all over the cities of this country. Many have had to be blown up and their residents rehoused in yet more green site development. There is ever yet greater danger of losing more countryside now that farmland, through over-production of grain, is 'set aside' on a subsidy, and becomes more economic as building land.

*Architecture Here and Now*, with its claim to be historic and prophetic is in the end simply 'here and now', very much a Thirties book, but nonetheless attractive and well worthwhile in its time as an exercise in popular education of the kind that would develop with Adult Education and the Open University after the war.

It is evident from this book, and from the process of its writing, that Clough's architectural interests were wider than his own projects might imply. For instance, there is a photograph and plan of the excellent Midland Hotel at Morecambe by Oliver Hill. It is a good example of what might be called British Modernism, perhaps what has come to be known as Art Deco. When Clough wished to extend the Dining Room at the Hotel in Portmeirion, he saw at once the stylistic and practical difficulties. Instead of reproducing the Victorian style of the original structure, Clough exploited a curved, highly glazed, plan of clearly Modern concept, and with great success. It works, it actually enhances the old building, and it is always welcoming. Yet it is reminiscent of Hill's Modern masterpiece at Morecambe.

In 1933, Clough's 'Fishponds' restaurant at Cobham in Kent was designed with masterly modernist flare. Even more so, the Morannedd Café, built by the sea at Cricieth in the late Fifties, exemplifies this brush with Modernism, and the boomerang-shaped plan is unique in Clough's canon. The great sweeping curves of glass under the flat roof show how easily Clough might have proceeded into Modernism, yet in the end, he maintained his Palladian aloofness and remained an unrepentant Traditionalist. He not only had the taste for it but the ability, and never fell into the traps of what has come to be called Post-Modernism, where certain elements remind us vaguely of tradition but in the end come to jar.

In one respect alone *Architecture Here and Now* must have been valuable in its time, for it condemns the prevailing muddle over all planning, and commends proper town, regional and national planning, all in simple, non-technical language. The authors advise that the architect can no longer develop his industrial site in isolation, but must work within a context, be it residential, industrial or rural. With the right attitude and will, architects can emulate the better attributes of eighteenth century towns like Bath and Harrogate, and even improve on them, since in building science and sanitation they are superior; 'it is in spiritual health and imaginative ingenuity that we lag behind'.

Again, it is indicative of its time that Russia is quoted as an example of national planning. 'Although we may often envy the way in which the Russians are able to plan their towns without argument or compromise, there is a great deal to be said for letting each man build what he likes — within limits.' Whether Clough and John Summerson would still put it quite like that is doubtful, for the collapse of Communism in Russia is surely indicative of the incipient chaos that was always there, though in a closed society like the old USSR, it was not be expressed or acknowledged.

Sometimes the views are almost embarrassingly naive from our own impeccable hindsight. Under a photograph of Lenin's tomb, the caption reads: 'Soviet Russia exalts simplicity and strength, and it is fitting that Lenin's tomb should exemplify a rugged fortitude'. On the other hand, under a drawing of the Euston Arch the authors write: 'Euston Arch, 1838, an impressive symbol of coming and going, was built before people had despaired of discovering beauty among machines. The idea is borrowed from Greece'. How sad that post-war planning has been the excuse for demolishing this splendid monument to our railway system, mostly doomed too. All of which demonstrates the urgency of forward planning on a national scale for the preservation and improvement of our towns and landscapes but with even more urgency than pioneers like Clough may have thought would ever be necessary.

These books are the chief items in Clough's writings between the wars, but there was much else, for he would lose no opportunity to write for what are now called the broadsheets, *The Manchester Guardian, The Times* and *The Telegraph*. He wrote a biography of Sir Lawrence Weaver, then *The Adventure of Building, Town and Country Planning*, and *Roads in the Landscape*. This might be seen as amply covering his chosen enthusiasms and mission but he also edited anthologies like *The Face of the Land* and *Britain and the Beast*. After the war there was *Headlong Down the Years* (with Amabel), a hugely satisfying satire in the Peacock style on the silly ploys and tactics of Electricity Board wallahs in general, but particularly in their quest to despoil Welsh valleys with a multiplicity of schemes as though the region were some compliant Mururoa to be trampled over. And after World War II Clough would extend his field by lecturing at home and abroad for organisations like the British Council and the Army. Altogether, he had a lifelong mission to raise public awareness of the problems, solutions and pleasures and miseries of the environment. Late in life this would extend further into the field of radio and television broadcasting for which he was a natural, and much beloved of camera and sound crews.

# Voyager

Clough had first learned to sail at Glasfryn as a boy of six. There he had messed about with a little old dinghy on the lake, with only a lug-sail, no keel and an oar for rudder. It was a good apprenticeship, rather like learning the vagaries of a coracle will fix you up for anything with oars.

In adult life, with his ancestral home in Meirionnydd near the coast, he was inevitably to return to sailing. It was in his blood and I believe that beyond architecture and family it was his only passion. Not long after the First World War he bought a small Hillyard sloop, *Twinkler*. In a pursuit like sailing, passion often comes before sense and he had two difficulties at once. First, he had not informed Amabel of his acquisition, and secondly, he had not thought out properly where to keep *Twinkler*.

As to the first, Amabel with her usual enthusiasm took to the role of deck hand at once. As to the second, it would set him on a trail of island- and peninsula-hopping that would eventually lead him to a site near Brondanw and to a momentous architectural decision.

After *Twinkler* had served its purpose, Clough searched in boatyards up and down the coast and eventually acquired a 15-ton Loch Fyne ketch, *Scott*. At first *Scott*, like a newly acquired puppy, presented certain problems. Every landfall involved a long and tiresome search by Customs. As with a puppy, a glance at the pedigree might have helped. *Scott* had a reputation as a smuggler's craft and Clough could never shake it off. However, the whole family sailed the coast of Wales and farther, and enjoyed the tussles with the sea and shoreline that sailors seem to like. Friends would ask why he endured such hardships, the cold and the wet, the occasional danger in a squall, and the uncomfortable quarters. To a land lubber it is inexplicable and he ceased trying to explain. But there *were* real dangers and anxiety, such as the occasion (as usual undated), when *Scott* was moored off one of the twin islands of St Tudwal off the Llŷn peninsula.

The islands had come up for sale round about 1930. Clough, anxious that they should not fall into the hands of some ruthless developer and ever interested in islands, purchased them. They would provide anchorage in Cardigan Bay, and also quarters, for the lighthouse was now automated and the Keeper's house vacated. One night Clough and Amabel decided to sleep aboard *Scott* while the children were snug in the Keeper's house. At dusk, making sure for the third time that everything was shipshape, they found that both anchors were dragging in a strong wind and tide. They managed to manoeuvre *Scott* to the lee side of the island, but even there they were dragging anchor. They were forced to run for Pwllheli, short of drifting out to sea. They knew the children were all right with ample rations in the house but it must have been alarming for both parties, the children abandoned for three days or so, the parents ashore, waiting for a quieter sea, and sick with anxiety. But all was well, and they were safely reunited.

On another occasion they encountered difficulties off Cherbourg and the engine died on them. Clough fired distress flares, but nobody ashore took the least notice. Clough had to manage as best he could and with his usual luck, a turn in the tide saw them safely into harbour, where a query about the absence of response to his rockets produced only a Gallic shrug of the shoulders. After a few days' sight-seeing Clough tried to revive the old engine, to no avail, so in a favourable wind they set sail out of Cherbourg for Dartmouth at midnight to work the tide. But the weather deteriorated and they had the most hair-raising voyage in steadily rising following seas. Clough was mightily relieved when at dawn he saw breakers ahead, but also worried that they might indicate the treacherous Casquets or some other hazard in the Alderney Race. It proved to be neither and Clough decided it must be the hallucinations of sheer fatigue. In the end they did not make Dartmouth at all, but Salcombe, some miles farther down the Devon coast, and considering the hazards of sailing the English Channel at its widest part, it was not a bad landfall. But Clough seems to have put wife and family at risk in some of his sea ventures and only a man with his luck could get away with it. Yet the last to charge him with recklessness would be the family.

Much later in life in the Spring of 1960, Clough chartered the yacht *Oronsay*, a 30-ton schooner out of Monaco. It had a most unusual and stimulating skipper, 'a somewhat Conrad-like figure', quite as ready to discuss Proust as great circle navigation. Their landfall was Calvi in Corsica. Their passengers were the Bretts and Elizabeth Beazley, the architectural historian.

The weather in the Mediterranean is not always plain-sailing and once or twice they were dependent for their survival on their professional skipper's skills. Once they were driven back with practically bare poles and briefly earned an honourable mention in the Italian Press and Radio. The previous evening they had sought anchor in the harbour of a small island. It proved to be inhabited by a penal colony, and one can imagine the governor's alarm at this excellent means of escape suddenly turning up. The harbour master refused to allow them even to lie alongside the quay until the skipper pulled rank on their behalf by declaring that Lionel Brett and Clough were English noblemen of the highest blood. (There had always been a strange respect for English nobility since Lord Byron's long and notorious sojourn in Venice and Pisa.)

They sailed on to Elba, to check on A.P. Herbert's book on Napoleon's exile there. Clough's one claim to any common characteristic with the Emperor was their mutual taste for town and country planning, for Napoleon had whiled away his lonely exile on the island by 'improving' it, much to Clough's taste.

On they went, up the coast of Italy, where they encountered one of those squalls that happen in that part of the Mediterranean and which had drowned Shelley off Lerici. They swept on past Carrara and might have moored in the little harbour of Portofino, had not Lionel Brett warned Clough that the place had altered greatly since Clough's visit forty years previously. It was better to pass by and retain the memory, which so informs the design of Portmeirion. And so, back to Monaco and home, much refreshed.

So much so that they decided to repeat the charter of the *Oronsay*, this time out of Messina, to circumnavigate Sicily, and with the Philip Hugh-Joneses aboard. The skipper once again was up to scratch and they completed the journey, point to point, in exactly the fourteen days of the charter. One moonlit night they were boarded by angry fishermen, who declared they had overrun and destroyed their tunny nets. It was too true, but Clough pointed out that they had cast their nets without lights at night. It took three hours to free the propeller. The dispute had to go before the British Consul. There seems no end to the hazards of sailing, but Clough would take it all in his stride. He was adept at turning flak from whatever quarter.

They landed from time to time to explore ruins and other sites at their leisure. It was indeed a fabulous way to spend a holiday, especially in the early Sixties when tourists were still probably less than half their present numbers.

In 1967 Clough, tempted by reading Norman Douglas's *South Wind*, proposed a visit to Capri, although he had been advised that it was already too late to visit that delectable island on account of the number of tourists swarming over it. But Jan Morris, that renowned traveller, insisted that it was such a 'Clough place' that he must visit it still, but in May, when it was suitably quiet, yet with perfect weather. They took her advice and found it was indeed bliss, as most Italian cities and islands are in May. And as far as taste went, Clough did find it a sort of Portmeirion writ large, with, for him, the added advantage of perpetual deep water, since tides are minimal. But this was always the ancient mariner brushing aside the aesthete, for the sands at Portmeirion are one of its glories, as anybody who has walked them at low tide on a sunny day will testify.

Exploring the Blue Grotto, Clough, blinded by the transition from brilliant sunlight to the dim light of the cave, stepped off a viewing platform straight into deep water with clothes, wallet and watch all soaked. Yet another of the charming girls he always seemed to meet arranged his drying out at a nearby café. He was a survivor time and time again. He had just recovered from a coronary. He borrowed a baggy but short pair of checked pantaloons from a chef while his own dried out in the kitchen, and he was no doubt briefly one of the sights of Capri. Over to Naples, which he found repellent, given his tastes, and he casually and cruelly averred that, 'for Naples, Vesuvius may now hold the only solution, as it did for Pompeii'.

In 1968, Clough and Amabel, wishing to fly to Corsica again, and having booked their direct flight months ahead, found themselves stranded by a French general strike associated with *les évenements* of that year. They could fly via Paris if they wished, stay the night in a hotel and make the most of the lost evening by exploring the city again, which Clough had earlier viewed with a somewhat jaundiced eye. Apparently his view on town planning did not accord with that of Baron Haussmann. But, taking a barge along the Seine, they revised their earlier view, proving yet again that there is no such thing as lost time, but rather wasted time.

Having enjoyed their second Corsica visit, again their flight was aborted. Instead (his lateral thinking again) Clough remembered seeing a rather fine steamer in the harbour, *Le Napoleon*, sailing out of Ajaccio for Marseilles. They secured a cabin and sailed for Marseilles. Stranded there by Sunday closing, they went out to see Le Corbusier's *Unite d'Habitation*, which might have been anathema, but in the event Clough found it 'slightly easier to take' than he had expected, except for its course texture and drab colour.

All this travel was part of an eager exploratory nature in Clough evident from the beginning in the boy impatient of confinement in nursery, classroom and school. He was a claustrophobe who was always happier out in the open air.

At the end of this life, Clough made a quite deliberate decision to retire from the sea, despite of dreams of some day being appointed an Elder of Trinity House, whose uniform and powers were the only honour he ever coveted. He recalled that he sold *Scott* to a scrap dealer, but I have often wondered about this, for on one occasion in the 1970s, the river Dwyryd at Portmeirion changed course yet again after a flood and the channel swirled in close to shore right under the hotel. As it did so, rapidly eating away at the sand, it exposed the timbers of some old craft that had been buried under the sands for years. I recall one evening after dinner, standing with Clough and Richard Hughes the writer, another neighbour with a nautical past, and talking about these timbers. I seem to recall Clough's references to them as those of his last craft. But it may just have been a general nostalgia for the sea, renewed by sight of the blackened timbers, still bearing the skeletal shape of a hull.

# Portmeirion

Just before the war in 1939, Christopher Hussey in *Country Life* commended Portmeirion as an example to those landowners who, either through indigence or inclination, did not wish to keep their inherited domain as their seat. The example became the more poignant after the war, when estates all over the country were being broken up and sold off in lots for speculative building. In many cases this involved the loss of a fine tract of landscape or the demolition of a building beyond the owner's pocket to maintain.

Clough was not quite in the position of the impoverished inheritor, for he actually chose (or rather it chose him) and purchased the peninsula of Aber Iâ (as it was formerly known) when it came on to the market. Nevertheless it stands as an example of self-development by a sympathetic and enlightened landowner. First of all Clough made no bones about building for commercial reasons, or to be more blunt, for profit. He would have to finance the development out of his own earnings from architectural projects (which must have been rising nicely in the Twenties and Thirties) and it would have to pay, as 'an appropriate site and a vivifying principle, a use, a job, that would make and keep it viable'; in this case, unashamedly tourism, 'a holiday retreat for the discerning'.

It was to be the culmination of the dream already nascent in the boy who, at Glasfryn, had responded to the warmth and grace of Tanrallt, and who, as a pupil at Oundle, had explored the old town and Kirby Hall, and had dreamed of building his own place, ideally on 'a vivifying principle'. It is this 'vivifying principle' that imbues Portmeirion — it is Clough, a highly personal and individual enterprise. No one else could have built Portmeirion. Another architect might have made it more ordered, better *planned*, more pure: yet another might have exploited a twentieth century style, perhaps a sort of Bauhaus village, and neither is a bad idea. But the charm of Portmeirion owes everything to its eclectic and eccentric designer. It is a delightful hotchpotch of sometimes disparate structures, Bavarian vernacular, Cornish weather-board, Jacobean, Regency, Strawberry Hill Gothic, and even Victorian Gothic. Some of it is even sham. A finial turns out to be painted on a sheet of steel, a stretch of water which normally denotes a sunken area, is merely raised on a former tennis court by building a low retaining wall to hold the water.

Yet it does work, and the impression at once, and also from long acquaintance (in my own case over forty years), is its charm.

Clough was the first to acknowledge the value of the site in
environmental terms. He had always enjoyed good luck, which in
any case is often a matter of pre-disposition. If his boyhood dream
were ever to be realised, then the principle criterion must be a site
of outstanding beauty, and given his nautical disposition, it ought
to be coastal. Having inherited Plas Brondanw, what greater good
fortune than to find, not five miles distant, an enchanting peninsula
suddenly available?

The peninsula has a strange and diverting history. An eccentric
lady tenant had jealously guarded the entire demesne like some
Miss Havisham in *Le Grand Meaulnes*. No one had been near the
place, nor been encouraged to be near, for a generation. Miss Haig
lived there with only a pack of dogs for company, and if she seems
to be forgotten, then her dogs are buried and well-remembered in
a group of elaborately worded headstones at the heart of the
Gwyllt, the wild landscape between the village and Tremadog
Bay:

Miss Haig's Beloved Dog
CLORAGH
How are the Dead raised up, and with what body do they come?
God giveth it a body as it hath pleased him, and to every seed
his own body: All flesh is not the same. Corinthians 1 Chapter 15.
So also is the Resurrection of the Dead.

The site satisfied another criterion, since Clough needed mooring for his yacht. He had cruised round the coast of Britain, rather
idly perusing this and that, dreaming perhaps of some island
paradise, yet realising that such a thing did not exist, since islands
by their very nature are inconvenient, have no amenities, are often
immured by storms and are inevitably remote.

The old and eccentric lady having died, the owner of Aber Iâ,
Sir Osmond Williams, sought a new tenant, or even buyer. Since
he was Clough's uncle by marriage, it was literally a matter of
nepotism, of the owner seeking his nephew's advice on who could
possibly want such a place following Miss Haig's tenancy. At the
time there were only the house of Aber Iâ and a stable complex.
The rest was wild, unkempt woodland, the haunt of a recluse who
had virtually renounced the world.

The peninsula was perfect in every way. On either side lay the
twin estuaries of Traeth Mawr and Traeth Bach, the former now
dry, alas, the other being the mouth of the Dwyryd, draining the
Vale of Maentwrog. Both estuaries had been used in a rather

primitive way for the loading of slates for export, with here and there the signs of an old quay hidden under furze and bramble at the water's edge.

Topographically the peninsula is one of a few in these islands that promise a sort of paradise for anyone fortunate enough to own and exploit in the appropriate manner. Its axis reaches from north-east to its south-west tip, ending in a beautiful sandy bay sheltered by a rocky point at either end. On its south-east facing side, the peninsula has its own micro-climate, facing away from the winter's north-westerlies. Traeth Bach is tidal, meaning a twice daily change in the conformation of the waters — at low tide an ever-changing series of sandbanks and channels, at high tide a stretch of shimmering water reaching over to Harlech, its castle in profile on the southern horizon. Even more, there is an island, Ynys Gifftan, rising from the waters like an ancient tumulus, and the whole faces the magnificent massif of Ardudwy, or the Harlech Dome, some of the oldest exposed rock in Britain. Finally, cutting laterally into this sheltered south-easterly side of the peninsula there is a deep dell, with a stream and cascade. This was to be the site of Portmeirion, building on the existing house and its immediate vicinity.

Sheltered on this south-easterly side, Aber Iâ is rare in its situation, and by its nature was extremely private, with adequate mooring for a yacht. This was a boyhood dream waiting to happen. The deal was struck between uncle and nephew, the place was Clough's and he was off the mark quickly, perhaps even recklessly, with building projects on the drawing board. This was an ideal place to exercise his principles of *improvement*. He was quick to spot an historic dimension to his demesne, for he had read Giraldus Cambrensis who in 1188 wrote of the 'newly erected castle of Deudraeth (literally "two estuaries") built by the son of Cynan'. One of my earliest commissions from Clough was to record this in an inscription under the belfry tower. It reads with some style and not a little tongue-in-cheek bombast:

> This tower, built in 1928 by Clough Williams-Ellis, Architect and Publican, embodies stones from the 12th Century Castle of his Ancestor Gruffydd ap Cynan King of North Wales that stood on an eminence 150 yards to the west. It was finally razed c. 1869 by Sir Wm Fothergill Cook inventor of the Electric Telegraph 'lest the ruins should become known and attract visitors to the place'. This 19th century affront to the 12th is thus piously redressed in the 20th.

Like many an old settlement in the more remote areas of Wales, the history of Aber Iâ is sketchy. Before the days of train and automobile, it would have been quite an excursion to reach Aber Iâ, and since the main coastal route crossed the neck of the peninsula, it would mostly have been by-passed. However, there has always been a history of ferries from either side of the peninsula, and certainly the painter J.M.W. Turner recorded one landing, Tŷ Gwyn, just opposite Portmeirion. Aber Iâ may have been just one of quite a few landing stages. It is known that a small settlement occupied the dell around 1790. There was a quay (now the terrace of the hotel), probably built for the transport of lead ore from the mine, which now serves as the hotel's wine cellar. Another dank tunnel farther along the Gwyllt was opened up for gold prospecting, but it was more prospect than reality for only one small nugget was unearthed.

Aber Iâ never developed as a self-supporting community. There were other ferries, like Abergafren a little higher up, and neither lead nor gold were worth the candle. What *did* happen however, around the eighteen-forties, was the arrival of the aforesaid Sir William Fothergill Cook and a Mr Westmacott (who built the house), both enthralled with the location, and it was they who first opened up its possibilities for Romantic development. Both these gentlemen spent fortunes on building and landscaping lawns, terraces and cascades.

There are days in a mild, damp November when Portmeirion takes on the air of a sub-tropical jungle: tangled fronds, exotic bushes and tall trees drip with a sort of warm fecundity. This is all due to one Caton Haig, who was typically 'Empire' and was an expert on Himalayan flora and arboriculture. Walking in the Gwyllt for many years, I often wondered if that other Himalayan expert, Miss Marianne North, has ever visited the place. Her little pavilion in Kew Gardens is covered from floor to ceiling with watercolour sketches of her travels in search of flora, with titles like 'Rhododendron, with distant view of Kanchenjunga'. Despite the largely eighteenth century taste of Clough's buildings, there is much about Portmeirion that reminds one of the Empire builders of the nineteenth century, when India was home to many British families. It is the early landscaping of Westmacott, Fothergill Cook and Caton Haig, that has left its mark on Portmeirion (or at least on its grounds), and so long as the *Ponticum* is kept at bay, Portmeirion will preserve this once secret garden of tall trees, exotica and hidden paths.

The latter might have become overgrown altogether during

Miss Haig's domicile, but after her death during World War I, a stag paced the woods and kept the paths open. How it came to be there is a mystery, but there are deer over on the other side in Ardudwy and the stag may have swum across the estuary, no great task at low tide, then found the exotica much to his taste. Anyway, it is largely due to the establishment of his territorial imperative that the miles of winding paths still exist, to offer endless delight to those who enjoy sudden vistas and viewpoints out of tangled growth.

Clough appreciated this particular heritage, and at one stage I drew and painted a map of all the paths and various features for him. It always hung outside the Gents toilet in the hotel, as though the terrain were too difficult for ladies even to contemplate. That map perished in the fire of 1981.

Clough disliked what he called the 'chilly sound' of the name Aber Iâ (literally Ice Mouth) and with his usual flair, he invented the perfect combination of Port (since it *was* a small port with moorings and a quay) and Meirion, the administrative area or hundred, to become Portmeirion. It struck a chord at once, for it owes not a little to one of Clough's favourite locations, Portofino in Italy to which he was introduced by the artist of Lawrence of Arabia's *Seven Pillars of Wisdom*, Eric Kennington. Cartographers, and in particular the Ordnance Survey, frown on such changes of name, but Clough felt he had been justified when some brilliantly detailed German invasion maps of the area were discovered during the war and bore the name 'Portmeirion'.

The transfer to Clough completed, he set about the task at once and by Easter of 1926, the old house had been refurbished to become a hotel (unlicensed). The matter of license would be a bone of contention with the local magistrates for some time, because in the Twenties the Temperance movement was very strong in North Wales and the opening of yet another den of iniquity horrified the local establishment.

Two cottages soon rose, the Angel and Neptune (1926). Both seem to me vintage Portmeirion, with their curving roofs of small rustic slates, the colour wash of the walls, all as typical of Clough as anything he ever built. There is nothing revolutionary about the design. They are traditional English country cottage vernacular, yet subtlely unlike anybody else's building. It is difficult to say quite why, but a glimpse at Cornwell village in North Oxfordshire gives an answer, for there Clough achieved his best vernacular in a given context. The cottages at Portmeirion provide its heart, and they hold their place against some of the more ambitious structures he later built.

Outside Angel stands a column, topped with an astrolabe. Its seat-level base of stone is often obscured by foliage, which is a pity, but if you move the leaves aside, you will find an inscription cut into the stone commemorating 'William Willetts, in gratitude'. Who he? many will ask, but Clough believed we should all be grateful to the man who confirmed our long summer evenings with the establishment of British Summer Time.

Next, the old gardener's cottage was refurbished to make Mermaid, and together these cottages are really the core of the village, enclosing the green. All this had to work for itself, had to earn bread and butter. The hotel had to pay its way, come what may. But that required an expertise quite outside Clough's competence or experience. A house-warming party of local notables and a celebrity or two, even a strange 'business man from outer space', was blessed with fine weather, and a good time was had by all. But the hotel's management creaked badly. The plumbing was cavalier, the general chaos of building debris still lay about, carpets were still to be laid, and if the invitees had to tolerate it, paying guests clearly had a right to complain and did. Clough's old friend A.P. Herbert lampooned the fiasco in *Punch*.

In the end, it required the recruitment of James Wyllie, painter, amiable socialite and restaurateur to get things right, and for many guests over the years till after Hitler's War his name was practically synonymous with Portmeirion, along with that of his illustrious successor in 1956, Michael Trevor Williams. With these two at the helm, along with Miss Betty Maxwell-Scott, success was assured, and it is no boast to declare that by now, with Clough's own grandson in charge, Portmeirion is a world site, attracting guests from every continent.

Just across the road from Angel and Mermaid, stands one of the dominant structures of Portmeirion, the Town Hall. This is not an original, or only in part, for most of it was acquired, the earliest of a series of what Clough called 'fallen buildings' which he rescued from an ignominious end, a task he went about with much the same zeal as Gladstone over 'fallen women' as the Victorians called them, with no mention ever of 'fallen men'.

In the Thirties Clough read in *Country Life* that Emral Hall in Flintshire was about to be demolished. The article amounted to an obituary. He had known the place in his youth and was aghast at the news, since he recalled in particular its unique barrel-vaulted ceiling of plaster in the ballroom, dating from the seventeenth century, and depicting the Labours of Hercules.

He alerted various possible saviours, such as the Victoria and

Albert Museum, but to no avail. Ardent compassion of that nature is not easily quelled and as the day approached of the sale of various lots prior to its demolition, Clough jumped on a train and reached Emral just as the sale was beginning.

The sale was piecemeal — doors, windows, panelling, plaster-work and so on. The Ballroom ceiling was the first lot to come up and since only Clough could imagine how to deal with its disman-tling and what to do with it ultimately, it was soon knocked down to him for £13. Having bought himself a ceiling, he felt obliged to bid for other items, the mullioned windows with their leaded glass, doors, panelling and so on.

Being so suddenly landed with this, he had to solve all sorts of logistical problems — dismantling the ceiling by sawing it into sections, numbering and crating it ready for transport in appalling weather conditions over the mountain passes, storing it all in a hired warehouse on Porthmadog quay, and then, not least, devising how best to use all this loot. But enthusiasm is such a spur to creativity that he was not long at the drawing board, and in consultation with his masons, the admirable Davies brothers, foundations were soon laid and building commenced. All this booty from Emral went into a new building designed specifically for the various items, but in particular for the ceiling. A public school headmaster patron of mine used to assess the various details of a building in terms of 'is it meant?'. Portmeirion's Town Hall has mellowed with the years and fits its immediate surround-ings well. Portmeirion would be diminished without it. Although strictly speaking it is a hybrid building, it looks very much 'meant'. A more recent addition to it to provide a restaurant is less happy in my opinion, with just a whiff of the Costa del Sol about it, which is a pity, especially since several fine tall beech trees had to be felled to make way for it.

Topping out of the Town Hall was achieved with a cupola made of an old copper pig-boiler turned upside down to support a crown. The pig-boiler has patinated so beautifully that, again, it looks absolutely 'meant'. A shield of arms flaunting the Red Hand of Ulster adorns the entrance. I am not sure what Ulstermen make of this, or whether or not it came from Emral like the rest, but it fits. Clough's motive would be purely aesthetic (I daresay the Papal Arms would have suited his purpose just as well — in short, no politics can ever be read into his statements in building).

The entrance up ascending steps is somewhat dark with, on the landing and straight in front of the visitor, a bronze portrait I made of Clough in 1969. To left and right are toilets, an inauspicious welcome, I always feel, but over the Gents is a beautiful little notice painted on a green tablet reading 'Gentlemen's Lavatory', the only remaining lettering that I know of by the original master Ralph Ellis, who had supplied much of the lettering for Portmeirion between the wars. All told, although the ceiling itself had cost Clough only £13, the entire project finally cost rather more than he had bargained for; yet, as I say, Portmeirion is unthinkable without it.

Gradually over the years, the rather austere name of Town Hall has given way to the name 'Hercules Hall' after the famous ceiling. Many happy parties have been held there over the years, a succession of Dragon Balls for charity, and occasions with their own particular flavour, such as the party to honour Miss Ingrid Bergman's stay there during the Sixties when she was filming Mark Robson's *Inn of the Sixth Happiness*. Robert Donat, only just surviving this his last role, for he died soon afterwards, was too ill to be present for more than a few moments. Outdoor sequences depicting rough mountainous terrain in China were filmed on the flanks of Snowdon in sometimes atrocious weather. One realised how arduous a film star's life can be, for Miss Bergman was up at crack of dawn for work on location, and was often back late in the evening. Yet, watching her chatting amiably with Bertrand Russell on a sofa in the Town Hall at the party was a touching sight. She looked so relaxed and took everything in such good part, when she might have been relaxing in her cottage with her children.

Although, as Clough readily admitted, it was a Town Hall still waiting for its town, the building has served its purpose well, if not as an administrative centre, as a tourist attraction. The deep relief of the barrel vaulted ceiling provides good acoustics, and concerts by musicians both famous and infamous have been held there with great success. It is used for many different functions: meetings of the Arts Council and of the British Council; exhibitions, balls, even Mass has been celebrated there. And no one would guess that the amazing ceiling arrived at Portmeirion in over a hundred pieces.

The Town Hall was the first rescue of a 'fallen building'. From then on, Clough acquired a reputation as a possible collector. But the buildings had to be right. My guess is that he refused quite as many as he accepted. He would receive various requests from all over the country, anxious to keep some beloved but redundant structure from destruction. But only a select minority have been 'adopted' and take their place in the family to happy effect.

Most notable of all is the Colonnade, which presides over the

Green as though it had always been there. It certainly demonstrates Clough's genius for placing buildings in their appropriate
context. The Colonnade certainly has its function beyond aesthetics
— it is a favourable place for a rest, with a view of the Green and
the Town Hall, and it provides a marvellous platform or band-
stand for outdoor performances by choirs and brass bands, serving
this purpose countless times.

It has a surprising pedigree, which Clough summed up in yet
another of his inscriptions:

> This Colonnade built circa 1760 by the Quaker copper
> smelter William Reeve, stood before his bath house at
> Arnos Court, Bristol. Damaged by bombs, it had fallen
> into decay and although scheduled as an ancient monument
> Her Majesty's Minister of Works approved its removal on
> condition that it should be here rescheduled.
>
> Admired by its alert contemporary Horace Walpole for
> its grace as a Classical Composition enriched by Gothick
> detail, it was also held in high esteem by the Council for
> the Preservation of Ancient Bristol whose good offices and
> the generosity of its former owners, the Bristol Tramways
> and Carriage Company, have made possible its preservation
> at Portmeirion.

At either end of the Colonnade, an ogee cupola is supported on
two corbels. One of these was missing when the drivers off-loaded,
so Clough asked me to carve one out of a blank in its place. He
gave me very little time, as usual, and I carved, as I thought, a
sketch portrait of Clough. It looks to me more like Noel Coward,
who would have 'simply adored' the idea of supporting an open
cupola in one of his favourite bolt-holes, where he wrote *Blithe
Spirit*.

The Colonnade was one of the structures built after the Second
World War. The war had brought all building to a halt. Supplies
were rationed, and the men were called up for service. Indeed, for
a while during the War, Portmeirion might not have belonged to
Clough at all, for the Air Ministry requisitioned it for the duration
as a rest centre for hard-pressed operational airmen on leave. This
rather shocked Clough. He worried that it might involve damage
to the delicate fabric of certain buildings which had been built far
below the specifications of military requirements. Meetings proceeded at the Ministry, drains and supplies were discussed and
everything minuted. Then the Civil Servants suddenly remembered that Portmeirion was a full day's journey from London and

that would make a hole of two days in an airman's leave. Just as precipitately the Ministry stopped the whole idea. However, Clough felt very strongly that fighting men on leave should have priority bookings should they still wish to come, and Jim Wyllie gave this his full support. Indeed, he proposed that while the war lasted, the hotel should remain open all the year round for just this purpose, and so, without requisitioning, Portmeirion became an unofficial leave-centre, much appreciated by a host of serving personnel, including Guy Gibson V.C., who spent his last leave at Portmeirion just before the raid on the Moehne Dam. Another familiar visitor during the war was Sir Kenneth Clark, there to supervise the conservation of the treasures of the National Gallery in air-conditioned underground chambers in the Blaenau Ffestiniog quarry complex.

Although building at Portmeirion came to a complete halt during the war, the place was very much alive during the five years of conflict. The war affected so many millions of lives that Clough, who knew first hand the devastation of war, would be the last to complain that it meant the almost complete cessation of building for nearly ten years, given that rationing of materials lasted into the ensuing peace. This was doubly irritating however, since the men were back and ready to proceed. But once rationing eased, building went ahead apace. Clough was constrained to maintain an uneasy balance between utility and indulgence in his building programme. While he had definite ideas about how Portmeirion should look and what features were to set off others, there were mundane things to attend to, drains to clear, servants' quarters to be extended, the hotel kitchen to be reorganised and extended. Clough managed to balance the two often opposing requirements by first attending to utility, then, feeling such an access of virtue, he would reward himself with the raising of some aesthetic morsel for his own satisfaction: an archway here, a statue there, a belvedere or a fountain.

Besides building, there was another factor which was to change the face of Portmeirion and that was the policy with regard to day visitors, who could be expected to increase with the expansion of movement in the car and also personal wealth. Before the war, a half-crown toll had been sufficient to deter most would-be visitors. Now, after what amounted to the emancipation of workers after the war, wages were relatively much higher so that a price toll would no longer deter. Yet Clough always felt that, whatever happened in this respect and without condescension, Portmeirion should have a 'remember where you are' feeling as he called it, otherwise its entire point would be lost. This involved several considerations, first litter, and in general the passing public seemed to respect this, though Clough himself nearly always patrolled the Gwyllt armed with his litter-picker for the occasional errant crisp packet; secondly, privacy, the segregation of certain areas so that residents should not be plagued by an endless procession of sightseers peering in front windows to see how they lived. Thirdly, as far as possible, a minimum of notices which would offend the eye and, most of all, no advertisements.

This 'remember where you are' feeling is cleverly achieved by the deep arch, almost a tunnel (with a Hans Feibusch ceiling mural) under the Gatehouse entrance, shortly after paying the toll. From the tree- and hydrangea-lined drive that gives access from the main road, the first segregation is the car park, which is *outside* the toll-gate so that Portmeirion, except for residents and deliveries, is virtually car-free. Even residents' cars are cunningly hidden behind the houses. So visitors at once begin walking towards the village, pay their toll, then proceed under the Gatehouse into another world, part fantasy, part practical building and astute use of colour, all laid out to the taste of one man.

A second gateway, Bridge House, built in 1958 at the original entrance to the village, further enhances this different world feeling. I recall two women entering and gazing down from Battery Square: 'Oh, it's just like Shangri La', said one, and though it is a romantic notion, it is understandable from somebody seeing Portmeirion for the first time after strolling past the gates from the outside world.

The first impact is Battery Square itself, a beautifully cobbled piazza of mainly weather-boarded houses, Toll House and Pilot House, vaguely reminiscent of Kentish building, especially Rye, and Bridge House, a more formal Palladian elevation topped by four urns. High on the right above Battery Square is the Pantheon, or the Dome as it is sometimes called, which makes such an impact seen from the Traeth at low tide. The Dome itself is a triumph of ingenuity, for domes are not lightly achieved. Through the ages, there have been all sorts of solutions to achieve a hemi-spherical structure atop a rectangular or octagonal base. Sometimes builders of large structures intended to be topped by a dome either lose nerve or run out of ideas of how to do it. When the building of the Duomo in Florence was in progress the proposed dome presented such problems that it was put out to competition, which was won by Brunelleschi. Domes are meant to dominate, literally to lord it over their neighbours, and Brunelleschi's dome does just that, as does Longhena's dome over the Salute in Venice. The Salute dome, which Clough knew well, gives such an impression of solidity, buttressed as it is by enormous scrolls of white Istrian stone. Yet the dome is merely a wooden structure, otherwise it is probable that nothing would have supported that expanse in stone.

Clough may have had this in mind when he consulted his master joiner Mr Smith, about springing the dome across the octagon which had been waiting for some time for this ultimate crowning. It is the great achievement of Mr Braund Smith, working to Clough's drawings. The dome quite properly dominates the village, with its admirable earlier structure the Belfry, as its ideal counterpoint. Yet the Pantheon is a building that seems never to have achieved a purpose. Clough's idea that it could take parties for which the Town Hall was too large and the Hotel too small, seems a lame excuse for building a dome that dominates the skyline. The real reason, the honest one, is that Portmeirion suffered from what Clough called 'dome deficiency'. In short, the Dome's purpose is purely aesthetic, and any practical use that may emerge will be purely gratuitous.

The same aesthetic reason lies behind the Campanile (1925) but it did at least have a reason for being built, namely, that Clough had acquired in the Twenties a 'splendid and melodious chiming clock from a demolished London brewery'. Seen from the Traeth, as I say, at low tide, the village clusters round these two features to marvellous effect. Any wise traveller opting to come by rail all the way and using the Cambrian Coast 'express' which circumnavigates Traeth Bach gets his or her first view of Portmeirion from across the water and the Dome and the Belfry are the immediate markers, with the dramatic backdrop of the mountains.

As the Dome reached completion and the ball was finally fixed on top of its lantern, Clough came along to my workshop and questioned me about the application of gold leaf, without specifying what for. 'Indoors or outdoors?' I asked, and upon hearing the answer told him it must be transfer gold leaf, rather than loose. The latter, though much superior in effect, would drift away in the slightest zephyr and fall like some expensive golden snowfall. Then what? We discussed what sort of gold-size, how the leaf is laid and so on. He then asked if I could get him some transfer leaf and some size. I told him I already had them in stock and he took them away like a boy raring to go.

When I visited the site about a week later, I saw a precarious looking ladder leading up to the lantern, and Clough himself (he was all of eighty at the time) busy laying on the leaf. He had obviously timed the drying out of the size to perfection, to just the right tackiness which takes the leaf and stays put. The ball gleams to this day, for gold neither weathers nor dims. Why he should do it himself, instead of allowing me or one of his staff I don't know, but I suspect the reason was twofold: first, not to risk anybody else's neck but his own on that rickety ladder at Portmeirion's second highest point, and secondly, to himself enjoy the craft of laying gold leaf and seeing the effect.

Although the Pantheon facade stands high over the Colonnade, again as though it had always been there, perhaps it is a little less acceptable in its detail. Clough confessed that it 'somewhat oddly fronts the Pantheon'. Like the Colonnade, it has a curious pedigree. It was designed by the illustrious Victorian/Edwardian architect Norman Shaw, generally regarded as a precursor of Modernism. No one would guess, it is such a wedding-cake of masonry topped by spreadeagles. And it is only the *upper half* of a music-room fireplace, built for Lord Ismay of the White Star line in 1883, the year of Clough's birth. It would have fitted perfectly into Orson Welles's *Xanadu*.

Nevertheless, despite any pure-minded reservations, it is fair to say that the Pantheon, and Portmeirion, would be diminished without this lowering feature presiding over the entire village. The Pantheon with its dome cried out for a front of some sort and Shaw's upper half of a music-room fireplace fits in scale, even if it *is* a little over-powering in texture.

This structure best illustrates Clough's honest, pragmatic approach to building. He once quoted his mentor Sir Laurence Weaver's dismissive comment as they both stood in front of Belfast's City Hall; 'Fair drips with drawing board, don't it?' So it may be that in the case of the music-room fireplace Norman Shaw dwelt too long at the drawing board and got carried away. Clough, by contrast, liked to leave the drawing board behind and get out on site with his masons, the excellent Davies brothers, to work things out on the spot, an afterthought here and a spare finial at hand to top it all off, or an urn or an astrolabe there. He had an unerring instinct for what would work and what not.

The fireplace is just one example of the junk he collected. He had an eye for what might just fit, even if it took years to do it. As you wander round the Gwyllt you will often come upon stray blocks of weathered stone, bits of masonry collected by Clough over many years, 'laid down to mature like father's port', he declared. While he was busy with an actual building or balustrade, he would remember these various bits and pieces, and would pluck whatever he thought might fit such and such a context, a moulding here, a parapet there, all from morsels donated by some conscience-stricken owner-demolitionist. Even Westminster Abbey off-loaded redundant stone, as can be seen at a parapet at the hairpin bend on the 'back drive' exit from the village.

Since Portmeirion was intended as a living folly, rather than a fossil, Clough was rather proud of its flora, though rather less of its fauna, which is unremarkable despite Sir Solly Zuckerman's attempt to introduce a species of green lizard. The lizards performed decently for a time, sunning themselves on the balustrade for the delectation of hotel guests, but not indecently enough to breed and renew themselves, and they eventually died out, probably of cold chastity. On the water the usual water birds are busy, especially with the incoming tide, but the only birds of possible interest to watchers or twitchers might be the divers, for even a Great Northern Diver has been observed.

There has always been a strain of Persian cats at Portmeirion, dating from the days when Maggie Owen cherished and generally nourished a couple. They rule the Green, but might be met on single hunting safaris well into the Gwyllt.

Then there was one terrifying beast, the parrot Agatha, who in pre-war life at Portmeirion was a menace and nosey parker who probed all goings-on with the zeal of Poirot on a case. Agatha was also a notorious predator on anything pickable, be it button or buttonhole, rubber windscreen wiper, bath plug, or felt hat. She dive-bombed cats and people mercilessly, taking the Stuka as her model, until one day she pulled out of her dive too near the face of one of her friends, a waitress, who in self-defence struck out vigorously with her umbrella and did for Agatha on the spot.

The flora is of much greater interest, though I have heard an eminent horticulturist say that Clough was no gardener. Certainly he would never have laid claim to the heights of gardening practice and lore that the R.H.S. would demand. He was more interested in the architectural layout than in species and as a garden planner he is among the greatest. Even a very early garden plan dated 1911 bears this out and Oare House is another celebrated garden owing much to his design.

The much vaunted rhododendron and azalea catalogue at Portmeirion is by now somewhat diluted, but the Gwyllt in Spring has to be seen to be believed, with cascades of blossom of all sorts on the trees and bushes. It is a sight missed by visitors in the high season of July and August. There are still the remains of the early

Victorian planting by Westmacott and Fothergill Cook. Then various friends of Clough, especially the Dorrien-Smiths of Tresco in the Scilly Isles, have contributed many valuable specimens.

If there is one weakness in the 'remember where you are' feeling, it is in the defence of plants. There can be few more respectable citizens than book-lovers and garden-lovers, but both have among their numbers a few who simply cannot resist the illicit acquisition of some much coveted specimen. Clough did take pride in Port-mcirion's specimens, and he cared passionately about the place of this or that tree or shrub in the scheme of things. He could be extremely stern with any miscreant caught in the act of stealing a cutting or taking a rooted specimen. On one occasion he caught a middle-aged man 'green-handed', so to speak, and was quite remorseless in exacting punishment. He required full expiation of some sort and was quite ready to invoke prosecution. The man happened to he a senior civil servant and was severely embarrassed. He pleaded there was nothing he would not do to remain anonymous — anything to avoid the publicity of a court case — the disgrace to his family, his career, etc etc. Clough was quite unmoved.

In the end, Clough, though fully understanding the man's plight and embarrassment, insisted on expiation, which took the form of an apology over the pseudonym 'Peccavi', to be inserted in local and national newspapers at the man's expense:

### EXPIATION

'I wish publicly and unreservedly to apologize for my ungrateful behaviour on the -th of last month when, yielding to sudden temptation, I uprooted and removed a valuable plant from the Portmeirion wild gardens, an act for which I now feel acute remorse, the more so as I realize that trespass such as mine would, unless checked, soon spoil the said gardens for those who now so much enjoy them. I am grateful for this opportunity for publicly expressing my regret as I am well aware that a prosecution would have been justified.'

'PECCAVI'

This text appeared in full and unamended in all the papers except *The Times* and *The Manchester Guardian,* who worried earnestly about this example of private justice instead of formal arraignment. But even there, the text was suitably amended and published, and the civil servant had to meet a considerable bill to preserve his anonymity. *The Daily Mail* even published a leader on the subject.

Clough was very much concerned for the future of Portmeirion. He was lectured by various financial pundits on the risks of capital venture into the hotel business. So many grand schemes had either failed altogether or had struggled to survive only after a series of bankruptcies. All this meant little to Clough, who simply wanted to build Portmeirion up to what he believed to be its true potential. In order to raise capital for further building he mortgaged what he had built, and remortgaged after building on the proceeds, and so on. In the end he proved to be as astute at business as he was at architecture, but owed much to the advice of son-in-law Euan Cooper-Willis.

Even more than these financial considerations, Clough was concerned that Portmeirion should retain its own especial aesthetic, that no addition by his heirs or others should betray the 'vivifying principle' that had inspired its foundation and early development.

I believe this concern has been amply answered by daughter Susan, who from the beginning of her career as artist and designer has understood the special needs of Portmeirion. For instance, the middle of the Gwyllt was for a long time a sort of wild morass that was neither proper wetland nor pond. To be frank, it was a mess as only nature can be where a hollow is neither properly drained nor dammed. Clough, whose prime purpose in life was always to build buildings, never seemed to get round to dealing with this mess, but towards the end he came to see its possibilities. He had it excavated, to form a couple of ponds. He planted accordingly; arum, reeds, nymphaea and so on, not long before he died.

Things seemed to rest there for a while, then Susan designed a Chinese bridge to connect one side of the upper pond with a knoll that juts out of the other side. Later still she designed a sort of decorative pagoda, with seats, all in steel, and in my opinion it is absolutely delightful, both seen from the far end of the pond, and as a viewpoint itself. It presides over the pond with the sort of authority that means its absence would now be felt keenly. Clough would have approved.

The management of Portmeirion has now passed into the third generation and Clough is probably applauding from the shades. But what, in the end, is one to make of Portmeirion? Opinions vary, naturally. For a start, it is unique. There is nothing quite like it. Clough's own delight in Port Grimaud on the Côte d'Azur, built on a similar 'vivifying principle' as a self-entire village by the sea, was genuine, but there was a difference. Perhaps it is the only comparison of a modern development, but it is not a very close one in the end.

The best summing-up was published by Clough's old colleague, Lewis Mumford in *The New Yorker* in January 1962. Mumford saw Portmeirion as 'an amusing array of politely incompatible, argumentative, but elegantly phrased buildings . . . Portmeirion is the fantastic collection of architectural relics and impish modern fantasies . . . .'

Mumford is careful to place all this in the context of Clough's concern for planning, improvement and conservation on a national scale, and he pays tribute *en passant*. Clough, he suggested, rather suffered at the thought of 'how constrictive and desiccated modern forms can become when the architect pays more attention to the mechanical formula or the exploitation of some newly fabricated material than to the visible human results'. 'In a sense,' Mumford goes on to say, 'Portmeirion is a gay, deliberately irresponsible reaction against the dull sterilities of so much that passes as modern architecture today.' He does sound a cautionary note, which even Clough probably heard and ignored. 'Though I prefer Williams-Ellis's work in his more sober moments of land-scaping and building I enjoy the spirit of nimble improvisation he has shown here.'

This preference for 'his more sober moments' is indicative. Clough was sometimes too self-indulgent at Portmeirion, too ready to adopt a 'fallen building' in a context where one of his 'more sober moments' might have served him better. So that in the end, *pace* Portmeirion and its maker's own fond regard for it as his special creation, many will judge him best remembered for his work at Cornwell, say, or in a house and garden like Oare, or in a country house like Dunwood in Yorkshire.

Yet, in the British Architectural Library of the RIBA, there is an early drawing for Portmeirion which indicates that Clough may indeed have had higher ideals for Portmeirion. Where the Gloriette now stands, in front of the original Salutation complex, he obviously had in mind a building of the proportions of Hercules Hall. It consists of a *piano nobile* supported on columns. The building is framed by two-storeyed houses in the same style, and the effect is all very much of a piece, which cannot be said of the present layout. This drawing is a grand concept of great beauty, of designing and building *ab initio*, unaffected by found parts and structures. Looking at this drawing, one cannot help regretting that it was never realised. But there was no way Clough could have afforded it. The dream could only be realised at other sites for wealthier patrons, in particular at places like Cornwell Manor or Oare House. It is a design along the lines of that 'water-conscious-ness' that he had commended so highly at his favourite village, for in the drawing he makes the utmost use of the original 'swimming pool' (now given over to aquatic plants and koi carp).

And yet, a second look at the drawing says something, if not a lot, for second thoughts, for had this design been realised, and the rest of Portmeirion been built to match (the bluff of the present Dolphin complex is likewise indicated for high treatment), it could all have veered into a sort of untouchable world of the absolutely perfect, of immaculate beauty beyond the reach of mere mortals. It might have appeared 'fossilised', an adjective he used of Williamsburg in the U.S.A.

As for dreams, there is another drawing in the collection which may or may not be by Clough. It is in very poor condition on brown paper, painted in body colour and is a sort of fantasy. The viewpoint is from the high bluff now occupied by the Watch Tower. Down below and solitary is the original Aber Iâ house, painted white. The estuary is recognisable, with Ynys Gifftan and the Ardudwy mountains clearly there. Hovering in the sky above the house two fantastic white doves sport madly with the air of willow pattern or Chagall. Out in the estuary, crossing the bar, a four-masted square-rigger sails blithely into port. Bottom left is the artist, a sort of Bloomsbury figure in stove pipe hat, sheltered from the sun by a Chinese parasol. He labours to capture the dream as the moon rises over the mountains.

I suspect the work is not by Clough but by some friend or visitor in the Twenties. I can understand why Clough kept it. It is no masterpiece, but it depicts a sort of dream. That is Portmeirion, the stuff of dreams, some never realised, others achieved against all the odds, and most compromised by the expedience of cost or the slight incompatibility of a 'fallen building'.

There must be many like me who simply love it, for what it is, for its maker, and for its ultimate harmony with nature. I say 'ultimate', for there are occasional details that jar — but the overall effect is of peace and an abiding beauty. People of all persuasions have admired and loved it, and have written about it. Since its mortality is by definition longer than that of mere humans, it will go on being admired like some old trouper. Fred Uhlman the painter and writer in his autobiography *The Making of an English-man* records how, during the war, he and his wife Diana learned of this fabulous village in North Wales, where Clough Williams-Ellis had built an example to the Welsh to brighten up the want of colour in their own villages. (Actually I think this was the last of Clough's criteria, but no matter.) Saving up their petrol coupons, they finally escaped from drab and bombed-out London, and found themselves in this fabulous environment and among the oddest of guests, the entire entourage, family and retainers of the royal family of Albania, waiting for the 'pipple' to welcome them back to Albania.

Portmeirion has always been popular with Stage and Screen. For the great figures of the Twenties and Thirties it was a favourite bolthole. Noel Coward, Yvonne Arnaud, Alistair Sim, Fabia Drake and many others were all regulars before the war. Privacy was guaranteed — no journalists or gossip columnists, no tele-photo-lens cameras. It was a very favourite playground and its entire ambience encouraged this. Rather as the Napoleonic wars cut off Grand Tours of the continent and opened up the Lake District and North Wales to Romantic Travellers, so in the last war Portmeirion offered refuge to those who had been used to the Côte d'Azur.

Film companies can be high-handed occasionally and once Clough arrived at Portmeirion to find a sort of Italian Grand Prix being filmed, with racing cars performing the most hair-raising circuits. He was not well-pleased, made that quite clear as only he could, but received no apology, despite the fact that one accident did take place, and residents were severely incommoded.

The greatest impact by film was the making of the television series *The Prisoner*, with Patrick McGoohan as its star and the late and beautiful Virginia Maskell. The village in general and its environment were shamelessly exploited in this very popular series and the filming took several months. But the impact was post-humous, so to speak, for the series caught on in a big way and became a cult. Such was the impression on a beguiled audience that people wanted to see this strange and beautiful scenario in the flesh. It was the odd mix of the film's claustrophobic 'meta-physics', the landscape and the elegant buildings. A Prisoner Society was formed and is now administered from Portmeirion by a permanent executive. By now, for many visitors Portmeirion is *The Prisoner*, completely identified with it in their minds. It has certainly had an impact on Portmeirion's fame and on the number of its day visitors.

Clough was always ready to receive the BBC and other television companies. Towards the end of his life, quite a few films were made of Clough and Portmeirion. Hywel Davies, Wynford Vaughan Thomas and Gethin Stoodley Thomas have all made films in

Portmeirion. Wynford Vaughan Thomas was among certain favourites with Clough, and I recall Wynford one evening composing a limerick on the spot on the difficult rhyme of Blaenau Ffestiniog. If anyone is intrigued to know what could possibly rhyme with Ffestiniog, Wynford had no trouble whatsoever, producing a very funny and rude limerick, using the Welsh word *Ceiniog* (penny) and what could be done with it.

Portmeirion is admired in different ways by different people, and even abhorred by a few strait-laced modernists. Clough lived to a great age and to the very end he was incorporating a great deal of differing material over the period 1926 to 1978. One of the most characteristic features is the mural painting by his old friend Hans Feibusch, whose Baroque figuration and colour blends so well with the fabric of Portmeirion. The tradition is being perpetuated by daughter Susan and grand-niece Bronwyn.

No one loved Portmeirion more than its begetter, as is appropriate. He cherished it, feared for its future. Fortunately it is safeguarded by law. In a speech on his ninetieth birthday, Clough gratefully referred to this:

> For my dread has been that some day some enterprising and misguided outsider might somehow intrude and expand the place beyond its natural limits — blowing up what had been conceived as an elegant little mouse into a bloated and clumsy cow. And now the Government itself has joined in the defence by scheduling the place as being of 'architectural and historic importance', and so not to be altered or interfered with by anyone without official approval — not lightly given — which of course delights me — even when I discovered that ANYONE included ME!

Yet there must have been occasions when he had second thoughts and after writing about the Pantheon in *Portmeirion, The Place and its Meaning,* he seems to sum up his conscience (was it the lack of function in the Pantheon?) about the village as a whole. The completion of the Pantheon, its dome, the gilded ball surmounting its lantern and that fantastic front, seems to have prompted reflection about the place in general. 'I might be accused of having merely indulged myself in an idiosyncratic, private architectural frolic of little general merit or interest or even utility.'

He hopes there is more to it than that. For Portmeirion is a protest, a *cri-de-coeur.* He quotes the strangest ally, Sir Herbert Read, arch apologist of Modernism, from his *Design and Tradition:*

'civilisation is no longer primarily human, but increasingly possessed by technology's idea of complete automation, cold, precise, imageless, repetitive, bloodless, nerveless, dead . . . the finest achievements of modern architecture do not compete with the finest achievements of the good styles of the past which display a richness, plenitude and splendour in dramatic contrast to the drabness and chaos of our own cities and buildings.' The aptness of this quotation, plucked from such a source, is revealing, for there is little doubt Clough *did* often feel the need to justify his self indulgence in Portmeirion.

He confessed to a low threshold of boredom. He would hate to bore anyone, but even more, himself. So, rather than risk boredom in one of his creations, he might possibly overdo things, risk vulgarity even. He confesses to feeling cheated if a building, for want of that little extra in feeling or adornment, is boring. He never ceased to spread a gospel that 'architectural good manners are also good business'.

Does Portmeirion answer this stern business criterion? The answer is surely a resounding 'yes'. He went on to enumerate the various kinds of people who had come to *use* the place, for what it was: a retreat, a place apart, a holiday resort of special character. Many writers have enjoyed both its special ambience and its seclusion — Bernard Shaw, H.G. Wells, Bertrand Russell, A.P. Herbert, Storm Jameson, and most famously of all for some reason, Noel Coward, who wrote his comedy *Blithe Spirit* from one Sunday to the next while staying in the Watch House. Rose Macaulay, Margaret Lane, Daphne du Maurier, Arthur Koestler, John Osborne and Thor Heyerdahl are a mere cross section to show how well it has suited writers. I think the reason it is so specially useful to writers is that in the hotel, and even more in any of the houses, it is possible to enjoy a feeling of absolute seclusion, and then, say, having achieved five hundred words, it is so easy to go outside and to enjoy at once that reinvigorating walk either on the sands at low tide or in the Gwyllt, and still to keep the world at bay.

Painters have not found it nearly so useful. For them, the light and colour of the Midi may be echoed on occasion in Portmeirion, but it is too contrived a retreat, too much of a stage set for them, too much gone over by Clough the artist already.

But for that very reason, film-makers and photographers (especially of *haute couture*) love the place. The epithet 'Italianate' is too often applied to Portmeirion, yet like all clichés it is in some ways apt. A producer on a tight budget for film or television can exploit corners of Portmeirion to such good effect that in the finished product you would believe it was Portofino itself.

One singular use of Portmeirion was that of pilgrims seeking to pay homage to a distinguished neighbour, Bertrand Russell, or 'Bertie', as Clough called him. They were old friends, both were acquainted with the earlier Bloomsbury years, and very nearly contemporaries. Russell spent his last years in Plas Penrhyn, a pleasant Regency house at the very crown of the peninsula, overlooking Traeth Mawr. People came from America, the Continent, and the English-speaking world in general to meet the philosopher, and many stayed at Portmeirion.

One day, out of the blue, another distinguished contemporary arrived at Portmeirion, of especial interest to Clough. Frank Lloyd Wright was of Welsh stock and he had come to Wales to receive an honorary doctorate from the University of Wales. What was Clough to make of such an international figure in his own world of architecture? More intriguing perhaps, what was Lloyd Wright to make of Clough and all his works?

First of all, the American was much taken with the landscape, its mountains, its rocks (much cantilevered) and its trees. 'For miniature majesty and general "style" only Japan could rival it.' He was impressed by Plas Brondanw, its 'somewhat austere four storeys' wrote Clough, 'of immensely solid masonry reared up on its terraced hillside, still much as my forebears first planted it some four centuries ago, and seeming to have the same "ten-fingered grip of the earth as its protecting oaks"'.

It is not difficult to see that as a description of Lloyd Wright's celebrated Falling Waters or Taliesin West, with a little adjustment in detail. 'But Portmeirion. That was quite another matter! Dare I let him loose on that?' Clough need not have feared — the American Welshman 'took it all without a blink', got the point of its frequent heresies, odd colour washes and faked perspectives.

In his book on the subject, Clough need not have apologised further, yet he did write at length about the number and variety of visitors using Portmeirion. For instance, after Venice, it must be one of the most favoured places for honeymooners. Portmeirion, from being a barely licensed premises during the season, is now a fully-blown establishment, able to book itself up all the year round with visitors from all quarters of the globe. So his 'good manners in architecture mean good business' is thoroughly vindicated and Clough need never have worried over it. Portmeirion is by now a beloved tract of landscape, a village and a legend. Each of its parts has a story of its own.

The village itself may be taken as extending from the Gatehouse to White Horses and the Camera Obscura tower out on the Quay beyond the hotel. White Horses is an original, low fisherman's cottage with a view directly over the water towards Harlech. It once belonged to a character known as Hwntw Mawr (literally Big Outsider, but in North Wales more specifically referring to a South Walian). His real name was Thomas Edwards and he had probably been employed by William Madocks on the making of the Cob. Hwntw Mawr was hanged at Dolgellau in 1813 for the murder of Mary Jones, the maid at Penrhyn Isaf farm just above Portmeirion, during a robbery.

Beyond White Horses a path leads to the extreme rocky point of the peninsula, with the 'lighthouse' (a fun structure with another upside-down pig-boiler standing in as a lantern). The high Spring tides race dramatically past this point and I have seen an old bull seal fishing there several times, and occasionally a porpoise on a mission. This is the place for a view of Tremadog Bay. It is a very particular area of the Irish Sea. Hilaire Belloc in *Cruise of the Nona* wrote affectionately about it:

> There is no corner of Europe that I know, not even the splendid amphitheatre standing in tiers of High Alpine wall around Udine, which so moves me with the awe and majesty of great things as does this mass of the northern Welsh mountains seen from this corner of their silent sea.

Back in the village, there are buildings of all styles, each with that distinct air of Clough about it. Because of the topography of the dell, it was not possible to number the houses, so each has a name, mostly referring to the sea: Pilot House, Watch House, Anchor, Dolphin, Neptune and Trinity House.

Government House was one of the earliest buildings and was so called because at the time of its building it dominated what there was of Portmeirion. Prior's Lodging got its name not because it is near the Belfry but because its first tenant was a Prior of the monastery of Caldy Island off Tenby in South-West Wales. Many years later another hotel guest told Clough that while he was exploring the upper reaches of the Amazon, he heard of a very holy man, living the life of a hermit deep in the jungle. He decided he must try to reach this holy man, and when he finally succeeded it was the same Prior. On his table among other books lay *Portmeirion: The Place and its meaning*.

The rest of the names merely reflect Clough's fancy. For example,

Angel called for an attractive sign (painted by daughter Susan). Chantry he simply liked as a name. Bridge House and Toll House are self-explanatory, though the latter has long since relinquished its function to the more recent Gatehouse and the little toll booth just outside it.

'Rest and be Thankful' might well be applied to Portmeirion, for Clough was astute at placing various halts, seats and rest areas. He never lost sight of that original vision of 'a holiday retreat for the discerning', and in that respect even the most outrageous follies are functional, in the sense that the fake lighthouse marks a rewarding viewpoint and heightens the impact.

One folly in particular gives enormous delight to children, though beyond that it is debatable it should be where it is, right in front of the hotel. *Les Amis Réunis* has the notional appearance of a ketch moored at the quay. Clough admitted it was neither building nor ship. But it does have a history.

As soon as he acquired Portmeirion, Clough bought an old trading ketch in Porthmadog harbour, had it towed over and moored by the quay in one and a half fathoms. It was a sort of houseboat, with water and electricity laid on, a ready residence where Clough and his friends might retire periodically. The Honorary Harbourmaster, Richard Hughes, the writer, used it. It gave the village an air of being in use, of work going on. Indeed, it was thought that it might attract further craft, or at least that was the idea for *Les Amis Réunis* being there, as a sort of decoy. But Traeth Bach is notorious for its shifting sands and the river's course is never the same two years running.

So *Les Amis Réunis* remained moored and alone, fulfilling her function of reuniting friends. It must have been great fun on a sparkling day in those early days at Portmeirion. But the time came for caulking and pitching, so she was laid over, first one side, then the other. However, before the job was complete, a gale blew up, the old ketch was carried along on the tide towards Ynys Gifftan and there was stranded on a deep shoal. She was soon filling with water and sand. No ingenuity or winches or manpower could move her and she became a wreck. She had to be abandoned as she became more and more engulfed in sand.

At the time, Clough was renewing the quay and he noticed that the quay wall just outside the hotel curved with much the same line as a ship's bulwarks. He salvaged what he could of the wreck: cabin, rails, masts, wheel etc, and incorporated these into a sort of ship-aground he built beside the quay, and there it is fulfilling the fantasies of generations of children and not a few adults.

Only Clough could have arrived at this dodge to retain a maritime flavour to Portmeirion. Not everybody approves. The naturalist and writer Edmund Vale was once shown round by Clough, ending up at *Les Amis Réunis*. Vale was a scholar and purist, and it is probable that Portmeirion did not meet with his entire approval. However, charity prevailed: 'I can forgive everything' Vale declared, 'but the ship'.

The Camera Obscura hard by White Horses recalls an early visit to Edinburgh, when Clough was shown Sir Patrick Geddes's historic lookout tower, incorporating a camera obscura. These structures were once the happy toy of scientifically-minded landowners all over the country, with the Victorian interest in optics. But they are now rare.

From his earliest days of garden planning and landscaping, Clough had collected statuary, and in his drawings he usually indicated their siting. The *Freya* from Stowe is beautifully sited at the foot of the steps below Dolphin. The most prominent statue must be *Hercules*, standing near Mermaid and the Gazebo. He is bowed down by his burden of the Earth, temporarily off-loaded by Atlas. He is the work of a Scottish sculptor, William Brodie of Edinburgh, around the middle of the last century. His plinth bears the legends of such good summers as we have enjoyed during the last forty or so years. In his long life (and by now my own too) Clough recalled 1959 as the best of all summers, when we basked in unbroken sunshine for month after month, and found it so heavenly that even the doom-watchers' predictions of impending drought could not deter us from exulting day after day in this glorious Mediterranean bounty. So Clough asked me to carve an inscription to mount on *Hercules'* plinth: *To the Summer of 1959 in honour of its splendour*. Since then, a few more medals have been awarded but nothing has quite rivalled 1959, which ended the much-maligned Fifties in a blaze of glory. The celebrated Sixties on the other hand, did not even warrant a 'mentioned in Dispatches', and indifferent summers persisted until 1974, with 1976 even rivalling 1959.

There is a welcoming *Apollo* (sadly an arm short) just beyond the toll booth. It is reputedly by Ruysbraek and I suspect is another acquisition from Stowe. The vagueness indicates that Portmeirion is already acquiring a history with suitable elisions. Then out on the quay, as though guarding all things maritime, stands Lord Nelson in full fig, a gift from an old friend, Sir Michael Duff. His colour is kept up with frequent cleanings and painting, but the propensity of the human race for laying on hands means that one part of his anatomy requires more frequent touching up. A sort of 'stand-in' Lady Hamilton at the opposite end of the quay is discreetly within his Lordship's sight without need for telescope.

Lately, and most prominently, two Burmese dancing girls in characteristic pose atop their tall columns grace the green below the Colonnade. For years they had withstood the weather and gradually taken on a rough grey patina quite out of character with their origins. They are carved out of a dark tropical hardwood. Now they have been smoothed to take gold leaf and they positively gleam. It is so typical of Portmeirion that these two unlikely oriental creatures should take their place without undue incongruity.

But Clough was sometimes unable to unearth, or to afford, the sort of item he wanted for such and such a placement, so he had no qualms about going along to Glaslyn Foundry in Porthmadog with a profile drawing of whatever god, nymph or putta he required to be cut out in sheet steel. Thereafter it was painted by whichever artist he happened to be in touch with at the time.

Then again, he would sometimes come along to my workshop and ask for stone carvings to adorn this or that. The problem was he often required intricate eighteenth century work that might require the work of many hands to accomplish in time. So I would say much of this work is below par. On the other hand, if you happened to be given enough time to do the job properly, he would then 'distress' it to his taste with a hammer or a blast from a shotgun.

There was never any question of installing an original or 'modern' work, and Portmeirion will never be one of those sculpture parks that are gradually emerging on certain estates like Bretton Hall in Yorkshire, or the proposed one at Powis Castle near Welshpool. Portmeirion is the work, or folly, of one man, and so it should stand, with the single exception of daughter Susan, who worked alongside Clough and has contributed admirable and appropriate items to the grounds. Indeed, she and her husband Euan have extended Portmeirion as a business enterprise especially with Portmeirion Potteries, in 1960.

The venture began as early as 1953, when Susan and Euan took responsibility for retail outlets at Portmeirion. This was extended in 1957 to a shop in Pont Street in London, so that in time, the word 'Portmeirion' has come to denote first the village itself, but also a range of goods and crafts that bear a distinct mark of their own, so distinct that for many people the word 'Portmeirion' will summon up that special and inimitable range of pottery designed mostly by Susan, but with contributions from her children and other associates in the craft.

At first, the pottery was produced by Gray's Pottery in Stoke, and though the designs were by Susan, it still bore the yellow ship backstamp of Gray's. Then in 1960 Susan and Euan took over Gray's altogether. Susan had trained at Chelsea School of Art, and the early *Dolphin* series reflected her expertise as an illustrator, but in 1961, after acquiring Kirkham's Pottery, she was able to expand her skills to shaping as well as decorating her series. *Totem* and *Serif, Cypher* and *Jupiter* followed, then in 1965 came *Samarkand, Montesol* and *Greek Key*. From then on, the range kept expanding, almost annually, but perhaps the most successful in both design and commercial terms is the *Botanic Garden* series, exploiting the neglected beauty of Victorian illustrations of flora and fruits. The adaptation of these beautiful motifs presented a technical problem, the solution of which demonstrated that the lateral thinking and ability to cut through technical obstacles had descended from father to daughter. Susan and Euan went to Germany to see the printers, who declared the designs would require at least seven separate sheets of transfer. Susan promptly got down on the floor and in the next three hours she demonstrated that it could all be filled on two sheets, thus making the venture both aesthetically and commercially viable. Still there were doubts. The owner of the printing works doubted if such an extraordinary pattern would sell. Susan would be the last to listen to such miserable advice. By the end of 1973 the series of *Botanic Garden* was complete and since then has been an enormous success. In fact the series represents over half of Portmeirion Potteries turnover, and one of the most successful ceramic patterns ever.

Another success is *Birds of Britain*. Susan found an incomplete copy of Edward Donovan's *Natural History of British Birds* of 1793, with its beautiful illustrations seemingly in mint condition. Only *Botanic Garden* outsells it. Over fifty birds adorn the series, which sell in countless countries. In Italy, one motif had to be omitted, the Owl, since it is regarded there as an omen of ill luck — surely right, since quite a number of the other fifty birds represent legitimate prey for the owl.

And still, in the 1990s, the range expands. Daughter Angharad Menna has based her *Welsh Dresser* motif on traditional hand-painted Llanelli ware. Her *Harvest Blue* of 1995 is based on eighteenth century still-life. Another daughter, Anwyl, produced the originals for the *Ladies' Flower Garden* series, based on a book of that name by a Miss Loudon around 1840. Anwyl went on to paint Welsh hillside flowers for yet another series, *Welsh Wild*

*Flowers*, and *Ancestral Jewels*, based on Celtic jewellery. With this third generation actively involved, Clough would have taken enormous pleasure in the thought that Portmeirion continued to be not only a commercial success, but was also a thriving centre of design.

The entire enterprise is a triumph of design, determination and business sense. Furthermore, the pottery as a whole is somehow inimitably Portmeirion. A small saddleback publication, *The Story of Portmeirion Potteries* by Victoria Stanton and Euan traces the history of all this enterprise and the illustrations do it justice. So successful is the Pottery in the export market that I have heard it said that in the U.S.A. the word Portmeirion denotes to most people the ceramics rather than the place, since the series, and especially *Botanic Garden*, can be found in any great American city.

# Hitler's War

Aside from the human suffering and loss of life occasioned by war, architecture is one of its chief victims. Architecture is about creativity, war is about destruction. When the Second World War began, Clough, like many of his colleagues, found his practice reduced to practically nothing. A major overhead, of course, was the large establishment in Hampstead, Romney's House, which had been justified by the size of Clough's architectural practice. Hitler's war cut the ground from under his feet. Clough was never one to dawdle, so he cut his losses, deciding that such commissions as came his way could be handled perfectly well from Brondanw. He let Romney's House to an odd religious guru and his followers, who thought the gallery would make an excellent chapel. After the war, Clough sold the house to Raymond Russell, a collector of musical instruments, who also liked the gallery for concert performances.

Back in North Wales, Clough volunteered once again for military employment and certainly regarded himself as fit as ever. But when he revealed his age, fifty-seven, he was told politely not to be silly and to go home. He cast around further for a staff job in some office, but in the end he became a member of the local Home Guard around the Porthmadog area, first as a private, then as captain, led by younger brother Martyn.

It is difficult, after fifty years of European peace, to convey the feeling of dread and danger that pervaded the first year or two of the war. Nobody knew what aerial bombardment might actually mean. Would the entire country be obliterated, like some wholesale Guernica? Gas-masks were carried everywhere. If the Nazis ever came to invade and occupy Britain, would there be a wholesale round-up of people with known and published anti-Nazi records? Amabel had been among the most outspoken in such work, but had wisely decided to publish under her married name rather than Strachey, for it was learned later that brother John Strachey, M.P., and oddly enough a remote cousin, Lytton Strachey, were both on the Nazi list for special investigation and treatment. So Clough and Amabel had good reason to be wary, and Brondanw provided a splendid retreat.

Yet even in distant Meirionnydd, no one felt quite safe. Brondanw is conspicuous on the narrow road up to Cwm Croesor. The family found a secret cave further up the valley, provisioned it just in case, and like the rest of the country, waited in dread for developments, for it would take four years before the Allies would regain a military foothold on the mainland of Europe, when the feeling of danger would recede.

Clough continued to offer his services in whatever capacity the authorities might think fit, but it became quite clear they would not be required. So he knuckled down to life in Brondanw and Portmeirion. The house was full of children evacuated from the Liverpool area, where the danger was very real, with mass bombing raids all the time. Much of the Lease-Lend supplies from America were off-loaded in Liverpool Docks, so it made sense to evacuate children. Brondanw must have seemed very heaven to them.

Architectural work was nearly at a standstill. In peacetime this would have had disastrous consequences for any practice, but in wartime it is amazing what can be put into cold storage and revived once again upon the outbreak of peace. Of course, the fabric of Portmeirion got steadily shabbier; building supplies and labour were in constant short supply, as we have seen. Both Clough's daughters were called to duty, and son Christopher was called to Clough's old regiment, the Welsh Guards.

Another national emergency was the important matter of tertiary education. That could not be held in cold storage indefinitely. The future depended on the up and coming generation now being called up for war service. University staff were depleted, education was offered in one form or another in the Forces themselves, especially based on a series of pamphlets known as ABCA (Army Bureau of Current Affairs). The Army even ended up with a definitive Force, the Educational Corps, dedicated mostly to continuing education of Army personnel, especially of those about to be demobilised, to prepare them for a return to peace-time formal education.

This often involved the recruitment of civilian lecturers in the full gamut of studies and, to this end, Clough was asked to address staff and students and public at Queen's University in Belfast. When architects in Dublin heard of this, they insisted that Clough should come up to Dublin to address them too. Ireland of course was neutral, and Clough was startled by the sudden absence of all the wartime restrictions of poor old Britain, especially the black-out. The lights were on, food was plentiful, and Clough always remembered the Dublin hospitality with a certain guilt, though also with warmth. He found it hard to tolerate the presence of the Swastika flag flying over the German Embassy. He returned to the dark of Britain with very mixed feelings and gave one of his first broadcasts, on 'Ireland Now'. Later, and especially when television came on the scene, he would become a practised and very popular broadcaster. He continued to broadcast throughout the war. All this extra-mural education would eventually develop into the establishment of the Open University, and abysmal ignorance would become more a matter of choice than of station or class.

Another movement in wartime was the employment of artists to record Britain, and Kenneth Rowntree, with his architect wife Diana, stayed as guests at Brondanw whilst recording Welsh subjects. They always recalled their stay with great pleasure. Kenneth painted Traeth Mawr and the Cob, and some of his paintings were later reproduced in a Penguin publication, *A Prospect of Wales*, now a collector's piece.

Education was not the only activity to be sustained against the odds during war. Clough and family had always enjoyed parties and celebrations, and were especially addicted to firework displays. Upon the occasion of Charlotte's twenty-first birthday, fireworks were surely called for, and Clough had quite a store left from before the war. But fireworks flaring in the dark, and especially rockets piercing the night sky, would have brought the entire local defence force down upon their heads. Clough the lateral thinker had a way round that. Brother Martyn owned a large slate mine in nearby Blaenau Ffestiniog, where enormous caverns had been dug out of the earth. So Charlotte's twenty-first birthday was celebrated grandly with an underground firework display, possibly the only one ever.

Sadly, the war was scarred also by deep personal tragedy, which was to mark both Clough and Amabel from then on. In the protracted and bloody battle of Monte Purgatorio in Italy, Christopher was killed in action. Clough confessed that whatever pleasure he derived from the armistice in 1945, the pain of this loss was almost unbearable. Christopher, prior to joining up, had been an undergraduate at King's College, Cambridge, where his room mate was Euan Cooper-Willis. Euan later married Susan.

Unlike some of the towns in England, Scotland and South Wales, there was little or no mark of the war in North Wales. There had been minor inconveniences like rationing, loss of personnel, coping with evacuees and so on. The Portmeirion drive had been blocked by concrete tank traps, and the Traeth itself was littered with poles driven into the sands, to prevent air landings and parachute descents. The concrete blocks were incorporated later into the foundations of the Pantheon, but the poles still sometimes emerge with the frequent changes in the river's course over the years.

It was 1947 when I first met Clough. My first impression was much the same as the scene in *Headlong Down the Years*, when Miss Minerva Headlong welcomes two antipodean visitors who have travelled the painfully long train journey from Paddington to a station on the Pwllheli line (presumably Penrhyndeudraeth): 'As she welcomed them she excused herself for having brought what she called the Little Lorry. One of the young gentlemen was obliged to ride in the back of this contraption, in the company of their own luggage, a consignment of fencing material, two good-sized statues, and also a small, vigorously protesting young pig in a tea chest.' Bar the pig, that was much the same as my first hair-raising ride in the back of a little pick-up truck with Clough at the wheel, on our way to discuss my renewing all the signage in Portmeirion.

If one crossed the Cob at Porthmadog and saw a vehicle approaching in the opposite direction with an eight feet by four feet sheet of hardboard flapping dangerously on its roof, that would be Clough. In his time he had been a keen motorist, not immune from classic models. Before the Second World War he owned a handsome Delage and Sir Osmond Williams recalls driving along the Portmeirion drive one day and meeting Clough driving in the opposite direction in this beautiful machine, Clough with both hands off the wheel, arms spread wide in greeting, all without any slackening of speed.

# Peace Again

After the second war-induced parenthesis in Clough's life and career, longer even than the first, there was peace again. In architecture and planning, lessons had been learned, and sometimes not. But one lesson did strike home and that was that the rehabilitation of the nation after the rigours and deprivations of war should not be neglected as after the First War, when the peace was a time of negative and neglectful political lassitude, ending in the Great Depression of the Thirties.

Two million homes had been either damaged or destroyed completely by bombing. In architecture, the accent would be on planning, in a way that had not happened before. It was not simply town planning, to rehabilitate towns and cities ravaged by bombing, but also rural planning and National Park planning. No building could be erected now without planning permission, and consultants were very much in demand for the scrutiny of applications for building permits. No longer could one selfish individual be allowed to wreck some immemorial site or view by development to the detriment of his fellow citizens.

One of Clough's earliest assignments in this was to advise in 1947 on the delicate issue of a holiday camp in North Wales. At the time, the proposed Butlin's Camp near Pwllheli divided people sharply. There were those for whom it meant trade, jobs and revival of the economy in a fairly impoverished area, and on the other side there were those who professed horror that such development should be allowed so near to a newly designated National Park of precious mountain landscapes. Both views, as usual, were understandable, but irreconcilable.

Clough was in the delicate position of being both Planning Consultant to Caernarfonshire County Council *and* Chairman of the Council for the Preservation of Rural Wales. The Government's inspector, Sir George Pepler, presided and asked Clough if he was representing both Councils, to which Clough replied that he was 'mis-representing' them, since he disagreed with both on this issue and was fully in favour of the Camp. This may sound difficult to understand in one so passionately devoted to the conservation of landscape, and so instrumental in the establishment of National Parks. Would it not mean 'undisciplined hordes' trampling that landscape to death, with more people than sheep?

Clough was quite hard-headed about it and he was proved right in the long run. He pointed out, first of all, that the County Council had already considered the plans before the war, when

Billy Butlin applied for permission to build his Camp near a pebbly beach at Afon Wen near Pwllheli in South Caernarfon-shire. But when war broke out, the Admiralty saw this as an ideal site for a service training camp and they were allowed to go ahead on condition that they handed it back intact on the cessation of hostilities. The Admiralty would lease the land for the duration, but the bargain seemed to have been forgotten in the heat of the debate. Clough believed this was a deal which should be hon-oured. Furthermore, he went on, the Butlin holidaymakers would most probably stick to the Camp with its many attractions, and not swarm all over the landscape as was claimed. In addition, now that the Admiralty was finished with their training camp, did the protesters variously wish to see the sort of wreckage and desolation that demolished military camps invariably left?

He was right on all counts. Butlin's holidaymakers did not as a rule head for the mountains, which were some twenty miles distant anyway. The coast at Afon Wen (the site of only a desolate railway halt and a few houses) was of no intrinsic beauty. The campers do, by and large, stick to the Camp with its countless amusements. Clough was far-sighted enough to realise what would happen once Peace got under way. There would be in-creased mobility, the holidaymakers would arrive anyway and it would be wiser if they were concentrated in one site well away from the centres of the National Park.

Clough's arguments made quite a few enemies among his own ranks of those who treasure the landscape, but time has proved him right. If there is any harm done to the mountains of Snowdonia, it is perpetuated by those who profess to love them, by climbing and hill-walking thoughtlessly and causing actual erosion, by their litter, their damage to drystone walls and so on. Only a minority are guilty of this, but the Campers are innocent. They tend to stick together within the Camp and Clough's advocacy was surely right. Nevertheless, even Dr Thomas Jones, the former Cabinet Secretary, fell out with Clough over it.

Another post-war assignment came along when Lord Silkin, Minister of Town and Country Planning, invited Clough to become Chairman of Stevenage Corporation, the first New Town. Clough was not appointed as planner or architect, but as administrator. Here again, Clough would have to face implacable hostility, including that of his old friend E.M. Forster, whose opposition to any development at Stevenage was based on the fact that the original house in *Howard's End*, Rook's Nest, was in the middle of the designated site for the New Town. Of course, individuals would suffer. There is no such thing, short of the most desolate areas in the Scottish Highlands, as an empty landscape where development will not disturb the existence, views and traditions of a few local inhabitants. It is now know as NIMBY, 'not in my back yard'. Forster felt sufficiently aggrieved about Rook's Nest Manor Farmhouse to insist Clough should meet some of the other local residents who shared his anxiety. Their hostility was the worst that Clough had experienced in a working life that occasionally had involved opposition of one sort or another from interested parties. Cherished privacy, the prospect of unwanted propinquity of complete strangers ('incomers' is another word that would evolve with such controversies) and the loss of favourite areas of landscape, even the threat to the value of local property — all these had to be considered and as Chairman, Clough had to face the music personally.

He pointed out first, that it was not he who had designated the area for a New Town, but the Ministry of Town and Country Planning. He went on to suggest that, with the booming post-war demand for land, the area would be open anyway to piecemeal speculative development of one sort or another. How much better that it be planned according to the criteria of the New Town legislation. No amount of argument would placate the protesters, but many years later, at Bertrand Russell's ninetieth birthday party, Clough had the satisfaction of hearing Forster admit that in the end he was 'well content' with Stevenage New Town.

In 1951, Clough produced for the British Council's 'The Arts in Britain' series a small but pithy booklet on *Town and Country Planning*. He proves absolute master of both his subject and of persuasion. Having established the need for planning he quotes supreme examples from the past of good planning, and once again castigates the industrial developers of the nineteenth century. In one illustration, of the Potteries, he makes his point admirably, or perhaps, infamously. Looking back one cannot help wondering how such widespread squalor was ever allowed to happen. Heavy smoke poured from chimneys and kilns, straight on to the pathetic terraces directly underneath. Less use of coal-fired kilns has since helped to clean up the atmosphere. Clough then quotes Nash's ambitious scheme for the development of Crown Lands in the West End, and the rational treatment of London's Georgian squares and of Regent Street (before it was pulled down after World War I).

He outlines the objectives of the 1946 New Towns Act and the 1947 Town and Country Planning Act and explains Abercrombie's plans for London and Greater London. This is Clough at his height as apologist and populariser in the field of national planning. The closing sentence of the booklet says it all: 'We are resolved that the new framework shall be worthy of the new life opening out before the people of Britain'.

This small booklet alone would make salutary reading for any incoming Minister of the Environment, of whatever party. Clough makes it abundantly clear that planning is not for the benefit of architects and planners (who are merely its instruments) but *for the people*.

The Stevenage chairmanship was the sort of public service that Clough was never wholly happy with. While a cause might enjoy his whole-hearted support, the actual committee work, worse still chairing it, was anathema to him. So he was glad when he was freed from that particular chore, as he saw it. He did not seem to recognise that all his writing and polemics in favour of planning had made him an obvious choice for such an onerous job. He was being given a chance to implement some of the very measures for which he had been pleading since he began practice.

Amabel, sensing his relief, thought she could safely insist on a visit to New Zealand where daughter Charlotte was expecting her first child. In the immediate post-war years, international travel was not yet fully organised to the extent that a trip to New Zealand would be merely a matter of turning up at Heathrow and then enduring a couple of days in flight. Passages were often booked far ahead. But Clough recalled his previous connection with Butterfield and Swire in Shanghai, and by 're-connecting' he quite shamelessly jumped the queue and he and Amabel enjoyed their voyage in one of Butterfield and Swire's 'admirable ships'. It was a simple case of what the Russians call 'protectzia'.

They disembarked first in Australia and swept round the continent for a few weeks, seeing as much as they could and meeting people, 'from academics and sheep-farmers to tycoons, and of course, architects'. Perhaps it was a member of the latter community who sparked off a journalist who waylaid Clough as they re-embarked at Sydney for New Zealand. What did Mr Williams-Ellis think of 'our great city and wonderful harbour?' Clough promised a reaction provided it was reported verbatim and unedited. It was:

> By God what a site!
> By Man what a mess.

Naturally offence was taken. Clough in his turn felt he had been

18. Portmeirion against the mountains of Snowdonia, access to, and the preservation of which, Clough Williams-Ellis campaigned to bring about

20. The Belfry and Battery Square

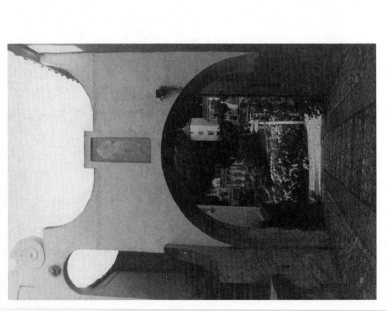

19. The cleverly designed entrance to Portmeirion

21. The Quay, looking towards Portmeirion, at which the mysterious remains of a boat were dis-covered

22. The Town Hall (Hercules Hall) and the statue of Hercules

23. The Gloriet, from which Clough Williams-Ellis would speak to assembled guests at the various anniversary and birthday celebrations which marked his later years

24-27. Portmeirion is remarkable for its perspectives. At the heart of the village lie the Dome (the top-most point of which an eighty-year-old Clough hand-gilded), the Colonnade and the Belfry; these photographs go some way to suggesting the variety of prospects at Portmeirion which just a few yards walk can create.

28. The Italianate roofs of Portmeirion

offended by the total disregard for any sort of planning whatsoever in Australia. As far as he could see, planning, or its lack, was simply a free-for-all access to anything anybody wanted. The most sublime and sometimes exotic landscape and coastline were often ruined by bungalows that he disliked so much.

There was no hiding from the public gaze, especially in what was still regarded in the home country as part of the British Empire. Clough was a celebrity — every word, every quote (especially if it might offend) would be blazoned across the front page of the Australian press. Such a thing would never deter Clough. Indeed, if it helped to advance the case for environmental planning, he would go out of his way to stir debate by any means.

In New Zealand he and the 'highly bellicose' Minister of Housing crossed swords at once, to the extent that the Press enjoyed a few days stirring things up with their usual glee. It became hot enough for the Prime Minister to intervene. He laid on a second official reception and offered Clough and Amabel a car and chauffeur to tour both islands. This clearly satisfied Clough's urge to explore, and South Island in particular impressed him. They circumnavigated the great lake of Wakatipu at Queenstown by launch and enjoyed a barbecue supper in a wooded bay.

Less enjoyable was the invasion of their hotel bedroom, while they slept, of a group of roistering drunks intent on toasting them. Clough, of course, was worried about the environment — would they be sick on the carpet? They were not lightly to be deterred, and when Clough discovered they were a group of undertakers enjoying their annual convention, he forgave all and by tact and persuasion managed at last to shoo them out.

There was a job for him too, at Stewart Island (at the southern tip of the country) where he was commissioned to plan a house for the daughter of New Zealand's first Surveyor-General. The setting was reminiscent of Scotland and the house was to replace one his hostess was presenting to the nation as a Prime Minister's retreat, rather like Chequers.

Such was his celebrity and perhaps even notoriety that New Zealand's architects asked him for some sort of testament before he left. He left six recorded talks, provocative and constructive as ever, pulling no punches, so that as they sailed homewards, first across the Pacific, then the Atlantic, he felt a pang of conscience (albeit brief) at this escape from any riposte to his barbed shafts. But there is no doubt that while he seems to have dismissed Australia very quickly from his mind he recalled New Zealand with a certain affection.

Back at home, Clough reflected on the progress (or lack) in architecture and planning in his own country, where he could be just as sharp-tongued as in the Antipodes. Now after all the years in practice, of enduring tedious committee work with planning luminaries like Sir Patrick Abercrombie and Lionel Brett, he decided that while architects could still find pleasure in their work, planners were still in somewhat deep water. It seemed pitifully little progress had been made. What he most enjoyed personally was being 'landowner, planner, architect, developer and paymaster all in one'. That rare status, of course, he held only at Portmeirion.

However, in 1961, he did find something for comfort and pleasure in the Festival of Britain, even if, as a member of the Welsh Committee, he found its contribution rather pathetic, for want of funds and 'patriotic fervour'. He seemed all too easily to forget that Governmental neglect of Wales, and of the valleys of the South in particular, left very little room for affection for London, as anybody would discover after a rugby international at Twickenham, when obscenities in Welsh on the road back from perhaps defeat did much to satisfy a quite different patriotic fervour from the kind Clough had in mind.

Nevertheless the forward-looking work of Hugh Casson's team gave Clough much pleasure and he exulted in particular at the stately pleasure dome installed at Battersea, all at the taxpayers' expense, which he found specially gratifying, for surely use of taxpayers' money denoted approval of a bright and beautiful architectural folly. So impressed was he by the whole joyous Festival that he always rated it 'the most significant and distinguished thing in the way of spectacle that we have attempted since the Field of the Cloth of Gold, far more important as an eye-educator, vastly more effective in influencing public taste through its very popularity'.

I would imagine few would agree, in retrospect, with that sanguine view, though at the time Clough was not alone in enjoying the general mood of optimism that prevailed during and after the Festival. Although the Festival Hall seems generally warm and welcoming, the general legacy of the South Bank has been pretty dismal and is in urgent need of refurbishment, which it is now receiving under the direction of Sir Richard Rogers.

But leaving aside the Festival, even as he registered his appreciation and his rather pious assessment of it, he found cause for deep concern nearer home on his very doorstep. The Central Electricity Board in 1951 proposed a scheme to harness many of North Wales's fast-flowing rivers, often in deep glaciated valleys easy to dam. Perhaps the most classic case was Cwm Croesor, the valley just above Plas Brondanw. It is a perfect U-shaped valley, the ideal of any engineer with a dam in mind.

To Clough, and to many others, this proposal seemed almost sacrilegious. Already certain valleys had been scarred by either dams or pipe-lines or pylons, notably Cwm Dyli, right under the southern flank of Snowdon. Llyn Trawsfynydd (before its atomic power station) although not so fine a stretch of water, was already dammed, with an unsightly pipe-line above Maentwrog. Many other valleys had been prospected, some of them wild and beautiful and unique in one way or another. The proposal was a multiple one of schemes large and small, all to be linked by power-lines to the National grid.

Living in this immemorial landscape, Clough was incensed, and he was not alone. There was a strong protest movement in which he was a key figure with a national profile. He was much regarded, perhaps even feared by the authorities proposing the scheme. I can remember large meetings in the mountains, and one in particular at Llyn Ogwen, when Clough spoke with passion, along with Sir Norman Birkett, to a crowd of walkers, residents and environmentalists. Clough, by this time sixty-eight, jumped athletically up on to the parapet that shields Llyn Ogwen from the A5 road that runs alongside. He spoke with his usual elegant turn of phrase, in passionate protest at this proposed act of philistinism. In retrospect, it is difficult to know what effect this sort of peaceful protest has on politicians, civil servants and government planners who, behind closed doors, cook up proposals.

In addition to this public participation, Clough, along with Amabel (its principal contributor) published the Peacockian satire, *Headlong Down the Years*. Clough's close friend the writer Richard Hughes introduced this 'absurd little tale' which starts off with Peacock's own Headlong Hall, then hares off hysterically into wit, sarcasm, satire, all the barbs imaginable to shoot down the Electricity Board. Although somewhat dated in its outrageous humour, it is still a very funny book. Richard Hughes places it firmly when he says: 'The personified Points-of-View, the stiff little stylised puppets they were handling began to wriggle their fingers with a life of their own, turned into living characters (often in the literal sense, and wearing disguises so diaphanous as to be scarcely even . . . decent)'. Certainly in the locality we enjoyed pulling off this thin disguise and recognising this or that figure. 'Mr Bo Dynmont, elegant in copper-coloured linen trousers and a lemon coloured shirt' was transparently Jim Wyllie, who managed Portmeirion at the time. The Squire of Headlong, leading his party but slowly, pointing out this and that to the newcomers — especially a series of what he called his 'nice little slums', was — well, need more be said? Several characters like Mrs Headlong and her sister-in-law Miss Minerva Headlong, are surely a composite portrait of Amabel herself, judging by the wit, intelligence and knowledge in the arguments. Place is important to the narrative and argument (more of the latter than the former), for the book's message, wrapped gleefully in satirical nonsense, is that place, landscape, is too precious to bear all the horrifying electrical developments proposed by government. 'Remember, too,' writes Hughes in the afterword, 'that the mountains of Snowdonia have something of the significance for Welshmen, all over the world, that Jerusalem has for Jews, all over the world.'

It worked. The whole scheme was abandoned (officially 'shelved') and no more was heard of electricity schemes until the advent of atomic power, when Trawsfynydd was chosen. Since it was already a spoiled lake, dammed many years before for electricity generation, and since strictly speaking it was outside the designated National Park, it was acceptable, but again, only after protest at a further few outrageous proposals, including one power station on Traeth Bach itself, where the tidal water was just the sort of thing the engineers were after for their cooling requirements.

When Trawsfynydd Atomic Power Station came to completion, a colleague of Clough's, the eminent landscape artist, the late Miss Sylvia Crowe, was commissioned to plant and landscape the station, which perhaps goes to show how sensitive the Electricity authorities were to environmental protest. But protest needs a national figure and Clough was just that. He never ceased to fight this sort of battle right to the end. One must, he always asserted, 'care passionately', as though to lie down and accept were to be only half alive. Surely he was right, and the preservation of Snowdonia from this comprehensive proposal is sufficient monument to that passionate care. It is imaginable that, without this sort of protest, the valleys of Snowdonia might have been cluttered with dams and power lines.

1951 was a landmark in Clough's life, and not always for the right reasons or reasons he would have chosen. At home on the evening of 10th December he set the alarm clock for 5 a.m. in order to catch the early morning train from Bangor to Euston for a meeting. It may have saved their lives, for there is little doubt that had the alarm been set for a more normal 7 a.m., both Clough and Amabel would have perished.

The alarm rang at 5 a.m. as bidden. Amabel seems to have been the first to speak: 'Someone must be burning paper — do have a look'. Clough rose, found the staircase filled with smoke. When he opened the drawing-room door and switched on the light, he was met by a blast of heat and smoke. Since there were no flames, he dashed downstairs through the smoke, opened the Library door and unleashed a blazing furnace. Pennant, his little terrier, lay dead on the threshold.

In an attempt to telephone, Clough almost fell through the half-burnt floor. The telephone line had perished in the heat. He sent off a messenger to the village (some two hundred yards) to summon the Porthmadog Fire Brigade, and while waiting, tried to tackle the rampant flames with antiquated fire extinguishers and old leather fire-buckets. For once his natural optimism had failed him.

The fire by now had taken a firm hold. As doors and windows collapsed in the heat and let in the air, the flames reached floor after floor, up into the attic. The roof fell in with a huge fountain of blazing sparks, and Clough and Amabel, clad only in night clothes and dressing gowns, watched from the garden below. In fact, those clothes were all that survived of their personal belongings. Spectacles, dentures, letters, files, books, drawings — everything had gone.

By mid-morning, the fire had consumed the whole interior and its contents, despite the best attentions of the Fire Brigade. Only the massive outer walls remained. Clough, conscious of his status as inheritor and guardian of all this, his patrimony, had concentrated what effort was possible on saving what he could of the fabric of the house, at the expense of salvaging individual items that might possibly have been rescued. In the end, only one table survived, and one book, albeit a precious one in Clough's eyes, Bickham's *Universal Penman*. He passed it on to me as it was for a while, its glorious old full-calf binding all scorched; both for temporary safe-keeping and for instruction, for he preferred Bickham's flowing eighteenth century penmanship to my own austere Gill-trained classical letter-forms for stone inscriptions.

The precious family silver, mostly eighteenth century and seldom used, had been stored in the attic and now was a blob of molten metal on the slate floor of the brewhouse.

The whole neighbourhood was shocked. Plas Brondanw had always been there, and Clough's imaginative refurbishment was much admired and loved. It seemed at first that it would remain a hollow ruin of blackened walls, empty window- and door-frames, all without a roof to keep out the weather. Looking at it on that bleak morning of the 11th, one could almost see the encroaching ivy inside and outside like many an old Welsh farmstead in the hills.

Sadly, the house had been inadequately insured, so any question of immediate salvage was out of the question. Clough had taken over the house as a young bachelor and had not thought of a mundane item like updating insurance. The whole prospect was dire indeed. Most people would have recoiled from such a blow and retired to some available cottage of character and made the best of it.

Not so Clough and Amabel. There were indomitable. One of their first actions was to ask me to carve a little memorial plaque to Pennant, to lie on his grave on the lawn below the house. The next, in this period of rationing of building materials, was to garner what was legally available in new materials and scout for old ones in the neighbouring quarries. Steel joists, for instance, were practically non-existent and Clough wished to rebuild against fire by introducing concrete floors with oak parquet. In the event, those floors are reinforced with old redundant tramway rails from the quarries. He bought and demolished Llanfrothen's old disused National School and used the dressed stone. He scoured places like Crowther's in London for eighteenth century doors and mantelpieces and all sorts of architectural impedimenta.

The rebuilding of Plas Brondanw was a major triumph of optimism in the face of adversity. To lose an only son, and then a home in a five-year spell would seem more than most people could bear, yet the 'revivification' of the old house was a miracle of hope, improvisation, energy and, lest it be forgotten, of architectural design, for Clough grasped the opportunity to implement certain new features that the old house had singularly lacked.

It took two years all told, and a tremendous house-warming party was held. Finally, to mark the occasion for perpetuity, Clough asked me to carve an inscription on a heavy old stone slab, to lie in front of an old urn he had stored away for some future occasion. It stands at the top of the avenue leading up from the gate of the house.

This flaming urn raised on the ashes of their home by Clough and Amabel Williams-Ellis celebrates the rebuilding of Plas Brondanw 1953 two years from its burning and the names of those to whom it owes its restoration, viz:

Wm. Davies, Tom Davies, Owen Edwardes, Harry Pike,
Hugh Owen, Robert Jones and R.O. Williams.

★ ★ ★

Every North Walian would recognise the burden of serving on a
Welsh national committee, for as Clough remarked, the meetings
were inevitably in Cardiff. Perhaps it is only for the comfort of the
civil servants involved. Clough was quite right in reminding them
that it was easier to get to London from North Wales than to Cardiff.
Yet he served faithfully on the Welsh Committee of the Festival of
Britain in 1951, and he advised Government Planning on reconstruction in Wales. The economy had to start again from scratch
with the docks and installations at Barry, Cardiff and Swansea all
severely damaged by German bombing. An impressive report
ensued and Clough remarked: 'although we were certainly out in
some of our pronouncements, we were right on target in others'.

Then an old friend, Sir Stafford Cripps, persuaded him against
his will to chair another committee, to investigate and report on
the British Glass Industry. Clough protested that he knew nothing
whatsoever about the glass industry, but Cripps was adamant. His
objective was to instil into the industry a new spirit of design, and
that would only come from designers *outside* the industry. Glass,
like many another British industry, was suspicious of Design,
which seemed to spell to them a sort of anarchic free-for-all.
Industry prefers to stick to old, tried and tested, traditional
designs. Introducing Clough to the industry would be rather like
letting a terrier loose among a colloquy of cats. His professional
colleagues on the committee were appalled when he dared to
question their perfect production of careful geometrical patterns.
Great skill, yes, but to what end? He even dared to declare a
preference for 'the natural simplicity of the jolly great flagons and
beakers of clouded glass, full of bubbles, presumably foreign
imports, still being sold at sixpence a time'. This, of course, was
heresy, but he made a good and constructive heretic always.

He was a valuable member of the Hobhouse Committee on
National Parks. Its members were an illustrious collection of
experts in various fields concerned with the environment: Sir Julian
Huxley as naturalist, Lord Chorley as legal adviser, and geologists,
agriculturalists, arboriculturalists, ecologists, with Clough as landscape amenity expert. He had already confirmed his championship of landscape by dipping into his own pocket to purchase the

mountain ridge overlooking Llyn Gwynant in Snowdonia and then presenting it to the National Trust to ensure its survival as an area of natural and original habitat. He was most certainly instrumental in the introduction of legislation to curb the outrageous appetite of advertisers for placing hoardings and billboards wherever they wished. Clough had noticed that local farmers in the most pronounced beauty spots did not always repair gaps in their fences. They then let off the gaps (usually in the most strategic places) to advertisers at a nice little rent. Deliberately to get something done, Clough planned to let the gaps in his own Hafod Llwyfog property, right under the flank of Snowdon, so that advertisers would have flocked to take up his offer. The result would have been so outrageous that it would offend and galvanise even the sleepiest legislator. Fortunately legislation was achieved before this was necessary.

In drawing up the proposed scheme for the Snowdonia National Park, Clough's colleagues queried his inclusion in the map of Cwm Croesor, his own stamping ground. His plea was that he, as an example of the local fauna, was justified in designating Cwm Croesor, and while it is true that the head of the valley has been much worked over for slate quarrying, nevertheless it is still a fine valley which has quickly reverted to its wild state. But he advised the exclusion of the area round Blaenau Ffestiniog, as beyond redemption with its overpowering waste tips. Yet that advice is debatable now. The great quarries are mostly worked out, have even become tourist attractions themselves. There is no objection to this, surely, but perhaps designation *within* the National Park might have prevented some of the more outrageous excesses in the name of tourism and profits.

Clough patently enjoyed the National Parks appointment and confessed that, apart from the Trunk Roads Committee, he never 'spent so long a time on any job more enjoyably or perhaps more usefully'. He was satisfied that the designation of the National Parks had been a success. He was critical that Government was in the end rather niggardly about providing funds. He regretted that subventions from a central fund would have assisted local initiatives in the way of enhancing specific sites and buildings in the parks. He regretted 'negative watchfulness' as not enough, but like all those who care about landscape, he was nevertheless gratified to have at least these National Parks laid down on the Statute Book for all time, and wrote:

A wide popularity and appreciation; a democratic good

will, an alert public opinion that would protect them from injury and maintain their integrity against the Philistine for our possibly more civilized successors, had somehow to be assured. The National Parks and their younger brothers, the Areas of Outstanding Natural Beauty, have gone a long way to fulfilling this task; they have helped in popularizing the enjoyment of their beauty by making lovely buildings and lovely places generally accessible, without somehow thereby impairing their distinctive characters.

As the world adjusted itself uneasily to Peace and manufactured new alignments Clough was by now a celebrity, much in demand all over the world. At the age of seventy he was still travelling and lecturing and would do so for a considerable number of years yet.

First there was a lecture tour in the British Zone in Germany. He and Amabel flew out in a converted bomber of whose airworthiness he was far from convinced. Apart from the actual lectures, he did his own special sight-seeing, with the accent on buildings, naturally. He was quick to note the immediate energy and resurgence of Germany after its catastrophic defeat, and reported at length in *The Manchester Guardian*. He was impressed by the conservation and restoration work, admired the detail and craftsmanship. Was this perhaps a lesson to be learnt back at home? The bombing devastation of areas of Hamburg and Hanover was so complete that he marvelled at the sheer will and effort to clear, not to wait for others to do it, and to simply get on with building by any means possible. One little town, where before the war he had enjoyed sketching, was quite flattened and he could only take heart at the way, phoenix-like, it was rising again from the ashes.

All this admiration from a man who had fought one dreadful war against the Germans and had lost his only son in another. Did he perhaps take it to a fault, this single-minded gaze at buildings, with little mention of people, whether British or German? Certainly the immediate post-war effort of the German people to restore their bombed-out towns was impressive, and perhaps Clough saw in this the answer to his constant prayer that his own people might care more and might aspire to the same sort of energy and determination in post-war reclamation.

He and Amabel forewent the return flight in the converted bomber, preferring the old Channel packet, but, clinging to the rails in a howling gale, with spume driving in their faces and less hardy passengers suffering *mal-de-mer* all round them, they wondered if they had been wise after all.

Then came a Middle East tour under the auspices of the War
Office and the British Council. Clough was surprised to find
himself snowbound in Damascus. It curtailed his programme
though he still lectured to Kurds in Mosul and to Iraqis in
Baghdad. With the verve of a young man he hopped from one
venue to another, and on one occasion was severely reprimanded
by the Council for thumbing a lift aboard a small unauthorised
plane from Cyprus to Beirut. He was warned that, had he not
survived the trip, he was not insured on that plane and his widow
would not have received a penny compensation. It was the sort of
thought that would never occur to Clough. Altogether, throughout his life, from morning prayers under father, the Architectural
Association, through Army and all the King's Regulations, to
Planning Officers and diplomats and civil servants of whatever ilk,
he was never easy to handle.

Egypt was another favourite stamping ground of British Council
personnel and guests, but there Clough had to suffer rather, as an
honorary member of the Brigadier's Mess in Ismailia, which was
a well-established watering-hole and oasis hard by the Suez Canal,
in days when Britain still regarded Egypt as more or less Empire.
There Clough met the Chief of Imperial Staff, Field Marshall
Slim, who ticked him off for painting too rosy a picture of post-war
development back home. These New Towns were all very well,
but mention of them made the chaps restless and homesick.

Naturally Clough did the sights, the Pyramids and the Sphinx
by moonlight. They were not altogether to his taste, but he was
greatly impressed by the treasures of Tutenkhamun in the
National Museum in Cairo. That city is not the place to explore
unaccompanied, unless keeping to established tourists trails.
Wander off into the labyrinthine old city alone and trouble may
ensue, as Clough soon discovered. Ever curious, he *did* wander
on his own and found himself accompanied by a mob offering
aphrodisiacs ('sent every fortnight to an English Duke whom they
named'). Clough's comment was understandable: 'I wonder if His
Grace knows or cares that he is being thus advertised as a satisfied
customer'. He escaped only after buying some expensive bottles
of scent of doubtful efficacy. He left Egypt on a final anti-climactic
note by seeing King Farouk in a nightclub. While I can imagine
the King, I wonder what the architect was doing there.

Fiji, Mexico, and another United States visit, all filled a busy
schedule that would have floored many half his age. At seventy
he ranged the world like the proverbial spring chicken, and
whereas other Welsh notables on lecture tours succumbed to the

blandishments of American hospitality (Dylan Thomas, who needed no encouragement, and John Cowper Powys who blamed his peptic ulcer on his U.S. lecture tours) Clough sailed blithely on, not only delivering his lectures but taking every opportunity to explore. He was not taken with the Pre-Colombian artefacts of Mexico, nor even by the Spanish Rococo, which he found extravagant.

Internal flights in the United States can sometimes be hazardous and on one flight his plane was diverted because of unfavourable weather conditions over their destination. As they eventually touched down at an alternative airfield, one 'hulking sore-head of a lawyer' berated the crew, accusing them of incompetence in thus diverting him from some important appointment. He shouted about breach of contract, threatened to sue the airline — all par for the course in a nation where sueing is a national sport. Clough was so outraged at the man's ingratitude and surliness that he took him on in single combat, verbally of course. With his patrician English he must have sounded like a chastising Duke of Wellington. It worked, and 'sore-head' sulked off, unappeased but no longer talking of sueing.

A trip to Williamsburg in Virginia must have given Clough particular pleasure. There was a Welsh connection, for the eighteenth century Welsh poet, Goronwy Owen, failing to achieve preferment in the Church in Wales, finally took up teaching in the Grammar School in Williamsburg and mourned his native Anglesey to the end, not without the occasional libation. Clough found the little town very much to his taste. In a way, of course, it invited comparison with Portmeirion. While Clough realised Williamsburg was a sort of fossil, and therefore somewhat artificial, he still commended it to his profession and to planners in general as an example of good manners in architecture. It was a term he used constantly in lectures and in print. Building and planning that offended in one way or another, but mostly visually, were assessed in terms or manners, just as one would assess people in their address to society. Portmeirion might be a folly, but compared to Williamsburg's time warp, it is a living organism.

Clough's flexibility of response to various developments was illustrated by his enthusiastism about one post-war development, uncompromisingly modern in aspect, in southern France. It was the brand new town of Port Grimaud, built by the French architect François Spoerry. The two architects exchanged visits like Heads of State, each envious of the other for some detail in their respective sites. Spoerry coveted what he called the verticality of Portmeirion, by which he meant the uneven terrain of its valleys and heights enabling complex siting. Although Clough had been Chairman of Stevenage New Town during its development, as administrator he had too little to do with its actual design. He had designed certain complexes like Portmeirion, Cushendun or Cornwell Village Street, but he had not been able to exploit his planning principles on a whole town. At Port Grimaud, which was developed on virgin salt-marshes at the head of the Gulf of St Tropez, he enjoyed the maritime flavour (no cars, like Venice), canals, bridges, terraces and clusters with little patio gardens, quays for mooring, and the centre island complex of social amenities like church, hotels, shopping centre and restaurants. It was a development after Clough's heart and it is a pity that, partly by lack of public patronage and partly by reluctance on his own side to get involved in bureaucracy, he never achieved a development of the dimensions of Port Grimaud. There was no doubt he would have liked to. His autobiographical note on Port Grimaud is a moving example of his despair at the lack of such adventure in his own country:

> Now whenever I need cheering up I just remind myself of this unlikely and so civilised happening on that otherwise dishonoured coast, when I immediately feel that all is not yet lost.

Another labour of love, and of dedication too, considering the amount of travel involved, was the volume *On Trust for the Nation*, published by Paul Elek in 1947. It is an apt title for a book devoted to properties owned or protected by the National Trust upon the occasion of its Jubilee. A glimpse at the folding map at the end of the book reveals the long distances Clough covered in those immediate post-war years, when at long last certain environmental legislation was laid down on the statute book, and it really looked for a while as though Britain might after all be heading for a brave new world.

The book celebrates much of the beauty that Clough had fought to preserve before the war. Here was one body which would protect all that he held most dear; not only grand country houses, but tracts of precious and unique landscape, oddities of history like the George Inn at Southwark, or some beautiful old thatched cottage with a history. Typically, he seizes the reader's attention at once, with a fanciful supposition:

> that by some miracle, all the lands and buildings possessed by the National Trust were to he uprooted and set adrift and then, by some further sorcery, reassembled into one

fabulous island. That would be magic indeed; the pith and
pick of England close-packed into a compass smaller
than that of the Isle of Wight, yet sampling all that we most
prize . . .

He goes on to develop the fancy, as only he could, imagining a
coast line made up of this or that piece of Trust coastland, a
shingle spit from Blakeney in Norfork, a river flowing past
Constable's Mill; inland a 'tempestuous territory' of assorted
lakes and mountains', and so on.

Then, just as dramatically, he arrests the fancy, by thanking God
that 'even a monster syndicate of maniacal millionaires could not
make it a reality or seduce the National Trust from its chartered
duty — the preserving of Beauty as and where it is'. He outlined
first, the scope and powers of the Trust, 'an entirely unofficial,
ungovernmental body founded and managed by private persons but
in the public interest'. His own interest, of course, is buildings
rather than people, and he makes no bones about it, confessing
to 'an instinctive, illogical and quite indefensible feeling that
seemly architecture and a gracious landscape are sufficient ends
in themselves, regardless of the social implications . . .'. He ties
himself in knots trying to justify himself, as though, given his head,
he would do without people except as figures in a landscape, like
some three-dimensional Claude Lorrain: 'That view . . . cannot,
I must own, be intellectually defended'. Then, having thus untied
himself he admits the condition of public accessibility — 'for the
greatest happiness of the greatest number'. He, the deviant
socialist, even condescends that 'with the overwhelming mass of
our teeming population town-bred, barbarously reared in far other
than splendid cities, having had little contact with beauty of any
kind and therefore knowing or caring very little for it, the introduction is a hazardous one'.

The first trek in *On Trust for the Nation* is a long one which takes
him all the way North to Lindisfarne on Holy Island, just off the
Northumberland coast. It is particularly memorable for him, since
the castle is a wholesale restoration by his old friend and hero Sir
Edwin Lutyens. Then, an oddity — he is grateful to the Trust for
taking on the preservation of the eighteenth century lime-kilns at
Beadnell, just farther down the coast. Then over to Alnwick
Castle, and Wellington, and on to Hadrian's Well, where the
Trust had an extensive section under its care at Housesteads Fort.

This Northumbrian safari is typical of the whole book, conveying
his obvious pleasure in the country and its treasures. He travels

over the Pennines to the Lake District where the Trust's holdings are predominantly tracts of dramatic landscape. He has time for a generous encomium to Wordsworth, poet of landscape if ever there were. And since much of the Trust's properties are enshrined in *Feng-shui* (Chinese for wind-water and its capacity to *shape* landscape) *en passant* he preaches a timely sermon on the proper treatment of *Feng-shui*, citing as a bad example the erection of a dam above the village of Dolgarrog in North Wales, which when the dam burst one stormy night in 1925, swept away much of the village with disastrous loss of life and property.

Perhaps these occasional 'sermons' are the real value of this book, for it is not simply a guide book by an admiring visitor for other visitors. It is also a textbook on the treatment of environment and amenity for those with the power to make or break a property, be it house or landscape tract. For example, the Forestry Commission is castigated for its unfeeling, regimented rows of alien conifers.

On to the Calf of Man. Clough thinks that perhaps it would be a good idea if all islands were preserved in trust 'for there is no *cordon sanitaire* like a salt water sound with a tide-rip'. He comes home to his own beloved North Wales, quoting, surprisingly, Hilaire Belloc, on its virtues: 'so magical are the mountain forms, so clear the lakes and tarns, so boldly break down to the sea the torrent-tongued ravines, so august is the pomp of the tides as they race inland up the rock-bound estuaries and fill the hollows of the hills with their sea-music'.

And it must be noted that he comes down firmly on the side of the people in a plea for a North Wales National Park, which in due course was implemented. 'The best things that are still left to us must now clearly be guarded not from the people but for them, else democracy is a farce and education and added leisure a heartless mockery.'

Derbyshire's Peak district, Lincolnshire's Tattershall Castle, and Blickling Hall in Norfolk are all visited, and their respective histories and virtues succinctly described. It is the sort of book, with its photographs, for example, of four-turretted Blickling seen across a lake, that makes one want to up sticks and travel round the land to see them.

He journeys down and down the country, extending southwards all the time. At the Wool Market in Chipping Campden in Gloucestershire, he buttonholes the reader: 'Regard it. So absolutely right, so happily a part of and at home in its superb grey setting — be humble before those who could build little towns so beautifully, blush for their crass descendants, your contemporaries, and be thankful for the Trust'.

West Wycombe delights him, not least because it provides such a stark and salutary contrast to its near neighbour, High Wycombe, which Clough had earlier excoriated to such an extent that he is grateful to find that *places* cannot be libelled. There is, too, West Wycombe Park, with its splendid colonnade, and it is noticeable that later, he would 'collect' one of the most distinguished colonnades for Portmeirion.

One property, whose aspect and history appealed specially to him, was St John's Jerusalem at Sutton-at-Home in Sussex. It was given to the Trust by Sir Stephen and Lady Tallents, who lived there at the time of his visit, and Clough is grateful to quote copiously from Sir Stephen's monograph on St John's, whose history dates from 1199, when the Knights Hospitallers took over this moated plot of land. He is grateful too, for the Trust's acquisition of the Seven Sisters, 'the White Cliffs of Albion', at a time when vast advertisements for gin and soap disfigured them — 'we have not been called a nation of shopkeepers for nothing'.

As for public access to Trust property, there is a touching warning on Clouds Hill, Dorset, the little tiled and colour-washed cottage that T.E. Lawrence (of Arabia) used as a retreat on leaving the Air Force as Aircraftsman Shaw. The upper room has a simple divan bed with all round, and within easy reach, shelves filled with Lawrence's library, which always appealed to me as a student as the ideal 'pad'. The whole place, with its contents, was handed over intact by his brother A.W. Lawrence. 'Alas,' Clough writes, 'all the books have been stolen by sneak thief souvenir hunters who have made away with much else that was movable.'

He ends appropriately with Land's End, recalling a splendid continental cruise in his ketch, when they passed the Longships Light, heading home for the next landfall of Milford Haven in Wales, and admiring the Mayon and Trevascan Cliffs by moonlight. *On Trust for the Nation* is a most engaging book, entertaining, informative, and amply filled with drawings by Barbara Jones and photographs.

All this committee work, writing, propaganda, cajoling a public largely indifferent to environmental concerns, brought him to the attention of a wider audience and even Government had taken note. By 1958, at the age of seventy-five, Clough was made a Commander of the British Empire, the first of several honours that came to him in old age.

# Eighties

At what he called the 'absurd age' of eighty, Clough was almost ready to think of, if not actually to take up, retirement. For him it was not so much a daunting prospect, end of the line, end of how to occupy the time, but rather a difficulty of conception. It is never easy for the self-employed, without the imposition of a third party to dispatch one to a sort of limbo. However he was just beginning to view the prospect of retirement, when an endearing couple whom he scarcely knew, telephoned him. They had inherited an old estate in Cumbria called Dalton Hall. The estate was overgrown and the house, though possibly romantic in certain eyes, was a rambling hulk, quite unmanageable without a huge complement of servants. The Mason-Hornbys were right to approach Clough. If he took on their proposals, it warded off once again the prospect of retirement, for better or worse. But from their point of view he had proved in the past how adept he was at facing and solving just the sort of comprehensive problem they had, of reconciling, if at all, the sentiment of preserving the past with the needs of the twentieth century.

Clough found the young couple irresistible; retirement could be deferred. He did not understand the concept in any case. Amabel admitted that taking on Dalton Hall gave him a new lease of life. Clough reflected that he was venerable enough to be the couple's grandfather and therefore the great-grandfather to their young children.

On inspecting the site he was horrified at the endless accretions to the original structure, much of it subject to dry rot. Even after discovering one or two likeable features, 'a quite scholarly dark Doric *porte-cochère*' for instance — he felt compelled to recommend that in the end only complete demolition would solve their problems. A new start altogether was the only answer.

At first the local community looked with disfavour on the wholesale demolition of their Hall, and Clough and the Mason-Hornbys had to ride quite a bit of local opposition and counter claims. The Hall had been there for generations — why could it not be refurbished and conserved, as other generations had kept it up? It is difficult to argue against history and appearances when they are riddled with dry rot. The trouble with dry rot is that its extent is mostly invisible and undemonstrable. In the end, Dalton Hall, Clough's last commission, gave both him and his young clients immense satisfaction. The final seal of approval is the affection of the neighbourhood for the new Hall.

Clough's career had stretched over some six decades, from Llangoed Hall in 1912 to Dalton Hall in 1969. In that time, he had had to recommend on several occasions either partial or wholesale demolition, a course he took with great reluctance, especially when he had witnessed, in other hands, the needless demolition of some fine edifice to make way for development of a housing estate of doubtful taste. He was gratified when 'listing' of cherished buildings was introduced, and by now some of his own have been listed and are therefore safe from the occasional indifferent owner and the speculative developer.

Certainly he cherished his own buildings and watched over them. When the urns were thoughtlessly removed from the facade of the Chapel at Bishop's Stortford College, he was quick to express his outrage. The authority responsible pleaded difficulty of maintenance, and only acceded to the return of the urns to their proper place at his own expense and not theirs. The urns are back and the building became the first by a living architect to be listed and thus protected.

Clough had every right to be outraged, for the facade of the Memorial Hall is one of his finest and the four urns are an integral part of the effect, the ultimate and logical adornment of the four ascending pilasters, owing much to Palladio, and perhaps most of all to the facade of San Giorgio Maggiore in Venice.

The threat of demolition of his first major project, Llangoed Hall, had caused him great distress and for a time its fate was in the balance. However, it has survived and is now a flourishing hotel on the main A470 route from North to South Wales. Sometimes he had to endure the opposite. *The Architectural Review* for December 1928 published a photograph of a country house he had built, Caversham Place, near Reading, for the Pereira family. It was a two-storey brick house, with a pedimented front, all built for £5,878 in 1924. Its shutters were painted in his favourite blue-green, a shade he would use a great deal at Portmeirion. The house stood in 22 acres of grounds, the sort of space beloved of speculative developers. Caversham Place is typical of Clough's art in his inter-war years, yet by 1951, it was up for sale with its grounds, demolished in haste, and a housing estate built in its stead. It was just the sort of action he deplored and it was a glaring example of the need for listing buildings of outstanding merit or history.

\* \* \*

Clough the dancing man had always enjoyed parties, but when he reached his eightieth birthday he almost cried off. First, he realised that reaching eighty is not the achievement it once was, and second, he and Amabel did not wish to be embarrassed with presents they did not need from friends and well-wishers. They tried to scotch all rumour about age or about the impending Golden Wedding just two years away. It was a sign of their popularity that in the end there was no question of not celebrating.

First, for his birthday, the Director of the Architectural Association, Bobby Carter, organised a grand party in the Harcourt Room in the House of Commons. The host was brother-in-law John Strachey. Speakers included Sir Robert Matthew, President of the Royal Institute of British Architects, A.P. Herbert (later knighted), Dilys Powell the doyenne of film critics, Lionel Esher, and of course Amabel herself. As an early feminist, she often suffered these predominantly male occasions with good grace, but was always ready with a waspish aside to any token woman companion who might be present, as she did once with my wife at a disgracefully male 'do' by the Gas Board at Portmeirion at which they were the only women present. I had just completed a commission for Wales Gas Board and perhaps they felt that the wife of the landlord of Portmeirion and my own wife were sufficient token.

Next, and patently more enjoyable, judging by Clough's own record, was a superb picnic, organised by an old friend, Christabel Lady Aberconway, at the Drum House, farther up the valley from Plas Brondanw. The Drum House was one of Clough's most felicitous conversions. In the past, the building had housed the drum or winding-gear that controlled the ascent and descent of trams bearing slate from the Croesor Quarries. The steep slope below it marked the lip of the U-shaped valley that the Electricity Board had had in its view for a hydro-electric dam earlier in the Fifties.

This was a perfect day. Despite his age, Clough was the life and soul of the party, absolutely indefatigable. Family and friends from all over the world turned up; local friends like the Marquis and Marchioness of Anglesey, and Sir Osmond and Lady Williams, Michael Burn the writer and his wife Mary, Michael Trevor Williams the Portmeirion manager and many others. From further afield, John Betjeman, who of course shared Clough's passion for conservation, lolled like a lump of England on the sheep-bitten Welsh turf.

Clough called this party the 'View Party' because as we sat on the steep grassy slope below the Drum House, quaffing wine and gossiping, spread out below us was Traeth Mawr and the Cob, with the waters of Tremadog Bay shimmering in the distance. It was all quite splendid, an occasion after Clough's heart, and it was the first of several such festivities in his old age, to celebrate either himself or Portmeirion, which itself by now was beginning to reach a respectable age.

Afterwards the high jinks transferred to Portmeirion, with bands, fireworks, floodlights picking out salient features in the fabric, and a gala dinner and ball. Clough's after-dinner speech was a triumph by all standards, and is worth recalling, not only for its deeply personal note but because it was a sort of testament, a retrospective credo, even an apologia, which was so touching in its sincerity and feeling that everybody recalled it with great warmth.

> True enough, I am undoubtedly eighty years old, but what of it? In these days there is nothing singular in that. Nor is there any merit in it, or so I had supposed. Yet, nonetheless, here is this honorific celebration dreamed up by a benevolent cabal of brother architects. For indulgent they certainly are in even countenancing, let alone embracing me, the un-qualified non-conformist, congenitally devia-tionist, rogue architect, that I am. I never sat for, still less passed, any examination of any kind; held no traffic what-soever with the Royal Institute until, one day it suddenly said: 'Hi! What are you up to out there — you'd better come inside as a Fellow'. And yet there is its most distin-guished president treating me not only as a man and a brother — but as though I were entirely respectable, indeed as an honoured colleague.
>
> And it's not as though I was an 'important' architect who just *had* to be recognised, because I am demonstrably and emphatically nothing of the kind — no great work of mine stands out against the sky in splendour to excite men's wonder. I shall never even appear in Banister Fletcher or any such reference work — I have merely had a perfectly lovely hobbyhorsical time designing and build-ing all sorts of lesser things that pleased me. Whence Portmeirion and such like trivia.
>
> Now in so far as I may be known at all, I think it is much less as a practical architect, landscape designer, town planner or whatever, than as propagandist of these ploys — books and texts and pamphlets and articles and years of lecturing and broadcasting and tub-thumping all over the place, my Milton's 'Farewell happy fields where joy forever dwells, hail horrors' — calling sinners to repentance, a

chord to which I felt inescapably compelled as in duty
bound.

One of my later books I began with: 'I dedicate this
book to all the beauty of my country, natural and other, in
gratitude and grief'. But really all my books should be
dedicated to my wife — to Amabel — for the first and best
we wrote together — *The Pleasures of Architecture* — pleasures
we have most happily shared ever since our very first
meeting when we immediately discovered a common
weakness of Strawberry Hill Gothic. That bond still persists — amongst all others.

He then quoted from his 'favourite philosopher' Don Marquis:

Artists are the only persons that should be listened to —
about anything; about education, government and the
government of life generally, which are of consequence
only in relation to the production of art and artists. The
main thing is to get more Shakespeares, another Leonardo,
a second Beethoven, that is all that matters in this world,
all else is extraneous or subsidiary. The purpose of the
universe is to play. The artists know that and that play and
art and creation are different names for the same — a thing
that is sweats and agonies and ecstasies . . . .

This self analysis places Clough perfectly in the unfolding history
of Architecture. At one moment he echoes Eliot's Prufrock — 'I
may not be a Hamlet, nor was meant to be' — and he knows full
well the baggage of Victorian and Edwardian upbringing he
inevitably carries, and he is well aware of the brave new world of
1963 and his anomalous position therein.

Letters poured in. Frederick Gibberd paid tribute by declaring
'it is rare to find an architect really sensitive to landscape . . .'.
From the House of Commons Megan Lloyd George telegraphed:
'Best wishes for at least twenty'. Clough looked so well and
indefatigable that many shared her view that 'another twenty' was
not beyond the realms of possibility.

Clough's readiness to help younger talent, whether in architecture or in some peripheral area like its history, was evident in John
Gloag's letter of thanks: 'You may not know it, but I owe you a
lot; I doubt if I should ever have started writing about architecture
had I not been inspired by *The Pleasures of Architecture* and one of
the highlights of my life was when, many years ago, you asked me
to contribute to *Britain and the Beast* . . .'.

Mary Burn echoed a complaint of many who were there: 'that

your lively and witty after dinner response to Roger's toast did not go on long enough'. Bertie Russell wrote: 'My dear young friend, Welcome to the happy company of the octogenarians which I have so lately deserted. May your ninth decade be prosperous, and your tenth, in due course, equally so. Logic forbids me to wish you many happy returns of either, but I feel most sincerely the analogous wish which logic does permit . . .'.

Naturally, Clough was easing off somewhat at his practice, but never ceased working at his desk in Brondanw. He was busy with three major projects: Nantclwyd, Voelas Hall and Dalton in Cumbria. Another interesting project in the Sixties was the restoration of Madocks's Town Hall in Tremadog. It had fallen into a dreadful state, the *piano nobile* upstairs in apparent terminal decay, the ground floor a dark space used only in summer by Bretons stringing onions which they brought over in bulk direct into Porthmadog Harbour. Clough's refurbishment returned this most distinguished building to its former glory as the focal point of the little town's fine square. I rented the ground floor as my studio and in 1968 Clough attended sittings for my portrait of him. Although he was eighty-five he was the most patient of sitters, and in marked contrast to Bertie Russell he talked very little. Two bronze casts were made, one for the National Library of Wales, the other for Hercules Hall in Portmeirion.

By 1971 Clough was taking a thoroughly retrospective view of his life and work in *Architect Errant*, published by Constable. In it his affectionate view of his upbringing, despite his grumbles at certain aspects, firmly established what was to affect him throughout his life and work. Looking back, he recognises the general claustrophobia whenever he was locked up, whether it be nursery, school, lecture room or office. Despite his coolness about life at Glasfryn, he recalls the beginnings of two great passions, for it was there on the lake that he first learned to sail, and it was from Glasfryn that he experienced the charm and elegance of Tanrallt and the Palladian grandeur of Glynllifon.

In the same year he breezed into my studio one day with the drawing for a carving I was to make for Portmeirion. He was in a hurry. 'I must be off,' he said. 'I'm off to be "Doctored" this afternoon at Aberystwyth'. At the venerable age of eighty-eight, Clough received an honorary degree from the University of Wales. Another eminent architect, Professor Dewi Thomas, read the citation:

> The year 1883 had its high points. It saw, for instance, the erection of the first steel-framed skyscraper in Chicago. In

it was installed one of the first electric elevators, but
horizontal travel would remain horse-drawn for another
twenty years or so, on roads, as it had been since before
the days of Rome . . . . The year 1883 also allowed the
signal honour of presenting to you, in 1971, the remarkable
Clough Williams-Ellis, 'Architect Errant' . . . . As a propagandist his voice has been unceasing and publications such
as *England and the Octopus* and *Britain and the Beast* gave
warning almost forty years ago of the spoliation and the
pollution which we now take seriously . . . .

Back at the drawing board, one large project, begun in 1956 but
proceeding well past 1970, continued to keep Clough happily
occupied and to give him great satisfaction. It was Nantclwyd Hall
in the Vale of Clwyd, undoubtedly one of his greatest achievements. The patron Sir Vivyan Naylor-Leyland had inherited a
rambling house and demesne which had suffered all sorts of
alterations and additions, ending up a complete muddle. Sir
Vivyan himself took a lively interest in a new design and contributed
a great deal to Clough's thinking on the matter. Clough was only
impressed by one wing dating from Charles II. The rest, he felt,
was beyond redemption, and his patron agreed whole-heartedly.
But Clough warned him that a major scheme to replace the old
Hall would involve merely a different kind of muddle, by bull-
dozer, for a decade or more. The owner was adamant. Clough
took it on. First there was the mess of wholesale demolition, which
at his age must have seemed a daunting prospect. The mere sight
of yet more muddle is surely enough to make retirement seem a
tempting prospect. But that was not the sort of thought that ever
entered his head. He preserved and refurbished the Charles II
wing, then turned the whole plan round from a north-facing
prospect towards one facing south, to look across magnificent
parkland full of possibilities for Clough's landscaping talents. An
abandoned railway line provided a new drive, and where it crossed
a rather sluggish stream, Clough had it widened and deepened in
order to do justice to two fine bridges he designed. These bridges
are late masterpieces, with low arches, a fine parapet adorned with
obelisks at either end and roundels in the cusps of the brick
masonry.

New vistas were arranged. There are four temples, an obelisk,
a round tower folly, a domed Doric rotunda reflected in the lake.
A monumental triple arched gateway gives access from the main
road with two side entrances, columns surmounted by eagles, and
a three-storeyed clock tower entrance to the garage yard. There

are even special Palladian kennels for the dogs. The sight of Stowe early in his career must have left its mark.

Amabel used to say that no boy ever had such a wonderful chance to indulge his hobby as Clough, and Nantclwyd Hall bore this out, for he patently enjoyed this chance to rebuild a great house from practically scratch and to deploy the parkland to his taste. The Hall itself presents one of Clough's best facades, with the central pediment topped by urns, and in the central of the three storeys a fine Venetian window. Once again, Clough's bold approach, turning the whole plan round from north- to south-facing, then designing the park to complement this move, is a late example of his lateral thinking. Far too often, conservation of an old fabric is not justified, for either aesthetic or financial reasons, yet piety often wins the day and an opportunity like Nantclwyd Hall is lost. Of course, there is no way of guaranteeing an architect of Clough's taste. In Nantclwyd Hall there is a lifetime of experience and sensibility and the whole scheme sits in its vale with the assurance of a master development.

# Nineties

Just upon Clough's ninetieth birthday, as though by prior arrangement, a most curious phenomenon occurred. As the tide ebbed opposite the Hotel, a large shiny object was left stranded about two hundred yards out. It was a six-feet long tunny fish which turned out to be four hundred pounds in weight. Clough made the most of this fortuitous event, for upon notifying the Marine Biology Department at Bangor University he was told that never before had such a fish, of any weight, been notified so far north in British waters. Clough was duly photographed with one foot on the fish, as though he had just landed his best ever catch. Later, in a speech, he would gratefully record the tunny's noble sacrifice, referring to 'the poor fish loyally advertising Portmeirion's enviable climate'.

If by his own admission he was not a 'great' architect (a point which many would dispute), there can never be any doubt about his passion for architecture, nor of his ability to convey this passion to a wide public. When F.R. Leavis declared in 1934 that the Sitwell siblings belonged to 'the history of publicity rather than of poetry', the same might be said of Clough. As wireless mutated into radio, and then black-and-white television mutated into colour, Clough was made for them all. Clough was a natural broadcaster, in both radio and on television. He made a broadcast on his ninetieth birthday and Woodrow Wyatt, on hearing it, telegraphed: 'Heard you in lively vigour on the wireless yesterday, which reminded me to salute your ninetieth birthday'. He sounded good, with his patrician voice and baroque prose, and he looked good, tall, stalking rather than walking, and his wardrobe ever so slightly *outré*. The long yellow stockings became his hallmark, until nobody remarked, because for him they were perfectly natural. The stockings, the waistcoat and the 'suspect felt hat' were a practical device, given the generally spartan conditions in which he often opted to live.

In his nineties Clough walked the Gwyllt as strongly as ever, if with a hint of frailty in his stride. Portmeirion occupied much of his time, for if you have not earned your leisure and pleasure at ninety, when shall you?

His mind was undiminished, and if he worked just a little less at the drawing-board, he found the energy to write one further volume, *Around the World in Ninety Years*. Here, after describing the almost total eclipse of architecture during Hitler's War, he once again (forgetting that he had already gone over it twice in print) lauds the post-war renaissance promised with the Festival of Britain and the New Towns, then regrets the impetus was not maintained. Slipped in, there is one retrospective amendment that is of significance, correcting earlier views in *Architecture Here and Now* and elsewhere: 'Far too many hapless citizens were rehoused in tower blocks that were were as extravagant to build as they were hateful to inhabit'.

But he does take pleasure in certain developments, if his pleasure is tinged with certain qualms which now loom large. For instance, he, one of the earliest motor-car enthusiasts at Cambridge before the First World War, came to see the unbridled expansion of the use of the car to proportions that are now virtually out of control. Even worse, perhaps, is another post-war phenomenon, vandalism, which is now pandemic. Clough in his youth had seen the expansion of the municipal parks movement, and now many of their amenities were becoming unusable because of this pestilential nuisance. He recalls being shown round the Wythenshaw development near Manchester and finds it 'immensely heartening'. It embodied so much that he had been advocating over the years. Later, revisiting the place as a member of the Trunk Road Advisory Committee, he is shocked to learn of a proposal to close off the elegant footbridge spanning the main road, the reason being 'to prevent the youth of the place hurling bottles and even old bedsteads on to passing cars'. This depressed him, as well it might. He had always maintained the civilizing effect of good surroundings on social conduct, yet here that thesis is being denied.

In publishing a book with a title like *Around the World in Ninety Years* he felt obliged to justify his claim that in his long and active life he had visited most corners of the world, or at least had had contact by 'remote control' as in the case of the Butterfield and Swire commissions in China.

He extols the blessed trade wind climate of the Caribbean in recalling his 1968 visit. He regrets the great expanses of sugar cane on Barbados (whose buildings his travelling companion Patrick Leigh Fermor described as 'bloodcurdlingly genteel'). But Clough admires some of the grand houses, built mostly from the wealth accrued from earlier slave labour. Bridgetown's remnants of Georgian building catch his eye and altogether he is an exceptional visitor in the sense that he takes in much more than the balmy beaches. He remembers cruising round the islands leisurely, even bumping into old friends like Philip and Hilary Hugh-Jones, frequent visitors to Portmeirion. Clough admired the streamlined elegance of Trinidad's oil installations (which might seem odd coming from him), but 'not her dismal pitch lake'.

Another well-favoured sun spot was Fiji, which enabled a meeting with daughter Dr Charlotte Wallace from New Zealand. From Fiji, Amabel travelled back to New Zealand with Charlotte, while Clough flew on to Mexico, where he was feted at an endless succession of cocktail parties given by the absurdly rich, who owned elegant mansions and gardens. Because of a very favourable exchange rate 'even the not so absurdly affluent could still afford pretty grand houses and lots of servants'. Bemused and more than a little befuddled by this endless hospitality, he asks one of his hosts: 'For goodness sake, what sort of place *is* this — I simply can't make it out?' His interlocutor promptly replies that it is a place in the sun for shady people.

Being Clough, he overdid things. Although repelled by Aztec, Mayan and Toltec remains, he simply had to climb to the top of one of the steep pyramids, forgetting they were at quite a high altitude above sea level. He collapsed and was revived by a friendly American stranger who offered him Coca-Cola — 'another experience never since repeated'.

Undeterred by this sharp reminder of mortality, he flew on to New York, where his host was an old Rhodes scholar friend, Joseph Brewer. He was invited to a party at the John Pierpoint Morgan Library, where another acquaintance, Lord Crawford, would deliver an address to mark the bestowal of his father's famous library on to the Morgan Collection.

Next came a meeting with his old colleague in Planning, Lewis Mumford, at his distant country cottage, practically buried in snow. Clough thought the weather-boarded structure looked frail and chilly, but inside, lined as it was with books, it was well insulated.

In his various voyages across the Pacific he 'found himself' as he put it, twice at Los Angeles. With his principles of planning, it is obvious the place set his teeth on edge, but he patently enjoyed some of the company there. One invitation from David Niven brought him into contact with a young actress. 'Maybe you know my grandfather, Frank Lloyd Wright?' she asked. When he replied in the affirmative, he went on to say how wonderful the old boy was at eighty-eight. She corrected him to say he was over ninety but never let it be known lest it deter clients.

If ever proof were needed that Clough was attractive to women, as he left the party, and searched his way through the shrubbery trying to find the highway, he met up with 'another exceedingly beautiful actress' trying likewise to find her way out. They continued the struggle together and then, eventually finding their exit, she said: 'On a night like this the lights of Hollywood look marvellous from high up on the hills — if you don't mind being seen with me in my rather vulgar raspberry-coloured convertible — might you care to come?' He made the most of this brief encounter. They went on to pay a late call on his very old friends Charles Laughton and Elsa Lanchester, and then his companion drove him back to his hotel in the small hours.

Wherever Clough and Amabel travelled, they seemed to meet and were entertained by friends. Hardly had they set foot in India at Bombay than they met Leonard Elmhirst (founder of Dartington Hall), and critic and writer Richard Church. They were intrigued to be in the audience at an occasion to celebrate Rabindranath Tagore the Indian poet and seer, being addressed by Pandit Nehru 'in flawless English'. There were obvious gaps in Clough's social and political sensibilities, for why should he remark on Nehru's 'flawless English', considering the British had ruled India for three centuries and English was the imposed language of government and social intercourse?

Clough was not in the least moved by the architecture of India and even less by its erotic sculptures, and was impressed only by the eighteenth and early nineteenth century official buildings of the Raj. He was duly impressed by Edwin Lutyens's more recent additions to this canon at New Delhi. And yet, magnificent though it was in both scale and design, it was the sort of massive project that Clough had avoided from early in his career, when he had deliberately curtailed his training at the Architectural Association and opted to go straight into building English country houses.

The Taj Mahal affected him not at all, and he even quoted Hugh Casson's caustic comment: 'this refugee from the mantelpiece'. 'But,' Clough concluded, 'we liked the monkeys.'

More to his taste was the British Cemetery, 'a truly wonderful outdoor architectural museum of funerary monuments, mostly of extreme elegance whether obelisks, columns, urns, altar-tombs, or little pavilions'. For him, this was the highlight of his visit to Calcutta, indeed to India, for he was moved not only by aesthetic response to the various monuments, but by the thought of the general youth of those commemorated, victims to the climate and disease.

Amabel was held back by broadcasting commitments in Bombay, so Clough hastened home on his own. Back at Brondanw, he was felled at once by a virulent infection and seemed near to death at one stage. A car was rushed from Wales to meet Amabel off the plane. Yet he rallied, only to suffer soon afterwards from a coronary thrombosis. It was all like trying to fell a tall poplar. He recovered. 'Oh, one of those things,' said Bertie Russell, 'I had one forty years ago in China and was none the worse for it.'

Another of Portmeirion's memorable parties celebrated Clough's ninetieth birthday. This was Portmeirion at its best; festive, decorative, thronged with old friends strolling about and meeting up on the lawn of the central piazza. The morning began with a colloquy of architects in the Pantheon, to pay tribute to their old colleague and indeed exemplar, given their present surroundings. Lord Harlech formally presented the Lion that now stands, or rather couches, beside the path leading down from Battery Square to the Town Hall. I carved the inscription to go under it:

> Presented to Portmeirion and its Founder
> Sir Clough Williams-Ellis
> by his friends and colleagues
> on his 90th Birthday
> May 28th 1973

Then followed dinner, and a ball in the Town Hall. But perhaps most memorable of all was the firework display, which many will remember as one of the finest at Portmeirion.

By now Clough had become a national monument, and he basked in this position. In 1976, when he was ninety-three, Portmeirion reached its Golden Jubilee and that was sufficient excuse for yet another grand occasion. 'The Chairman of the Council for the Protection of Rural Wales and the Directors of Portmeirion request the pleasure of the company of . . . .'

He felt constrained to decline an invitation from the Royal Institute of British Architects to a dinner in London to celebrate this auspicious occasion. If Mohammed would not come to the mountain, then the mountain must come to Mohammed, and the Council came up with a counter proposal to visit Portmeirion and dine with him there. He took the opportunity when they came to show off the RIBA Arms, painted on a blank panel in the Orangery at Plas Brondanw by great-niece Bronwyn.

Congratulations poured in afterwards. Michael Burn the writer in his thanks afterwards wrote perhaps the best tribute: 'Versailles without the pomposity, the Duchess of Richmond's ball but no Waterloo, Ranelagh, Battersea all rolled into one . . . and as for your own speech Jeremy Thorpe was unashamedly envious'. Hans

Feibusch, whose mural paintings do so much for Portmeirion,
wrote '. . . Now I go home, full of wonderful pictures (and good
food), but chiefly remembering you addressing us from the chancel
of the Dome and from the balcony in the garden like Prospero
himself, the great wizard of the West . . .'.

His old friend, Fabia Drake the actress wrote: 'I cannot go away
without leaving a little letter of delight at what Noel must surely
have been anticipating when he wrote the song: 'I've been to a
Mar-vellous Party!'

Aside from major projects like Nantclwyd Hall, Clough still
enjoyed designing monuments and follies. Late in life he designed
a Classical temple for a chain of lakes at Hatton Grange in
Shropshire. It became a multiple product in the sense that the new
epoxy resin method of casting allowed as many repeats as were
deemed necessary or prudent, rather like a sculptor's plaster cast
acts as model for a limited edition of bronze casts. In this case the
pillars were made of simulated Portland Stone, i.e. pulverised
stone dust set in resin to achieve a fair resemblance to the original
stone. The dome was of patinated copper. The whole thing was
so successful that he had several casts made for clients (and one
for the Gwyllt at Portmeirion), and he called it his 'Stop me and
buy one Folly'.

The architect John Taylor about this time was busy planning
his own folly, Castell Gyrn near Ruthin in Clwyd, and sought
Clough's advice when planning difficulties cropped up. At ninety,
many a man would have opted out and referred Taylor to some
younger colleague perhaps. Not Clough. He was passionately
engaged, especially since the project was the sort he would heartily
approve anyway. His visual acuity, whether viewing a site or a
drawing, was as brilliant as ever. His advice is detailed and
exacting:

> I think the plan reads logically and very well and that the
> East elevation is excellent, but the West one less so, largely
> owing to the large windows — so desirable from within.
> Perhaps the big ground floor one could be dissembled by
> being recessed so that it might more resemble a gateway.
> On the 1st and 2nd floors I should like to see the 3 light
> windows reduced to 2 lights — that being compensated for
> by the little side-lights I have suggested on the plan with a
> question mark — which should add interest both inside
> and out. I assume that mullions would be of stone match-
> ing the general masonry as near as may be and not too
> finely wrought.

The term 'not too finely wrought' is significant. He goes on to describe his own own on-site method of building:

> I should be delighted to show you my outlook tower
> here, where slight irregularities and a general ruggedness
> sufficiently deceived an Ancient Buildings survey team to
> start measuring it up officially! So far as I know, no plans
> or drawings of it exist anywhere as I simply marked out its
> outline on the rock on which it stands and then personally
> supervised my estate masons as it rose stone by stone —
> mostly from an old cow-byre and unwanted field-walls
> adjoining, all beautifully weathered and of all sizes from
> that of a suitcase down to a cigar box.

After that came another bun fight, this time to celebrate the 150th anniversary of the Athenaeum, of which Clough was now 'father'. He replied to the invitation — 'To have received a tribute from the Chairman and Fellow Members of the Athenaeum on my absurd antiquity makes me feel venerable indeed, whilst to find myself the Father of so august an institution merely through a 1918 election seems enjoyably absurd'. He seems to have enjoyed this note of absurdity throughout old age.

Upon receiving greetings from the Royal Institute of British Architects, he replied to the President, Alex Gordon: 'I was ever a loner, and I am afraid did very little at any stage in aid of our organisation. I thank it the more for its friendly greeting'. He was, you might say, a professional non-joiner.

In 1974 he was invited by Lord Butler, Master of Trinity, to its forthcoming 'feast', an occasion he seems to have enjoyed enormously. It had been over seventy years since his time there as a freshman. He found fellow guest Willie Whitelaw most amiable.

Then came 1975, when Clough and Amabel celebrated their Diamond Wedding. It gathered together not only their many distant friends, but also the locality, one or two of whom were still able to remember that first homecoming after the wedding in St Martha's Chapel on a Surrey hilltop back in 1915.

In one press notice of the general festivities he was referred to as 'the late'; 'Must strive to live that libel down', was his comment. But the tall poplar was bending in the wind. He still strode in the Gwyllt, but the old vigour was fading and it was sad to witness. Not that *he* ever uttered a word of complaint. The summer could still be enjoyed, and the winter endured. But the winter of 1977-78 was hard on Clough. Yet he would have been the first to declare it had been worse for many others. Then he slipped on ice and fractured his femur, a frequent injury in the very old. He knocked himself unconscious and was taken by ambulance to Bangor. As the vehicle was halfway there and passing through Penygroes, he came round, asked where he was, and ordered the nurse to take him back home at once. Of course, with such a helpless casualty the nurse had no choice but to persist with the journey.

At the hospital in intensive care, Clough turned his face to the wall, refusing to cooperate or to eat. He was beyond what doctors can offer, and probably knew it — except that when Amabel informed him that there was a fifty-fifty chance of success if he was operated on, 'Yes' was the prompt reply. The operation was a success, Clough was returned to his beloved Brondanw according to his wish and in very short time he was receiving friends again and even toddling around his room on his aluminium pulpit.

A week before he died, I managed with his secretary Richard Haslam to help him outside, where he and I sat in a rare hour of April sunshine, sipping sherry before lunch. That was Clough, exulting in the sun, reminiscing and reprimanding, laughing and even for a few moments singing. We tripped heavily (given the awful timbre of our respective voices) through one or two 'Twenties' hits. He remembered the words of a few Coward numbers better than I did. Tone deaf as we both were The Master would have been horrified.

We expressed gratitude for the bright morning after the rigours of the hard winter. The singing came to an end, whether for want of breath or repertoire I would not care to say. He suddenly quietened, then declared, provocatively: 'I've decided after all these years that I'm an atheist!' I loved him for that, because of the courage, defiance and, of course, the implicit doubt of seven or eight decades, for his father, being a cleric, must at the very least have initiated the internal debate, and Clough had decided against, at a moment when you might expect the opposite.

Although he had seen the legislation for the 'listing' of buildings and sites of outstanding historical or aesthetic quality, some of Clough's work has already suffered. I am glad he cannot see additions and site alterations even within a few miles of Brondanw. His beautiful church hall (1955) at Pentrefelin near Cricieth is now hidden behind an unimpressive bungalow. At Llanystumdwy a little further along the road to Pwllheli, the urns have gone from the gate piers of his Moriah chapel. Worst of all, at the Lloyd George grave, so highly praised by Lewis Mumford and now a world heritage site, an unprepossessing rectangular slate plaque with ghastly lettering has been placed over the arch. This mausoleum is one of Clough's most beautiful concepts in stone, without a straight line in it. While its legend is commendable celebrating the 50th anniversary of Lloyd George's death, that nasty little rectangle now ruins the whole effect.

His monument, despite his many great houses, must be Portmeirion. Puritanical critics might decry it, but he built it with passionate conviction and very little money. It is among the most enjoyable things around these days in a very naughty world as far as environment goes. John Cowper Powys from his eyrie further up the valley in Blaenau Ffestiniog described it well in a letter to Louis Wilkinson, though his nomenclature is wobbly:

> . . . the most extraordinary place three or four miles large along the sea shore called Port Merrion & built or invented by that daring Architect Mister William Clough-Ellis. Phyllis describes it as a Ballet Stage Setting on the everlasting Sands of Time . . . . It is Faked-Antiquity or Pseudo-Romance, but the more intelligent you are the more you cotton to it. It's like a 'Folly' in the time of Horace Walpole painted by Gainsborough. Fake-Fake Pseudo-Pseudo, but so highly decorative that it is like some Petit Trianon of Versailles — False light, fake pseudo airy fairy, but a pure pleasure!

Like most cultural attractions, Portmeirion is suffering today from the very tourists it attracts, as with Florence or the Parthenon, all in danger of being trampled underfoot by the sheer numbers of their admirers. The present ease of transport makes everything so very accessible. Yet the paradox in all this is that Portmeirion would probably fall down but for the tourist income. Maintenance of property is an expensive business.

The scale of Portmeirion is deceiving. Everything is just that little less than one thinks. You find yourself stooping slightly to negotiate an arch which, from a distance, appears to be in firm human scale but is in fact just a little less. This was not so much a matter of economy (he was not rich and had no illusions that Portmeirion was a self-indulgence), as to accommodate the fabric to the confines of the little dell in which the village is situated.

Portmeirion started off as a fine dream and it was gradually eroded, by life, by time, and by the gradual contraction of all our dreams following the war. The original intention that it should provide a retreat for artists and writers soon faded, artists and writers being what they are, refusing to conform, chary of arranged retreats and preferring to search out their own or even fleeing from any idea of retreat.

Clough was great fun. He enjoyed the macabre and belonged to that rare breed like Horace Walpole and Thomas Love Peacock who kept a foot in both the Classical and Romantic worlds. I would place Clough with a few rare spirits among the best company to enjoy. He wrote as felicitously as he drew and built, and perhaps he talked even better. What was unique about him was his appearance, he stalked through the gardens on his long thin legs clad in britches and yellow stockings without the least affectation.

He loved Wales. It was typical of him when he was showing King George VI round Eryri that he should point up to a peak opposite Snowdon with his cane and say, in answer to a royal query: 'Actually that bit belongs to me but you can keep that under your crown'.

His defiance of architectural trends is in many ways now justified. Many of his buildings, like Capel Moriah in Llanystumdwy stand the test of time better than most contemporary buildings. Nor was his design necessarily expensive. At an early period in his career, he declared he could build a worker's cottage for one hundred and ten pounds and it was true at the time and he did it. He was a great patron of the young and I owed a great deal to his patronage when I returned from war service and sought to establish myself as artist and craftsman in Gwynedd in those austere post-war years.

His comment that he had 'few if any close friends that he would much miss' might be construed as the jaundiced view of an old buffer with little time for people. Yet that is not always the impression he left behind. People still talk of him with great affection and there were countless words and little acts of kindness on his part which belie these words. John Gloag's letter of appreciation would be echoed by many.

The three Mason-Hornby children, aged 10, 11 and 12, wrote to congratulate him on his ninetieth birthday. Clough wrote back personally 'Dear Francis, Christopher and Catherine, Thank you all three for your birthday letters. You're all a long way off ninety, but it's quite fun when you get there. I like to think of you growing up at Dalton, which it is nice to hear you approve of — so do I! All I'm waiting for now is to see the garden catching up with the house, and I hope all three of you will enjoy seeing your home becoming more and more beautiful . . .'.

He held that vision of beauty to the very end. And praise be,

Dalton and its garden are in good hands and Clough's dream is now reality. He never betrayed that vision of beauty. Like his exemplar Palladio he was animated by the dictum of Vitruvius . . . *firmitas, utilitas, venustas,* which Sir Henry Wotton in 1624 translated as 'Firmness, Commodity and Delight'. That Delight is evident not only in the many fine houses and gardens Clough created, and in Portmeirion, but also implicit in the stalwart work on various committees whose ultimate objective was to assure that Delight for the rest of us in the shape of the National Parks, the National Trust, the New Towns, and all the liberating dismantling of nineteenth century industrial squalor. Clough would be the last to declare the struggle was over. Indeed, it has barely begun, but Clough was among the great initiators.

François Spoerry in his book *A Gentle Architecture* pays a fitting tribute: 'He died in 1978 leaving the world a poorer place; for men like Clough Williams-Ellis are rare and special people'.

He had all the qualities required for the good life. He was an indefatigable survivor. Life might have ended for him in the Great War, as it did for so many millions of men, but his luck held even there. Who but he could survive a serious car accident in his late eighties? He was well liked by men and adored of women. He loved nature and its gentle submission to the ministrations of a sympathetic gardener or architect, and he had the good sense to grasp what opportunities life offered him and to make the most of them. He had a grotesque sense of humour, of spoof, and some of it goes into his buildings. To hide an ugly central heating chimney in Chantry Row he designed a sheet metal vertical *half* of an onion dome. The flèche of the Town Hall is beautifully topped by a pig boiler. And anything else would be wrong.

He treated death as lightly as he treated life. Discussing with Lady Aberconway how he could get her ashes into an urn on top of a tall column he planned to build for her, his solution came promptly: 'There will be a tube from bottom to top and we'll blow them up by bellows'. His last wish was that his own ashes should be sent up by rocket over the beautiful Dwyryd estuary.

The day before he died, Clough still managed to steal the show. He loved to quote fatuous lines like 'backing into the limelight'. Another favourite was that such and such a body was 'a hotbed of cold feet'. BBC2 visited me one day to record my impressions of another neighbour, Richard Hughes (or Diccon, as we all knew him). I completed my stint, then asked whom they were recording next. They replied that it was Amabel, for Amabel did indeed know as much as anybody about Diccon's early days. When the crew got to Brondanw, they found Clough sprawling on a couch, obviously not far from death, and more or less comatose. But the presence of a camera or recording outfit would alert him to the very end. He declared he had something to say about Diccon. A few months later, while we were still feeling the pain of his death, tears pricked my eyes as we heard that booming voice from the grave, speaking most eloquently on his impressions of Diccon. It was as he would have wished, to go out working to the very end, still backing into the limelight. After that recording, as though it was a last supreme effort, he relapsed into sleep and never woke again, unless in some Portmeirion in the heaven in which he firmly did not believe — or did he?

That is something we never know of one another — where we stand *sub specie aeternitatis*. But I cannot resist appending a letter written late in life to another peninsular eccentric, Captain Henry Winch, dated November 25, 1971:

> Thanks for notice dear Henry — but Harlech Meeting on the 4th Dec — Alas! not possible, I think (Amabel in London at moment) But we shall scarcely be back in time from Devon — where that day a monument of mine is being dedicated by the Arch Bish of Canterbury. A 4 engined jet is touching down for us at Llanbedr (with his Grace on board!) & will deliver us back that evening.
> We should make the headlines if we crash!
> yrs
> Clough.

Among his surviving papers there was one fugitive bit of nonsense which he must have written towards the end of his life in a fit of rueful but humorous introspection. It is a sort of school report on his life and character and is so revealing that it is worth quoting in full:

> Report on X
> A vigorous extrovert with a lively but limited intelligence. Introspection is unknown to him and although genial and friendly enough has few if any close friends that he would much miss. He has no aptitude whatsoever for an intimate téte-téte & would be far happier and more effective making a public speech.
> He is narrowly *un*-emotional and even-tempered — only twice in his life having contrived to make a show of temper by deliberate intent. His dominating interests are visual, natural scenery — preferably dramatic, and architecture,

in which latter, though academically ill-equipped, he none
the less claims to have a natural instinct for responding to
a site or a buildings requirements appropriately, and to
have a judgement of proportions, particularly, that is unerring.

His reading is slow and fairly miscelaneous, makes little
of poetry & is allergic to 'Permissiveness'. He writes readily
and rapidly in his own somewhat coloquial and free-wheeling
style but dispite his almost entirely visual memory is an
erratic speller.

In the matter of religion he has declined (or advanced)
from a mild and formal Christianity derived from an
orthodox home & school through agnosticism to a reason-
ably firm atheism, but is not deeply concerned anyway any
more than with philosophy generally.

He is probably considered by some to be something of
a snob because he certainly has a distaste for most 'regional' accents whilst positively enjoying a pleasant voice
speaking educated 'upper-class' English with an adequate
vocabulary almost regardless of the sense (or nonsense)
conveyed.

He also certainly has a weakness for splendour &
display & believes that even if he were reduced to penury
himself he would still hope to be cheered by the sight of
un-inhibited lavishness & splendour unconfined *somewhere*
— He would recognise the absurdity of another King
Ludwig II of Bavaria or even a Lord Lonsdale in To-days
world, as inconceivable as latter-day Cleopatras or Prince
Regents, which is why he feels that Copenhagens Tivoli
Gardens or something like them should be spread around
the civilized world giving everyone a taste of lavishness,
gaiety and cultivated design. [sic]

Amabel survived a further six years, dying in 1984, simply of
old age. She had kept her vow, had never ceased to write, even
towards the end producing her autobiography *All Stracheys Are
Cousins* the year before her death. Science had always fascinated
her, and she sought answers that might explain the universe, then,
not finding them, she explored the intricacies of Buddhism, even
to going out to an ashram in Khatmandu for enlightenment, no
mean exploit for a woman of seventy-nine.

In the Thirties she had been at the heart of much of the soul
searching of the Left in politics, during the rise of Fascism. She
had been undeviating in her views, saw Fascism from the
beginning for what it was and viewed the Government of the day,
and also the Labour opposition with dismay. She watched her

brother John cross the floor from Conservative to Labour, then flirt with Mosley and his New Party before Mosley sank into Fascism. That seemed to bring John to his senses.

Certainly Amabel had known intimately many of the Left's luminaries, like Aneurin Bevan and Jennie Lee, and she toured the Rhondda when it was at its poorest in the Thirties, trying to understand and to help where she could. It must have been a daunting experience for the girl from Newlands Corner.

She never ceased her searching, and is most discerning about Clough on this: 'Looking back, what seems peculiar is that such a search never engaged Clough in the least; such speculations seemed never to cross his mind. He was perhaps like Wordsworth's "Happy Warrior" who even into old age relies "upon a genial sense of youth". I walked shoulder to shoulder with him; we were married for sixty-three years'.

Seeing her the day before she died brought to mind Bishop King's lines,

> Stay for me there: I will not fail
> To meet thee in that hollow vale.
> And think not much of my delay:
> I am already on the way . . .

# Acknowledgements

Since Clough Williams-Ellis and his wife Amabel both wrote copiously, I am deeply indebted to them both, for a long personal friendship and for their published works.

For access to copyright material I am deeply indebted to their surviving family, and in particular to daughters Susan and Charlotte, to son-in-law Euan Cooper-Willis, and especially to grandson Robin Llywelyn.

I would also like to thank Sir Osmond Williams, and Lady Williams, Michael Burn, John Taylor, Michael Bevington, Pyrs Gruffudd, Tom Owen, Henry Keswick, Paul Cox at the National Portrait Gallery; Jill Lever and staff at the British Architectural Library, Cecily Mason-Horby, Michael Trevor Williams, Canon William Jones, Hans Feibusch, John and Bethan Jones, Lord Esher, Tony Bianchi at the Arts Council of Wales, Muriel Wilson formerly of the British Council, Sir Bernard Ashley, Robert Evans and staff at the Department of Manuscripts and Records of the National Library of Wales, Sir Philip Naylor Leyland, Michael Watts for much of the photography, and Matthew Farrah for his proofreading and work on the index.

Finally, I thank my wife Judith Maro, especially for her memory where mine erred; and my daughter Naomi for patiently housing me in her studios with my army of wrecked typewriters. I mourn the passing of the ever-so-durable manual typewriter. Old fingers do not take lightly to electronic gadgetry. So a last word of thanks to Mick Felton, who accepted with good grace a manuscript in four different faces and declared it would 'scan', whatever that may mean.

Jonah Jones

# Illustration Acknowledgements

Numbers 5, 8, 9, 10, 11, 14, 16, 17, 19, 21, 22, 23, 27 and 28 courtesy of Jonah Jones; 3 courtesy of the National Portrait Gallery; 15 courtesy of Cecily Mason-Hornby; 1 and 2 courtesy of the Estate of Clough Williams-Ellis; 18, 20, 24 and 26 courtesy of Richard Tilbrook.

# Select Bibliography

*Books by Clough Williams-Ellis*

(with Amabel Williams-Ellis), *The Pleasures of Architecture* (London: Jonathan Cape, 1924)
*England and the Octopus* (London: Geoffrey Bles, 1928)
*The D.I.A. Cautionary Guide to St Albans* (London: Design and Industries Association, 1929)
(with Lady Weaver), *Lawrence Weaver* (London: Geoffrey Bles, 1933)
(with John Summerson), *Architecture Here and Now* (London: Nelson, 1934)
*On Trust for the Nation* (London: Paul Elek, 1947)
(with Amabel Williams-Ellis and Richard Hughes), *Headlong Down the Years* (Liverpool: Liverpool University Press, 1951)
*Portmeirion: The Place and its Meaning* (London: Faber, 1963)
*Roads in the Landscape* (London: HMSO, 1967)
*Architect Errant* (London: Constable, 1971)
*Around the World in Ninety Years* (Portmeirion and Glasgow: Golden Dragon Books, 1978)

*Books and Articles on Clough Williams-Ellis*

Anon., 'Cold Blow, Oare, Wiltshire', *Country Life* LIII (1923), 195-6
Fry, E. Maxwell, 'Portmeirion', *Architects' Journal* LXV (1928), 871-84
Hussey, Christopher, 'Oare House, Wiltshire', *Country Life* LXIII (1928), 334-41
Hussey, Christopher, 'Cornwell Manor', *Country Life* LXXXIX (1941), 432-36, 454-57, 476-79
Hussey, Christopher, 'Plas Brondanw, Merioneth', *Country Life* CXXII (1957), 434-37, 488-91
Rattenbury, Arnold, *Catalogue of Memorial Exhibition*, Portmeirion, 1981 (unpublished)
Haslam, Richard, 'Nantclwyd Hall', *Country Life* CLXXXII (1988), 58-63

# Index